Solaris™ 8 Essential Reference

Other Titles by New Riders

Solaris Advanced System Administrator's Guide, 2E
Janice Windsor,
ISBN: 1-57870-039-6

Solaris System Administrator's Guide, 2E
Janice Windsor,
ISBN: 1-57870-040-X

Solaris System Management
John Philcox,
ISBN: 0-7357-1018-X

Inside Linux
Michael Tobler,
ISBN: 0-7357-0940-8

Inside XML
Steve Holzner,
ISBN: 0-7357-1020-1

Linux System Administration
M Carling, Jim Dennis, Stephen Degler,
ISBN: 1-56205-934-3

Linux Firewalls
Robert Ziegler,
ISBN: 0-7357-0900-9

Linux Essential Reference
Ed Petron,
ISBN: 0-7357-852-5

Vi iMproved (VIM)
Steve Oualline,
ISBN: 0-7357-1001-5

Networking Linux: A Practical Guide to TCP/IP
Pat Eyler,
ISBN: 0-7357-1031-7

KDE Application Development
Uwe Thiem,
ISBN: 1-57870-201-1

GTK+/Gnome Application Development
Havoc Pennington,
ISBN: 0-7357-0078-8

MySQL
Paul DuBois,
ISBN: 0-7357-0921-1

Berkeley DB
Sleepycat Software, Inc.,
ISBN: 0-7357-1064-3

MCSE Essential Reference: Core Exams
Matthew Shepker,
ISBN: 0-7357-0006-0

Developing Linux Applications
Eric Harlow,
ISBN: 0-7357-0021-4

Solaris™ 8 Essential Reference

John P. Mulligan

201 West 103rd Street, Indianapolis, IN 46290

Solaris 8 Essential Reference

SECOND EDITION: *January, 2001*

International Standard Book Number: 0-7357-1007-4

Library of Congress Catalog Card Number: 00-102951

04 03 02 01 7 6 5 4 3 2 1

Interpretation of the printing code: The rightmost double-digit number is the year of the book's printing; the rightmost single-digit number is the number of the book's printing. For example, the printing code 01-1 shows that the first printing of the book occurred in 2001.

Printed in the United States of America

Trademarks

All terms mentioned in this book that are known to be trademarks or service marks have been appropriately capitalized. New Riders Publishing cannot attest to the accuracy of this information. Use of a term in this book should not be regarded as affecting the validity of any trademark or service mark.

Solaris is a trademark of Sun Microsystems, Inc.

Warning and Disclaimer

This book is designed to provide information about Solaris 8. Every effort has been made to make this book as complete and as accurate as possible, but no warranty or fitness is implied.

The information is provided on an as-is basis. The authors and New Riders Publishing shall have neither liability nor responsibility to any person or entity with respect to any loss or damages arising from the information contained in this book.

Publisher
David Dwyer

Associate Publisher
Al Valvano

Executive Editor
Stephanie Wall

Managing Editor
Gina Brown

Product Marketing Manager
Stephanie Layton

Publicity Manager
Susan Nixon

Acquisitions Editor
Ann Quinn

Development Editor
Laura Loveall

Senior Editor
Lori A. Lyons

Copy Editor
Kelli Brooks

Indexer
Christine Karpeles

Manufacturing Coordinator
Jim Conway

Proofreader
Marcia Deboy

Composition
Amy Parker
Suzanne Pettypiece

Contents

Part II Developer Reference

About the Author

John P. Mulligan is the creator and co-editor of SolarisGuide (`http://SolarisGuide.com`), the leading online information resource about Sun Microsystem's Solaris operating environment, featuring technical manuals, FAQs, news, and more. Started as an informal collection of Solaris information while he was a student at Lafayette College, SolarisGuide has since been acquired by Internet.com Corporation and is now the premiere source for Solaris news and information for professionals worldwide.

John spent three years working in the Computer Support Services department at Lafayette College working on just about every aspect of UNIX system administration and management. He was responsible for migrating all the college Sun systems from SunOS 4.x to SunOS 5.x (a.k.a. Solaris 2). During that time, he also worked on a research project involving the mathematical modeling of microfluidic flows on Sun Solaris workstations.

He is also the author of the first edition of *Solaris Essential Reference* and now the second edition, updated for Solaris 8. *Solaris Essential Reference* remains a concise and efficient reference available for the Solaris Operating Environment.

John currently lives in East Berlin, Pennsylvania, and works at P.H. Glatfelter Company as an environmental engineer. He can be reached at `john@thinkhole.org`.

About the Technical Reviewers

These reviewers contributed their considerable hands-on expertise to the entire development process for *Solaris 8 Essential Reference*. As the book was being written, these dedicated professionals reviewed all the material for technical content, organization, and flow. Their feedback was critical to ensuring that *Solaris 8 Essential Reference* fits our reader's need for the highest quality technical information.

Jeffrey Meltzer has served as the Senior Network Administrator for VillageWorld.com, Inc. for the past five years, which specializes in setting up Private Label, Community-based, and Franchised ISPs. Jeffrey is responsible for the installation and maintenance of more than 100 Sun servers running versions of Solaris from SunOS 4.1.4 through Solaris 8 at Village World.com. He also serves as Co-Editor for SolarisGuide.com, a leading online information resource about the Solaris Operating Environment. Other online projects Jeffrey is involved in are PublicNAP.net, where he is the Postmaster and Webmaster for a site that assists Network Administrators in finding out more about the Public Exchange Points worldwide, and the FreeCert Project, which is attempting to provide free SSL certificates to qualifying organizations. Jeffrey currently resides in Long Island, New York; he can be reached at `jeffrey@meltzer.org`.

Nojan Moshiri's experience with UNIX administration dates to the late 1980s in parallel to the rise of the modern Internet. Over the past 10 years, Nojan has been both a student and teacher of these technologies—including various flavors of UNIX—to colleagues at the University of California and in private industry.

Currently, Nojan maintains his enthusiasm for new technologies with R&D in Internet commerce. Advocating standards and UNIX-based approaches to commerce's round-the-clock needs, Nojan has preached this message to Silicon Valley companies such as Apple Computer, Cisco Systems, and other leading startups.

Dedication

I would like to dedicate this book to Phil Kostenbader.
Thanks, Phil, for being a great boss, mentor, and friend.

Acknowledgments

First, I want to thank my parents—my dad for giving me a love of science and technology, and my mom for giving me the writing skills to be able to put my thoughts into words. Mom and Dad, you have always been there for me, supporting me in everything I have ever done. I can never thank you enough. I also need to thank my brother, Eddie, who is always there for me when I just need to have a long conversation about computers, technology, and other geeky things that no one else wants to hear about.

Thanks also go to everyone I worked with at New Riders: Ann Quinn, Stacey Beheler, Laura Loveall, and Lori Lyons. They helped me turn my ideas into an actual book while displaying amazing amounts of patience. You all deserve a raise after working with me! I also would like to thank the technical reviewers, Jeffrey Meltzer and Nojan Moshiri, who helped to check my technical information.

There are many other people that I need to thank as well. Thanks, Jaime, for everything—being excited for me, listening to me, laughing with me, and always being there for me. Thanks, Uncle Jimmy, for giving me the motivation to write something as large as a reference book and sharing your writing experience with me along the way. Thanks, Aunt Mary, for just being my Aunt Mary. Thanks go to Matt, Mike, Chad, Maia, Amanda, Tony, and Jeff for always providing great diversions from writing. And to everyone else who in some way supported my efforts—thank you.

Tell Us What You Think

As the reader of this book, you are the most important critic and commentator. We value your opinion and want to know what we're doing right, what we could do better, what areas you'd like to see us publish in, and any other words of wisdom you're willing to pass our way.

As an Executive Editor at New Riders Publishing, I welcome your comments. You can fax, email, or write me directly to let me know what you did or didn't like about this book—as well as what we can do to make our books stronger.

Please note that I cannot help you with technical problems related to the topic of this book, and that due to the high volume of mail I receive, I might not be able to reply to every message.

When you write, please be sure to include this book's title and author as well as your name and phone or fax number. I will carefully review your comments and share them with the author and editors who worked on the book.

Fax: 317-581-4663

Email: `stephanie.wall@newriders.com`

Mail: Stephanie Wall
Executive Editor
New Riders Publishing
201 West 103rd Street
Indianapolis, IN 46290 USA

Introduction

This book is designed to be the ideal reference for Solaris users who know what they want to do, but just need to know how to do it. This reference assumes that the reader is well-versed in general UNIX skills and is simply in need of some pointers on how to get the most out of Solaris. Rather than a lengthy tutorial that holds the user's hand, this book serves as a desktop reference of everything an experienced user will need to know to use Solaris.

This edition has been updated to include the use of Solaris 8. However, even though Solaris 8 is a significant update compared to the previous versions of Solaris, this book is still an excellent reference for previous versions of Solaris, including Solaris 2.x and Solaris 7. One change in the Solaris 8 release is the inclusion of GNU software and utilities on a companion CD-ROM that accompanies the Solaris 8 program. The most important of these GNU utilities are covered in this book, as they are essential tools for system administrators and users. There is a list of some of the key new features of Solaris 8 in Appendix A, "Solaris Version Changes."

I have placed the emphasis of this reference on the essentials of using the SunOS 5.x operating system rather than using the Open Window environment. The general rule is that anything that can be done from a graphical user interface (GUI) in Solaris can also be done from the command line. Using the command-line interface (CLI) rather than a GUI allows users and administrators to have full access to Solaris computers even when they are not using a terminal that supports graphics. Therefore, the commands and explanations in this reference can be used over remote logins, over corporate LANs, across the Internet, at the actual computer console, or over a serial terminal connection—regardless of what type of monitor or frame buffer is present (if any).

Book Conventions

This book has been designed to facilitate quick searches. The best way you can speed up your searches is to understand the layout of this book. The following example can help you do this.

The first page of most chapters will have two jump-tables. The table on the left is a list of all the specific commands, utilities, and so on, that are featured in the chapter, in alphabetical order, with respective page numbers. The right jump-table reflects the order of the chapter as it actually appears. Each line in bold indicates the "highest" or "broadest" header. The following is an example of this level of chapter header.

Informational Utilities

The specific commands, tasks, utilities, and so on are listed in smaller headers, as follows.

`finger`

Following these smaller headers will be a consistent flow of information found throughout the book, including the syntax, description, options, commands, special elements and/or information, and relevant cross references.

```
/usr/bin/finger [options] {user]
```

The description of `finger`.

Option	Description
`-b`	Do not show home directories and shells in the information given.
`-z`	Not an actual option. This is simply to display that information is listed in alphabetical order, if it is deemed useful to present it this way.

In-Depth Information or Special Warnings

These elements can be skipped, but usually include useful, *extra* information.

▶ **See Also** `whois` (page 86)

There are also several typographical conventions that are used in this book. They are as follows:

Convention	**Description**	**Example**
Commands and scripts	Solaris commands, command lines, and shell scripts are shown in a monospaced font.	`/usr/ucb/ps -auxw | grep inetd`
Variables	Variables that hold the place for substitutions are shown in italic and a monospaced font.	`cat` *`filename`*
Optional syntax	Optional items in a command's syntax appear in brackets.	`finger [`*`options`*`] [`*`host`*`]`
Keystrokes	Keystrokes and keystroke combinations appear in bold.	**CTRL+Z**

I

General Usage Reference

1
Text Utilities

Sorting

sort

sort

```
/usr/bin/sort [options] [files]
/usr/xpg4/bin/sort [options] [files]
```

Sort, reorder, and list the lines of a text file or stream. Temporary files are written to `/var/tmp/stm*`.

Option	Description
`+n.m`	If only *n* (an integer) is given, skip *n* fields before sorting. If *n.m* (both integers) is given, start at character *n* of the *m*th field.
`-b`	Ignore blanks, spaces, and tabs.
`-c`	Produce output only if the file is not already sorted. The xpg4 version produces no output under any circumstances.
`-d`	Use only letters, digits, and spaces for sorting. All other characters are ignored (dictionary sort).
`-f`	Case-insensitive sort. Ignore difference between upper- and lowercase characters (folding).
`-i`	Ignore non-printable ASCII characters.
`-k keydef`	Restricted key sorting. Sorting is restricted to a portion of the line.
`-m`	Assume the file is already sorted and merge them.
`-M`	Sort as months using the first three non-blank characters (`-b` is implied).
`-n`	Sort by number (arithmetic value). Leading zeros are ignored.
`-o file`	Redirect the output to a file—either new or the input file itself.
`-r`	Reverse the sort.
`-t char`	Redefine the delimiter to `char`. The delimiters are spaces and tabs by default.
`-T directory`	Define temporary file directory. Use `/var/tmp` by default if not specified.
`-u`	Non-unique (repeated) lines appear only once.

continues >>

continued

Option	Description
`-y` *kmem*	Set the amount of main memory to be used by `sort`. If `-y` is given without an amount (*kmem*), the maximum amount of memory is used.

Example	Task
`sort -b userlist > ➥userlist.sorted`	Sort a list of usernames, ignoring leading spaces and tabs, outputting to a file.
`repquota -a | sort +2n`	Sort the output of a quota report by disk usage.
`sort hostlog | uniq -c`	Sort a list of hostnames, removing duplicates, and count the frequency of each one.

▸**See Also** `join` (8), `uniq` (5)

uniq

`/usr/bin/uniq [options] [files]`

uniq

Find, count, and delete repeated lines in text files or streams. If the repeated lines are not adjacent, they will not be detected. Therefore, it is recommended that the text be sorted first.

Option	Description
`-c`	Frequency count of each line.
`-d`	Do not output unique lines.
`-f` *fields*	Ignore the first *fields* fields when comparing lines. Also, `-`*fields* can be used with the same effect.
`-s` *chars*	Ignore the first *chars* characters when comparing lines. Also, `+`*chars* can be used with the same effect.
`-u`	Do not output non-unique lines.

Example	Task
`last | awk '{print $1}' ➥| sort | uniq -c`	Determine how many times users have logged in.
`sort hostlog | uniq -c ➥| sort -rn`	Sort hosts in a log file by frequency in decreasing order.
`uniq -c datafile`	Perform a simple frequency count of data.

▸**See Also** `sort` (4)

Formatting

cut

cut `/usr/bin/cut options [files]`

Select columns or fields out of a file. Either `-b`, `-c`, or `-f` must be used. Works well when used with `paste`.

Option	Description
`-b list`	Specify columns by byte size.
`-c list`	Specify columns by character positions.
`-d delim`	Use the character following `-d` as the delimiter. Spaces must be in quotes.
`-f list`	Specify what fields to cut using delimiter defined by `-d`.
`-n`	Do not split characters.
`-s`	Do not output lines that do not contain the delimiter specified with `-d`.

Example	Task
`cut -c2`	Show only the second column of a file.
`cut -d: -f1,6 ➥/etc/passwd`	Display usernames and their home directories.
`cut -d" " ➥-f2 file`	Show second column of a space delimited file.

▶See Also awk (19), join (8), newform (8), paste (10)

fmt

fmt `/usr/bin/fmt [options] [files]`

Generic text formatting utility to create lines of the same length. Blank lines and spacing are not altered during the formatting.

Option	Description
`-c`	Align the left margins of a paragraph with the line after the initial indentation.
`-s`	Do not join lines. Useful when formatting code and text.
`-w width`	Fill lines to *width*.

Example	Task
`cat myfile	fmt -c >` `➥alignedfile.txt`	Align the left margins of a text.
`cat myfile	fmt -w >` `➥filledtext.txt`	Fill lines of text to 80 columns.

▸**See Also** `newform` (8)

fold

`/usr/bin/fold [options] [files]`

fold

This utility can be used to fold lines. This is done by inserting newline characters at a specified place in each line. Words will not be broken if a text file is folded.

Option	Description
`-b`	Measure the width in bytes.
`-s`	Break lines at blank characters.
`-w width`	Specifies maximum line width in characters. Default is 80.

Example	Task
`fold -b 32 myfile.txt`	Fold a text file to 32 bytes.
`fold -s myfile.txt >` `➥myfile2.txt`	Insert newline characters into the text where there are blank characters; send the output to a new file.

▸**See Also** `cut` (6), `fmt` (6), `paste` (10)

iconv

iconv

`/usr/bin/iconv [options] [file]`

Convert characters of one code (such as 8859 or 646fr) to another code. Output is sent to standard output.

Option	Description
`-f code`	Sets the input code set.
`-t`	Sets the output code set.

▸**See Also** `fmt` (6), `newform` (8)

join

join

`/usr/bin/join [options] [files]`

A relational command that can be used to join two files.

Option	Description
`-1 field`	Join on the specified field of file 1.
`-2 field`	Join on the specified field of file 2.
`-a number`	Output a line for each unpairable line in the file specified by the number.
`-e string`	Replace blank output with the specified string.
`-j field`	Same as `-1 field -2 field`.
`-j1 field`	Same as `-1 field`.
`-j2 field`	Same as `-2 field`.
`-o list`	Output lines contain the fields specified in the list. If the fields specified in the list are not in the input, they are treated as blank fields.
`-t char`	Use the specified character as the separator.
`-v filenumber`	Output only unpairable lines in specified file.

▸**See Also** awk (19), cut (6), paste (10), sort (4), uniq (5)

newform

newform

`/usr/bin/newform [options] [files]`

Utility to reformat text in a variety of ways, reading from files or from standard input. Note that command-line options are processed in the order given. Similar to `cut` and `paste`.

Option	Description
`-a n`	Append *n* characters to the end of each line to obtain the line length specified by `-l`.
`-b n`	Trim *n* characters from the beginning of each line. If no *n* is given, the lines are truncated to the effective line length.
`-c char`	Change the character used by `-a` or `-p` to *char*.
`-e n`	Trim *n* characters from the end of each line.

continues >>

continued

Option	Description
`-f`	Show the tab specification used by `-o`.
`-i` *spec*	Replace tabs with spaces using the given tab specification. (Opposite of `-o`)
`-l` *n*	Set the effective line length to *n* characters. Default is 72 if no value is given.
`-o` *tabspec*	Replace spaces with tabs using the given tab specification. (Opposite of `-i`)
`-p` *n*	Prepend *n* characters to the beginning of each line to obtain the length specified by `-l`.
`-s`	Remove leading character from each line up to the first tab, moving the first eight characters to the end of the line. Characters beyond the first eight are replaced by `*`.

▸**See Also** `fmt` (6)

nl

```
/usr/bin/nl [options] [files]
/usr/xpg4/bin/nl [options] [files]
```


Add line numbers to text either from a file or from standard input. Line numbers are added to the left side of the text and reset at the top of each page.

Option	Description
`-b` *type*	Page numbering specification, which can be one of the following: ■ `a`: Number all lines ■ `n`: No line numbers ■ `t`: Number all non-empty lines ■ `p` *exp*: Number only lines matching regular expression *exp*
`-d` *chars*	Specify the two-character delimiter to be used for logical page breaks. If only one character is entered, the second is assumed to be a colon.
`-f` *type*	Page numbering specification for footer. Types are the same as `-b`.
`-h` *type*	Page numbering specification for header. Types are the same as `-f` and `-b`.

continues >>

>>continued

Option	Description
-i *n*	Increment page numbers by *n*.
-l *n*	Number of consecutive blank lines to count as a single line.
-n *format*	Line numbering format: ■ ln: Left justified, no leading zeros ■ rn: Right justified, no leading zeros ■ rz: Right justified Default is right justified with no leading zeros (rn).
-p	Do not reset page numbering at page breaks.
-s *sep*	Separating character between the line number and the text. By default, the separator is a tab.
-v *n*	Starting page number.
-w *n*	Width of page numbers. Default is 6.

Example	Task
nl source.c	Add line numbers to a source code file.
ls | nl	Add line numbers to a directory listing.

►**See Also** fmt (6), sort (4), uniq (5)

paste

paste

/usr/bin/paste [*options*] [*files*]

The paste command joins specific lines of text contained in two files. This is done by replacing the newline character at the end of each line in the first file with a tab. The newline characters at the end of each line in the second file are not changed.

Options

Option	Description
-d *delims*	The -d option is used to specify alternate delimiters for use when pasting two files. Delimiters are given in a list (with no spaces) in place of *delims*. Tabs can be specified as \t, and newline characters can be specified as \n.

Example	Task
paste *file1 file2*	Join two corresponding lines in two files.

►**See Also** awk (19), cut (6), join (8), newform (8)

Editors

ed


```
/usr/bin/ed
/usr/bin/red
/usr/xpg4/bin
```

Command–line-based text editor for UNIX operating systems. The `red` command is the restricted version of `ed`. Using `red` allows the user to edit only those files in the current directory, and the use of shell commands (`!`) is prohibited.

When executing shell commands, `/usr/bin/ed` uses `/usr/bin/sh` as the command interpreter. `/usr/xpg4/bin/ed` uses a `ksh`-compliant shell.

Commands

Commands are of the following form unless otherwise noted:

`[address][command]`

Command	Description
`! command-line`	The given command line is sent to the command shell and executed. The character `!` will be replaced by the current filename.
`!!`	Repeat the last executed shell command.
`a text`	Append *text* after the addressed line.
addr	Output the specified address (*addr*) to standard output.
`c text`	Delete the addressed line and replace it with *text*.
`d`	Delete the addressed line(s).
`e file`	Empty the buffer and load *file* info into the buffer. The current line is set to the last line of the file. `ed` first checks to see if the current file has been saved since the last changes.
`E file`	Same as `e file`, except that no check is made to see if the current file has been saved since the last change.
`f file`	Change the current filename in use to *file*, regardless of whether *file* exists. All subsequent changes are written to *file*.

continues >>

>>continued

Command	Description
`G/`*`regexpr`*`/`	Similar to the `g` command. Each line that matches the regular expression *`regexpr`* is displayed, and a single command can be entered. That command is then executed on the displayed line. (Known as the *interactive global* command.)
`g/`*`regexpr`* ➥`/`*`command`*	Execute *`command`* on every line in the buffer matching the regular expression specified by *`regexpr`*. (Known as the *global command*.)
`h`	Help. Displays a short message to explain the most recent diagnostic.
`H`	Help mode. All subsequent diagnostics produce error messages.
`i` *`text`*	Insert *`text`* before the addressed line.
`j`	Join lines between the two specified addresses. Newline characters are removed.
`k`*`char`*	Mark the addressed line with the character specified by *`char`*.
`l`	Write the addressed lines to standard output, showing all control characters and non-printable characters.
`m`*`addr`*	Move the addressed line to the address specified by *`addr`*.
`n`	Display the addressed lines with line numbers shown.
`newline`	Output the next line in the buffer to standard output.
`p`	Output the addressed lines to standard output.
`P`	Toggle prompting. If prompting is on, an asterisk is given on the line when waiting for a command. No addresses are required for this command.
`q`	Quit. If changes have been made since the last time the buffer has been saved, a warning is given.
`Q`	Quit without checking for unsaved changes.
`r` *`file`*	Read *`file`* into the current buffer without changing the current filename.
`s/`*`regexpr`*`/` ➥*`text`*`/`	Search the buffer for text matching the regular expression specified by *`regexpr`* and replace the first occurrence with *`text`*.
`s/`*`regexpr`*`/` ➥*`text`*`/g`	Similar to `s/`*`regexpr`*`/`*`text`*`/`, but replaces all occurrences.

continues >>

Command	Description
s/*regexpr*/ ➥*text*/l	Similar to s/*regexpr*/*text*/, but outputs to standard output the last line in which the replacement was made.
s/*regexpr*/ ➥*text*/*n*	Similar to s/*regexpr*/*text*/, but only replaces the *n*th occurrence.
s/*regexpr*/ ➥*text*/*n*	Similar to s/*regexpr*/*text*/l, but outputs the last line in which a substitution was made in the format specified by *n*.
s/*regexpr*/ ➥*text*/p	Similar to s/*regexpr*/*text*/l, but outputs the first line in which the substitution was made.
t*addr*	Same as the move command (m). However, the addressed lines are copied after the address specified by *addr*.
u	Undo the last change made to the buffer.
v/*regexpr*/ ➥*command*	Run *command* on all lines not matching the regular expression specified by *regexpr*.
w *file*	Write the addressed lines to the file specified by *file*. The file is created (mode 666) if it does not already exist.
W *file*	Append the addressed lines to the files specified by *file*. The file is created (mode 666) if it does not already exist.
X *key*	Toggle encryption on or off. Encryption is performed using the key specified by *key*. If a key is not given, encryption is turned off.

LIMITS

- 512 characters per line
- 256 characters in a command line (excluding ! commands)
- 255 characters in a pathname and/or filename (including slashes)

vi

vi

```
/usr/bin/vi [options] [files]
/usr/bin/view [options] [files]
/usr/bin/vedit [options] [files]
/usr/xpg4/bin/vi [options] [files]
/usr/xpg/bin/view [options] [files]
/usr/xpg/bin/vedit [options] [files]
```

Edit and reformat text using a full-screen editor (visual editor), based on the ex editor. Using view instead of vi causes the text file to be opened in read-only mode.

Option	Description
+command	Execute *command* when `vi` is started.
`-C`	Encryption mode. Same as `-x`, except that all text read is assumed to be encrypted.
`-l`	Configure `vi` to edit LISP programs.
`-L`	Report all saved files after `vi` was improperly shut down (editor crash or system crash).
`-R`	Read-only mode.
`-r` *filename*	Recover a file left in the buffer after a system crash.
`-s`	Run in non-interactive mode (suppress feedback). This mode should be used when running non-interactive scripts.
`-t` *tag*	Edit the file that contains *tag* and position the editor at its definition.
`-v`	Use `vi` in the display editing state.
`-V`	Verbose mode, sending output to standard error. Useful for debugging scripts when used in conjunction with `-s`.
`-w` *n*	Set the default window size to *n* characters wide.
`-x`	Encryption mode. The user is prompted for a key that will be used for encryption and decryption. Temporary buffers are encrypted as well.

Modes

	How to Enter Mode	How to Terminate Mode	Description
Command Mode	Start `vi` or exit other mode	**q**	This is the normal mode for `vi`, and the mode that is entered upon starting the editor. When other modes are finished or exited, `vi` returns to Command mode. Pressing **ESC** cancels a command before it is executed.
Input Mode	**`A`**, **`I`**, **`O`**, **`C`**, **`S`** (upper- or lowercase), or **`R`**	**ESC**	Text may be entered in this mode.

Canceling Commands

Command Keystroke	Description Effect
ESC	Terminate Input mode or cancel a command before it is executed.
DEL	Interrupt.

File Manipulation

Command	Description
`ZZ`	If the current file has been changed, save and exit. Otherwise, just exit.
`:w`	Save changes. (Write-out.)
`:q`	Quit without saving changes.
`:e_file`	Edit *file*.
`:e!`	Reopen file for editing, discarding any previous changes.
`:w file`	Save *file*.
`:w! file`	Save *file*, overwriting if it already exists.
`:sh`	Start shell and then return to `vi` when done.
`:! command`	Run *command* and return to `vi`.
`:n`	Specify new argument list.
`^G`	Report the current filename and line.
`:ta tag`	Position cursor to the *tag*.

Movement and Positioning

Command	Description
`^f`	Forward one screen.
`^b`	Back one screen.
`^u`	Scroll up half screen.
`^d`	Scroll down half screen.
*n*G	Go to the beginning of line number *n*.
/*pattern*	Go to the next occurrence matching the specified pattern.
?*pattern*	Go to the last occurrence matching the specified pattern.
`n`	Repeat the last ? or / search.
`N`	Reverse the last / or ? search.

continues >>

>>continued

Command	Description
/pattern/+n	Go to the nth line after the specified pattern.
?pattern?-n	Go to the nth line before the specified pattern.
`]]`	Next section.
`[[`	Previous section.
`(`	Go to the beginning of the current sentence.
`)`	Go to the end of the current sentence.
`{`	Go to the beginning of the paragraph.
`}`	Go to the end of the paragraph.
`%`	Find pairs of brackets or parentheses.
`H`	Go to the top (head) of the screen.
`L`	Go to the bottom (last line) of the screen.
`M`	Go to the middle of the screen.
`+`	Next line.
`-`	Previous line.
Carriage return	Same as `+`.
`v` or `j`	Next line but stay in the same column.
`^` or `k`	Previous line but stay in the same column.
`^`	Go to the first non-blank character.
`0`	Beginning of line.
`$`	End of line.
`:$`	Go to the end of the file.
`l`, **Space** →	Forward one character.
`h`, **CTRL+H** ←	Back one character.
F*x*	Find next occurrence of *x*.
F*x*	Find previous *x*.
T*x*	Move to the character just before the next *x*.
T*x*	Move to the character directly following *x*.
`;`	Repeat the last `f`, `F`, `t`, or `T` command issued.
`,`	Repeat the inverse of the last `f`, `F`, `t`, or `T` command issued.

continues >>

ontinued

Command	Description
n|	Move to column *n*.
W	Forward one word.
B	Back one word.
E	Go to the end of the word.
W	Forward one blank-delimited word.
B	Back one blank-delimited word.
e	Go to the last character of a blank-delimited word.

Marking Text

Command	Description
M*x*	Mark current position (with an *x*).
`*x*	Go to next mark.
'*x*	Move cursor to first character (non-space) in the marked line.

Inserting and Replacing Text

Command	Description
^H	Delete previous character (**Backspace**).
^W	Delete the previous word.
Erase *character*	Same as **Backspace**.
Kill *character*	Delete current line.
\	Display the current kill and erase characters.
^D	Backtab one character and reset left margin.
CTRL+D	Backtab to the beginning of the line without resetting left margin.
0^D	Backtab to the beginning of the line and reset the left margin.
^V	Quote a non-printable character.
A	Append text after the current position.
A	Append text at the end of the current line.
II	Insert text before current position.
I	Insert text before the first non-blank character.

continues >>

>>continued

Command	Description
R*char*	Replace a single character with the specified character, *char*.
R*chars*ESC	Replace multiple characters specified by *chars*.

Operators

`vi` can also be controlled using operators. To use any of the following operators, type the given operator followed by a cursor movement. The following example "yanks" the subsequent sentence to the buffer:

```
y)
```

Operator	Action
!	Filter the text through a command.
<	Shift left.
>	Shift right.
c	Change.
C	Change an entire line of text.
d	Delete.
D	Delete an entire line of text.
J	Join lines.
s	Substitute characters.
S	Substitute whole lines.
U	Undo last change.
x	Delete characters.
X	Delete characters before current position.
y	Copy to buffer (also called *yanking*).
Y	Copy lines (*yank*).
p	Put yanked lines before current position.
P	Put yanked lines after current position.

►**See Also** awk (19), ed (11), sed (32)

Advanced Text Tools

awk

`/usr/bin/awk [options] [files]`

A text utility that uses a scripting language.

Option	Description
`-f file`	Use *file* as the program file to use.
`-Fchar`	Use *char* as the field separator.

Predefined Variables

Variable	Description
FILENAME	Current filename.
FS	Current field separator. Can be changed on the command line with `-F`.
NF	Number of fields in the current record.
NR	Number of the current record.
OFMT	Number format. Default is `%.6g`.
OFS	Field separator to use for output. Default is blank.
ORS	Field separator to use for records. Default is newline.
RS	Input record field separator. Default is newline.

Actions and Functions

Action/ Function	Description
`Break`	Break out of a loop.
`Continue`	Go directly to the next iteration of a loop.
`Exit`	Stop reading input and exit.
`exp(x)`	Return the value of e^x.

continues >>

>>continued

Action/ Function	Description
`for(`*`expr1`*`:` ➥*`expr2`*`: `*`expr3`*`)` ➥*`command`*	Three expressions control the `for` loop: ■ *`expr1`* initializes the loop. ■ *`expr2`* is the test case. ■ *`expr3`* is used to change the loop variable. For example, to increment a variable to a certain number: `for(i=0; i<10; i++)` *`command`* Also, to run a command for each record in an array: `for (`*`record`*` in `*`array`*`)` *`command`*
`Getline`	Read the next record from the current input file.
`index` ➥`(`*`string1`*`,` ➥*`string2`*`)`	Give the position of *`string1`* in *`string2`*. Zero is returned if *`string1`* is not found.
`int(`*`n`*`)`	Convert *`n`* to an integer by truncation.
`length(`*`string`*`)`	Return the length of string.
`match(`*`string`*`,` ➥*`egexpr`*`)`	Give the position of the regular expression *`regexpr`* in the given string.
`next`	Go to the next line of input.
`print`	Print the arguments to standard output. To print fields (separated by the field separator `FS`), use `$`*`fieldnumber`* (for example, `print $3` would print the third field). Redirection and pipes can be used with print statements.
`printf`	Same as print, but uses `C printf` formatting. Valid formats include the following: ■ Decimal number: `%d` ■ Strings: `%s` ■ Floating Point Numbers: `%`*`x`*`.`*`y`*`f` (in which *`x`* is the total number of digits, and *`y`* is the number of digits after the decimal point)
`split (`*`string`*`,` ➥*`a`*`,`*`fs`*`)`	Split *`string`* into an array specified by *`a`* using *`fs`* as the field separator. The array has elements of *`a`*`[1]`, *`a`*`[2]` ... *`a`*`[`*`n`*`]`.
`sprintf(`*`format`*`,` ➥*`expr`*`,`*`expr`*`)`	Format the expressions in a similar manner to `printf`.
`substr` ➥`(`*`string`*`,`*`m`*`,`*`n`*`)`	Return the first *`n`* characters of *`string`*, that begin at position *`m`*.

▸**See Also** `ed` (21), `sed` (32), `vi` (13)

ex


```
/usr/bin/ex [options] [files]
/usr/xpg4/bin/ex [options] [files]
```

Text editor based on the `ed` editor and related to the `vi` editor.

Option	Description
`+command`	Same as `-c command`.
`-C`	Same as the `x` option, but all text read is assumed to be encrypted.
`-c command`	Execute `command` upon startup.
`-l`	Use LISP mode for editing.
`-L`	Display the names of all files saved after the editor was improperly exited.
`-R`	Read-only mode. No changes are made to the file.
`-r file`	Recover and edit `file` that was left in the buffer after `ex` was improperly shut down.
`-s`	Do not output anything. Useful when used in scripts where no user feedback is required.
`-v`	Use in visual editing mode. Same as running `vi`.
`-V`	Verbose output.
`-wn`	Set the screen size to *n* characters wide.
`-x`	Encrypted mode. This option prompts the user for an encryption key.

Modes

Mode	Description
Command	Normal state. `ex` starts up in this mode. A `:` is shown as a command prompt.
Insert	Type **a**, **c**, or **i** to enter Insert mode. Enter a **.** on a line to exit to Command mode.
Visual	Type **vi** to enter Visual mode. Type **Q** to exit to Command mode.

Commands

Task	Command	Description
Abbreviate	`ab [string1][string2]`	After issuing this command, whenever *string1* is typed it is replaced with *string2*.
Adjust Window	`[addr] z [option][n]`	Print the lines starting at the addressed line and going *n* lines, in an adjusted window. Options are as follows: ■ -: Addressed line at bottom ■ .: Addressed line at center ■ +: Addressed line at top ■ ^: Previous window ■ =: Set current line to addressed line and place it at the center of the window
Append	`[addr] a[!]text`	Insert *text* after the addressed lines. The use of ! toggles autoindenting.
Arguments	`ar`	Display files that are being edited.
Change	`[addr] c[!]text`	Replace the addressed lines with *text*. The use of ! toggles autoindenting.
Change Directory	`cd directory`	Change the current directory to *directory*.
Copy	`[addr1] co [addr2]`	Copy the text addressed by *addr1* to *addr2*.
Delete	`[addr] d [buffer]`	Delete the addressed text. If a buffer is specified, copy the deleted text to *buffer*.

continues >>

>continued

Task	Command	Description
Edit	`e[!] [+line] [file]`	Edit the file specified by *file* at line *line*. If ! is used, the current file is not saved before closing.
Encryption	`X`	Using encryption, attempt to determine if input is encrypted or not.
Escape	`[addr] !command`	Execute command on the addressed lines replacing them with the output. If no address is given, the command simply runs and sends the output to standard output.
File	`f [file]`	If no filename is specified, just display the current filename. If a filename is specified, change the current filename to *file*.
Forced Encryption	`C`	Assume all input is encrypted text.
Global	`[addr] g[!]/pattern/` ➥`[command]`	If lines are addressed, execute command on all addressed lines. If no lines are addressed, the command is run on lines matching the pattern. If no command is given, the lines are sent to standard output. ! reverses the matching pattern (commands are lines that do not match the pattern).
Insert	`[addr] i[!]text`	Insert text before the addressed lines. ! toggles autoindenting.

continues >>

>>continued

Task	Command	Description
Join	[*addr*] j[!][*count*][*flags*]	Join addressed lines into a single line, putting two spaces after a period. ! joins the lines without adding spaces.
List	[*addr*] l	List addressed lines, printing tabs (^I) and newlines ($).
Map	*map*[!] [*macro commands*]	Create a macro named *macro* that will perform the commands specified by *commands*.
Mark	[*addr*] ma [*mark*]	Mark the addressed lines with the character *mark*.
Move	[*addr1*] m [*addr2*]	Move the lines addressed by *addr1* to *addr2*.
Next	*n*[!] [*files*]	Begin editing the next file in the file list. If a file list is specified by *files*, the current file list is ignored. ! current changes are not saved.
Number	[*addr*] nu [*n*]	Display the addressed lines with line numbers. If a number *n* is given, *n* lines are shown starting with the addressed line.
Open	[addr] o [/*pattern*/]	vi mode is entered (single line vi commands can be used) starting at the text addressed by *addr* or matched by *pattern*.
Preserve	pre	Save the current file to the system save area.

continues >>

continued

Task	Command	Description
Print	[*addr*] p [*n*]	Print *n* lines starting at the address specified by *addr*.
Print Next	<newline>	Print the next line to standard output.
Put	[*addr*] pu [*buffer*]	Put the contents of buffer at the address specified by *addr*.
Quit	q[!]	Quit. ! quits without saving any changes.
Read	[*addr*] r [*file*]	Insert the text from *file* after the addressed lines. A command can be used in place of a file by typing !*command*.
Recover	rec [*file*]	Recover *file* from system save area. Refer to Preserve, earlier in this table.
Rewind	rew[!]	Rewind to the first file in the file list. ! changes to the first file without saving changes.
Shell	sh	Use a new shell and edit after it exits.
Shell Escape	!	Go to shell.
Shift Left	[*addr*] < [*n*]	Shift addressed lines *n* characters left.
Shift Right	[*addr*] > [*n*]	Shift addressed lines *n* characters right.
Source	so *script*	Run an ex script specified by *script*.

continues >>

>>continued

Task	Command	Description
Substitute	`[addr] s [/pattern/ ➥text/][opt][n]`	Substitute text matching *pattern* with *text* starting at the addressed line and going *n* lines. Options are as follows: ■ c: Confirm each substitution ■ g: Global substitution ■ p: Print the last line that was substituted
Tag	`ta tag`	Begin editing the file that contains the tag specified by *tag*.
Unabbreviate	`una string`	Unabbreviate *string*. Refer to Abbreviate, earlier in this table.
Undo	`u`	Undo last change.
Unmap	`unm[!] macro`	Unmap the macro specified by the character *macro*. ! removes input mode macros.
Version	`ve`	Display ex current version number.
Visual	`[address] vi [winsize]`	Edit using visual mode starting at the addressed lines using a window size of *winsize*.
Write	`[addr] w[!][>>][file]`	Write the addressed lines to file. If >> is used, the lines are appended to file. ! causes ex to overwrite the file.
Write and Quit	`wq`	Write and quit. ! ensures that none of the current contents of the current file are overwritten.

continues >>

continued

Task	Command	Description
Yank	`[addr] ya [buffer][n]`	Yank *n* lines to ***buffer*** starting at the addressed lines. The general buffer is used if none is specified.

Editing Options

Task	Option	Description
Autoindent	`Ai`	Automatically indent lines.
Autowrite Directory	`Aw`	Always save changes before changing files.
Exrc	`Ex`	Read `.exrc` on startup.
Ignore Case	`Ic`	Ignore the case when doing pattern matching.
List	`List`	Display tabs (`^I`) and newlines (`$`).
Magic	`magic`	Treat `.`, `[`, and `*` as special characters in patterns.
Mode Lines	`modelines`	First and last five lines are executed as `ex` commands. They must be in one of the following forms: ■ `ex:`*`command`*`:` ■ `vi:`*`command`*`:`
Number	`Nu`	Show line numbers.
Paragraphs	`Para`	Use first character of each paragraph as a macro.
Redraw	`Redraw`	Attempt to use terminal as if it were a smart terminal.
Report	`Report`	If the last command modified more commands than the report variable, the user is notified.
Scroll	`Scroll`	Command mode lines.
Section	`Sect`	Section starting macros.
Show Mode	`Smd`	Show `vi` Insert mode.

continues >>

>>continued

Task	Option	Description
Slow Open	slow	Do not update during inserts.
Terminal	term	Sets terminal type.
Window	window	Visual mode lines.
Wrap Margins	wm	Automatically wrap (split) lines at margins.
Wrap Searches	ws	Searches wrap when the end of the file is reached.

►See Also awk (19), ed (11), sed (32), vi (13)

grep

grep

`/usr/bin/grep [options] pattern [file]`

The grep text utility is used to find specific strings or patterns within a file. The default behavior of grep is to print all lines of text that match the given pattern or contain a specified string. The utility can also accept input from standard input if no file is specified.

Option	Description
-b	Print block numbers for each line.
-c	Print the number of lines that match the pattern.
-h	When searching multiple files, do not print the filename before each line.
-i	Perform a case-insensitive search.
-l	List the files in which the pattern is matched. If the pattern is found more than once in a file, the filename is printed only once.
-n	Show line numbers for each line printed.
-s	Do not show any error messages.
-v	Inverse. Print all lines that do not match the pattern.

Example	Task
grep smith /etc/passwd	Print all occurrences of the name smith in the system password file.
grep security *	Print the filenames and lines containing the word security in all files in the current directory.

continues >>

continued

Example	Task
/usr/ucb/ps -auxw | ➥grep smithj	Display all the processes currently owned by smithj.
grep -v false *file2*	Print all the lines that do not contain the word false in the file.

nawk

```
/usr/bin/nawk [options] ['program']
/usr/xpg4/bin/awk [options] ['program']
```

nawk

A text utility that uses a scripting language. nawk can do everything that awk can do, but more.

Option	Description
-f *file*	Use *file* as the program file to use. If multiple -f options are used, the specified files are joined and used as a single program.
-F*char*	Use *char* as the field separator. A regular expression can also be used in place of *char*.

Predefined Variables

Variable	Description
ARGC	Number of command-line arguments.
ARGV	Array of command-line arguments. ARGV[1]...ARGV[ARGC]
CONVFMT	Number conversion format. Used for printf number converting only—not output statements.
FILENAME	Current filename.
FNR	Relative number of the current record.
FS	Current field separator. Can be changed on the command line with -F.
LENGTH	The length of the string matched by the match command.
NF	Number of fields in the current record.
NR	Number of the current record.
OFMT	Number format. Default is %.6g.

continues >>

>>continued

Variable	Description
`OFMT`	Current number format. Default is `%.6g`.
`OFS`	Field separator to use for output. Default is blank.
`ORS`	Field separator to use for records. Default is newline.
`RS`	Input record field separator. Default is newline.
`RSTART`	The position of the first character in the string matched by the match function.
`SUBSEP`	Array subscript separator.

Actions and Functions

Action/ Function	Description
`atan2(`*`x`*`,`*`y`*`)`	Arctangent of *`x`*`/`*`y`*.
`Break`	Break out of a loop.
`close(`*`expr`*`)`	Close the file or pipe specified by *`expr`*.
`Continue`	Go directly to the next iteration of a loop.
`cos(`*`x`*`)`	Cosine of *`x`*.
`Do` *`Statements`* ➥`while(`*`expr`*`)`	Loop. Statements in the body of the loop (statements) are executed until the expression *`expr`* is true. The `while` command can also be used by itself. (`while(`*`expr`*`)` *`statement`*`)`
`Exit`	Stop reading input and exit.
`exp(`*`x`*`)`	Return the value of e^x.
`expr` `| getline`	The return value of *`expr`* is sent to `getline`.
`for(`*`expr1`*`:` ➥*`expr2`*`:` *`expr3`*`)` ➥*`command`*	Three expressions control the `for` loop: ■ *`expr1`* initialized the loop. ■ *`expr2`* is the test case. ■ *`expr3`* is used to change the loop variable. A common example is to increment a variable to a certain number: `for(i=0; i<10; i++)`*`command`*
`for(`*`record`* `in` ➥*`array`*`)` *`command`*	Run *`command`* for each *`record`* in *`array`*.

continues >>

continued

Action/ Function	Description
function *fname* ➥(*args*) ➥{*statements*}	User-defined functions: ■ *fname* is the function name. ■ *args* are any arguments to be passed to the function. ■ *statements* are the function statements enclosed in braces.
Getline	Read the next record from the current input file.
getline < *expr*	Evaluate *expr* and treat the return value as a filename. The input is then taken from that filename.
getline *variable*	Assign the value of the next line of input to *variable*.
gsub(regexpr, ➥*index* ➥(*string1*, ➥*string2*))	Give the position of *string1* in *string2*. Zero is returned if *string1* is not found.
int(*n*)	Convert *n* to an integer by truncation.
length(*string*)	Return the length of string.
log(*x*)	Natural log of *x*.
match(*string*, ➥*regexpr*)	Give the position of the regular expression *regexpr* in the given *string*.
Next	Go to the next line of input.
print	Print the arguments to standard output. To print fields (separated by the field separator FS), use $*fieldnumber* (for example, print $3 would print the third field). Redirection and pipes can be used with print statements.
printf	Same as print, but uses C printf formatting. Valid formats include the following: ■ Decimal number: %*d* ■ Strings: %*s* ■ Floating Point Numbers: %*x*.*y*f (in which *x* is the total number of digits, and *y* is the number of digits after the decimal point)
rand()	Return a random number between 0 and 1.
sin(*x*)	Sine of *x*.

continues >>

>>*continued*

Action/ Function	Description
`split` ➥`(string,a,fs)`	Split *string* into an array specified by `a` using *fs* as the field separator. The array has elements of `a[1], a[2] ... a[n]`.
`sprintf` ➥`(format,expr,` ➥`expr)`	Format the expressions in a similar manner to `printf`.
`sqrt(x)`	Square root of *x*.
`srand(n)`	Seed the random number generator (`rand()`) with *n*. If *n* is omitted, the time of day is used.
`sub(regexp,` ➥`string)`	Replace the text that is matched by the regular expression with *string*.
`substr` ➥`(string,m,n)`	Return the first *n* characters of *string*, that begin at position *m*.
`system(expr)`	Execute the command name returned by the evaluation of the expression specified by *expr*. Similar to the `system() C` function.
`tolower(string)`	Return *string* in all lowercase letters.
`toupper(string)`	Return *string* in all uppercase letters.

▸**See Also** `ed` (11), `sed` (32), `vi` (13)

sed

sed

```
/usr/bin/sed [option] [file]
/usr/xpg4/sed [options] [file]
```

Text utility to edit/modify streams and files.

Option	Description
`-e` *command*	Run the edit command specified by *command*. More than one `-e` can be specified from the command line.
`-f` *file*	Take the editing commands from the script file specified by *file*.
`-n`	No output.

Edit Commands

Edit commands are very similar to the command-line usage of the `ed` editor. They take the following form:

```
[addresses] command [arguments]
```

Command	Description
! *command*	Run *command* on the lines *not* addressed.
#	Comment. If a # is the first character of any line, that line is treated as a comment and ignored. See #n.
#*n*	If a # directly followed by an *n* are the first two characters of any line, the output for the rest of the script is suppressed.
:*label*	Assign a label called *label* for use in a script. By itself, this command does nothing.
{*commands*}	Execute *commands* on the addresses specified.
{*commands*}}	Execute *commands* on the selected pattern space.
=}	Print the current line number to standard output.
a *text*	Append *text* after each addressed line. Results are sent to standard output.
b *label*	Go directly to :*label* in the script. The command directly following :*label* is the next to be executed.
c *text*	Replace the addressed text with *text*.
d	Delete the addressed text.
D	Delete a multi-part pattern up to the first newline. Multi-part patterns are formed by using the N command.
g	Replace the pattern space with the hold space. The hold space is set by using the h or H command. Similar to pasting from a Clipboard.
G	Similar to g, but the hold space is appended to the pattern rather than replacing it. Similar to pasting from a Clipboard.
h	Copy the pattern space to the hold space. Similar to copying something to a Clipboard. Previous contents of hold space are replaced.
H	Similar to h, but the pattern space is appended to the hold space, rather than replacing it.

continues >>

>>continued

Command	Description
`i text`	Insert ***text*** before each addressed line. Results are sent to standard output.
`L`	Print the pattern space on standard output, including control characters and non-printable characters.
`n`	Replace the pattern space with the next line of text. Results are sent to standard output.
`N`	Similar to `n`, but the next line is appended to the pattern space rather than replacing it.
`p`	Print the pattern space to standard output up to the next newline.
`P`	Print the pattern space to standard output.
`Q`	Quit. If an address is given, the addressed line is sent to standard output before exiting.
`r file`	Append the contents of the file specified by ***file*** directly after the pattern space.
`s/regexp/text/`	Substitute. Substitute the text for ***flags*** with the regular expression specified by ***regexpr***. The following flags change the behavior of the substitution: ■ `n`: If an integer *n* is used, only the nth match is substituted (*n*=1...512). ■ `g`: Global substitution. Substitute all matches. ■ `p`: Print the pattern space for substitutions made. ■ `w file`: If any substitutions are made, they are written to file. Using `w` erases the current contents of ***file*** if it already exists, and all substitutions are appended to the file.
`t label`	If any changes have been made to the addressed lines, go to `:label` in the script.
`w file`	Write the pattern space to the file specified by file. The pattern space is appended to the end of the file.
`X`	Same as `h`. Exchange the pattern space and hold space contents.

Command	Description
y/*string1*/ ➥*string2*	Transform the characters of two equal-length strings. *String1* must have the same number of characters as *string2*.

Example	Description
s/thinkhole/meltzer/g db.foo	Globally substitute meltzer in place of thinkhole in the file db.foo.

▶**See Also** awk (19), ed (11), ex (21), grep (28), nawk (29)

2
Shell Scripting

continues >>

Page Contents

>>continued

Shell Summary

Shell Name	Path	Startup Files
Bourne Shell (sh)	/sbin/sh	.profile

Built-in Commands bg, break, case, cd, chdir, continue, echo, eval, exec, exit, export, fg, for, getopts, hash, if, jobs, kill, login, logout, newgrp, pwd, read, readonly, return, set, shift, stop, suspend, test, times, trap, type, ulimit, umask, unset, until, wait, while

Standard Environment Variables HOME, PATH, CDPATH, MAIL, MAILCHECK, MAILPATH, PS1, PS2, IFS, SHACCT, SHELL, LC_CTYPE, LC_MESSAGES

Shell Name	Path	Startup Files
C Shell (csh)	/usr/bin/csh	.cshrc

Built-in Commands alias, bg, break, case, cd, chdir, continue, dirs, echo, eval, exec, exit, fg, foreach, glob, goto, hashstat, history, if, jobs, kill, limit, login, logout, nice, notify, onintr, popd, pushd, rehash, prepeat, set, setenv, shift, source, stop, suspend, switch, time, umask, unalias, unhash, unlimit, unset, unsetenv, wait, while

Standard Environment Variables ARGV, CDPATH, CWD, ECHO, FIGNORE, FILEC, HARDPATHS, HISTCHARS, HISTORY, HOME, IGNOREEOF, MAIL, NOBEEP, NOCLOBBER, NOGLOB, NONOMATCH, NOTIFY, PATH, PROMPT, SAVEHIST, SHELL, STATUS, TIME, VERBOSE

Shell Name	Path	Startup Files
Korn Shell (ksh)	/usr/bin/ksh	.profile

Built-in Commands alias, bg, break, case, cd, continue, echo, eval, exec, exit, export, fc, fg, for, function, getopts, hash, if, jobs, kill, let, login, logout, newgrp, print, pwd, read, readonly, return, select, set, shift, stop, suspend, test, times, trap, type, typeset, unlimit, umask, unalias, unset, until, wait, whence, while

Standard Environment Variables ERRNO, OLDPWD, OPTARG, OPTIND, PPID, PWD, RANDOM, REPLY, SECONDS, CDPATH, COLUMNS, EDITOR, ENV, FCEDIT, FPATH, IFS, HISTFILE, HISTSIZE, HOME, LC_ALL, LC_COLLATE, LC_CTYPE, LC_MESSAGES, LANG, LINENO, LINES, MAIL, MAILCHECK, MAILPATH, NLSPATH, PATH, PPID, PS1, PS2, PS3, PS4, SHELL, TMOUT, VISUAL

Executing Scripts and Commands

eval sh csh ksh

eval

`eval argument`

The `eval` command reads the subsequent arguments into the shell and executes them as commands. This is useful for executing command lines that are generated by another program, such as another shell script.

▶ **See Also** `exec` (40), `source` (40)

exec sh csh ksh

exec

`exec command [command arguments]`

The `exec` command is used to run a command without starting a new process. The new command will take the place of the current shell until it has terminated. Input and output from the command being executed may affect the current shell. Arguments can be sent to the command specifying them after the command name. The syntax of this command is the same for all the shells: `sh`, `ksh`, and `csh`.

▶ **See Also** `eval` (40), `source` (40)

source csh

source

`source [options] filename`

The `source` command is available only in the `csh` shell. It reads the file specified and executes the commands. This command is useful for rereading a user's `.cshrc` file if something has been changed in it, such as a `PATH`.

Example	Task
`source .cshrc`	Update environment after changing the startup file.

▶ **See Also** `eval` (40), `exec` (40)

Setting and Unsetting Environment Variables

export sh ksh

The set command does not necessarily make variables available for subsequent commands to use. This is done by using the export command. The export command sends the variable and its value to the shell environment, causing its value to be set and used by all other commands until it is unset. The csh shell does not use the export command. It uses the setenv command instead.

export

sh Syntax

```
export [variable]
```

ksh Syntax

```
export [variable [=value]]
```

Example	**Task**
`export score1`	Export the variable *score1* using the sh shell.
`export score1=100`	Export the variable *score1* and set it to 100 using the ksh shell.

▸ **See Also** set (41), setenv (43), unset (44), unsetenv (44)

set sh csh ksh

The set command is one of the commands used to set environment variables. In the case of the csh and ksh shells, the arguments of the set command are variables that will be assigned the null value. Alternatively, the csh command can also be used to assign a specific value to a variable using an equal sign. For the sh shell, the environment values $1, $2, $3, and so on are assigned the values of the first, second, and third arguments, respectively. In all cases, if the set command is issued with no arguments, the values of all environment variables are displayed.

set

sh Syntax

```
set [options] [arguments]
```

Option	Description
—	Treat all options as arguments. (Necessary to set a variable to a dash.)
-a	Variables that are to be exported are noted.
-e	If an error is encountered (a non-zero exit status), exit immediately.
-f	Suppress filename generation.
-k	All keywords are treated as arguments, not just those after the command.
-n	Do not execute any commands.
-t	Read and execute only one command.
-u	If the variable is currently unset, return an error code.
-v	Verbose. Print all command lines when they are read.
-x	Verbose. Print all command lines when they are executed.

csh Syntax

```
set [variable [=variable]]
```

ksh Syntax

```
set [options] [arguments]
```

Option	Description
—	Ignore all other options.
-A	Treat the first argument as a variable name. Unset any previously assigned value and make the variable an array. The remaining arguments are assigned to each element of the array in order.
-a	Automatically export all variables.
-e	If an error is encountered (a non-zero exit status), exit.
-f	Suppress filename generation.
-k	All keywords are treated as arguments, not just those after the command.

continues >>

continued

Option	Description
-m	Display a status message when background jobs are running and when they finish.
-n	Do not execute any commands. Command lines are checked for errors.
-t	Read and execute only one command.
-u	If the variable is currently unset, return an error code.
-v	Verbose. Print all shell command lines when they are executed.

Example	Task
`set foo=2`	Set the variable `foo` to the value of `2` using the `csh` shell.
`set cat`	Set the environment variable `$1` to the value of `cat` using the `sh` shell.
`set test1 test2`	Clear the values of the variables test1 and test2.

▶ **See Also** `export` (41), `setenv` (43), `unset` (44), `unsetenv` (44)

setenv csh

`setenv [variable [value]]`

setenv

The `setenv` command is similar to the `export` command of the `sh` and `csh` shells. It sets and exports a variable to the shell environment. After the `setenv` command has been used on a variable, the variable and its value are available for use by all other subsequent commands. If no arguments are specified, all the currently set environment variables and their values will be displayed.

Example	Task
`setenv`	Show all environment variables and their values.
`setenv PATH $PATH':/usr/sbin'`	Add `/usr/sbin` to the current `PATH` variable in the `csh` shell.

▶ **See Also** `export` (41), `set` (41), `unset` (44), `unsetenv` (44)

unset sh csh ksh

unset

The unset command is used to clear the value of environment variables. For the sh and ksh shells, the behavior is the same. The csh unset command works in a similar fashion but can also use wildcards (*) to do pattern matching. It should be noted that accidentally typing unset * in the csh shell will unset all environment variables and can cause problems.

sh Syntax

```
unset [variables]
```

csh Syntax

```
unset [variables]
```

ksh Syntax

```
unset [options] [variables]
```

Option	Description
-f	Unset the variable even if it is a function name, such as ERRNO or TMOUT.

Example	Task
`unset test1 test2 test3`	Unset three variables using the sh shell.
`unset test1`	Unset the variable called *test1* using the csh shell.
`unset -f ERRNO`	Unset the ERRNO function variable using the ksh shell.
`unset cat*`	Unset all variables that begin with cat using the csh shell.

▶ **See Also** export (41), set (41), setenv (43), unsetenv (44)

unsetenv csh

unsetenv

The unsetenv command is used to unset the environment variables in the csh shell. The command behaves much like the unset command of the sh and ksh shells.

csh Syntax

```
unsetenv variable
```

Example	Task
`unsetenv TOPO`	Unset the environment variable called TOPO.

▶ **See Also** export (41), set (41), setenv (43), unset (44)

RC File Environment Variables

HISTORY csh

HISTORY specifies the number of lines to be stored in the command history. By default this is set to 1. The ksh shell uses the fc command to execute and edit previous commands.

HISTORY

Example	Description
`set HISTORY=20`	Set the history to 20 command lines.

LD_LIBRARY_PATH sh csh ksh

LD_LIBRARY_PATH is the search path for dynamically linked libraries. Although this is not specific to any command shell, it is important in many cases. If a needed path is missing from this environment variable, an error similar to the following will be returned upon executing a command.

LD_LIBRARY_PATH

```
fatal: libfoo.so.2: can't open file: errno=2
```

To fix this problem, find the location of the necessary library (for example, libfoo.so.2) and add that path to LD_LIBRARY_PATH.

Example	Description
`set LD_LIBRARY_PATH=/usr/X11R6.1/lib:/usr/dt/lib`	Set the dynamically loading library path.

EDITOR sh csh ksh

Defines what editor to use when called by certain programs. For example, crontab will use the editor defined in EDITOR to edit the crontab file. If no editor is specified by the user, the default is ed.

EDITOR

Example	Description
`set EDITOR=/usr/` `➥local/bin/pico`	Set the default editor to `pico`.
`set EDITOR=/usr/bin/vi`	Set the default editor to the `vi` editor included in Solaris.

IFS sh ksh

IFS

`IFS` specifies the internal field separator for the shell. The `IFS` character is used as the delimeter to interpret command lines. More than one character can be specified. `IFS` is set to SPACE, TAB, and NEWLINE by default. This can be useful when parsing text files. For example, when parsing the password file, it is useful to set the `IFS` to a colon (:).

Example	Description
`set IFS=':'`	Set the internal field separator to a colon.

PATH sh csh ksh

PATH

PATH defines the search path for commands. If a command line begins with `/`, it is taken to be a fully qualified path name and PATH is ignored. Otherwise, the paths specified are searched in order until the command is found. If no matching command is found in the PATH, an error is returned. A dot (.) in the path causes the current working directory to be included in the path. For security reasons, the dot (if included) should always be last in the path list, or preferably not included at all.

Example	Description
`set PATH=/usr/bin:/usr/` `ucb:/usr/local/bin:.`	Set a simple user PATH variable.

PROMPT csh

PROMPT

Sets the prompt used for command lines. By default, this is set to `%`.

Example	Description
`set PROMPT="'hostname':"`	Use a prompt that displays the current hostname and the current shell level.

Input and Output

Command-Line Arguments

It is possible to use command-line arguments when writing shell scripts. This is done by using $1, $2, $3, and so on, in the script. The script name, as executed, is $0. The first argument is $1, and so on.

Command-Line Arguments

Example

Consider the following command line:

```
myscript apple cow monkey
$0 = myscript
$1 = apple
$2 = cow
$3 = monkey
```

Suppose a line in the script reads as follows:

```
echo "The second argument is $2."
```

As a result, the following line will print:

```
The second argument is cow.
```

echo sh csh ksh

Print text to standard output. By default, the text is terminated with a newline when displayed.

echo

Option	Description
-n	Suppress newlines. A newline is not added to the end of output.

Example	Description
`echo -n "Waiting 10 seconds..." sleep 10 echo "done."`	Print the first line, wait 10 seconds, and then print "done" on the same line.

read sh ksh

read

Read from standard input and assign to variables.

ksh Options

Option	Description
`-p`	Take input from the output of a coprocess.
`-r`	Raw. Do not allow newlines to be escaped to continue lines (e.g. adding \ at the end of a line).
`-s`	Save. Input read is saved to the command history.
`-u` *`descrip`*	Input is read from the file descriptor specified by *`descrip`*.

Example	Description
`read` *`id contents capacity`*	Assign the first field (delimited by `IFS`) to `$`*`id`*, the second to `$`*`contents`*, and the third to `$`*`capacity`*.

Redirection

|

|

Action: Pipe. Sends the standard output of one command or script to another command.

<table>
<tr><th>Example</th><th>Description</th></tr>
<tr><td><code>myscript.sh | mail ➥foo@foo.com</code></td><td>Mail the output of the script to <code>foo@foo.com</code>.</td></tr>
</table>

<

<

Reads from a file, sending the contents to the standard input of a command.

Example	Description
`mail foo@foo.com < ➥report.txt`	Mail the file `report.txt` to `foo@foo.com`.
`myprogram < commands.txt`	Send the contents of a file to the standard input of a program.

>

Sends the output of a command to a file. If the file does not exist, it is created. If it already exists, an error is returned.

>

Example	Description
`grep "com" domains.txt > commercial.txt`	Find all lines that contain `"com"` in the file called `domains.txt` and put them in a file called `commercial.txt`.
`myprogram > output.txt`	Send the output of a program to a file.

>>

Appends the output of a command or script to a file. If the file does not exist, an error is returned.

>>

Example	Description
`echo "The last line." >>` `➥somefile.txt`	Echo a string and append it to the end of a file.
`myprogram &>>` `➥myprogram.out`	Append all output including `stderr` to a file.

tee

`/usr/bin/tee [options] [files]`

tee

The `tee` utility acts like a tee in plumbing: It effectively splits standard output into two streams. This command can be useful in some cases, especially those in which the input from a program must be viewed on the screen and sent to a file at the same time. The output can also be appended to more than one file by specifying multiple files on the command line. The output of `tee` is not buffered. If the file specified exists and the `-a` option is not given, the file will be overwritten.

Option	Description
`-a`	Append. The output of tee is appended to the specified file rather than overwriting it.
`-I`	Interrupts are ignored.

Example	Description
`csh	tee -a logfile &`	Record a log of a command shell.
`myscript.sh	tee ➥-a myscript.out`	Send the output of a shell script to the screen and a file.

Logical Operations

case/switch

case/switch

Choose from among a list of options. Usually a variable is read in using `read`, and then `case` is used to act, depending on what the value of `read` was. Options can also be complex expressions, such as *`option1|option2`* (*`option1`* or *`option2`*).

sh Syntax

```
case $VARIABLE in
        option1)                action1;;
        option2)                action2;;
        option3)                action3;;
        optionn)                actionn;;
esac
```

csh Syntax

```
switch ($VARIABLE)
        case option1:
                                action1
                                breaksw
        case option2:
                                action2
                                breaksw
        case optionn:
                                actionn
                                endsw
endsw
```

ksh Syntax

```
case $VARIABLE in
        option1)                action1;;
        option2)                action2;;
        option3)                action3;;
        optionn)                actionn;;
esac
```

csh Example

The following is an example of how to use the switch command in the csh shell. The example would echo the full department name based on a key letter.

```
switch ($DEPT)
               case "S":
                              echo "Sales Department"
                              breaksw
               case "M":
                              echo "Marketing Department"
                              breaksw
               case default:
                              echo "Invalid dept. code"
                              endsw
endsw
```

if-then-else

Test a condition or expression and perform an action based on the results. The if statement can be simple, or it can use else statements to provide more alternative actions.

if-then-else

sh Syntax

```
if condition; then action; fi
or
if condition; then action; else action2; fi
```

csh Syntax

```
if (condition1) then
action
else if (condition2) then
action2
else
action3
endif
```

ksh Syntax

```
if condition; then action; fi
or
if condition; then action; else action2; fi
```

Example	Task
`if [ $A -gt $B ]`	Test if the variable *A* is greater than the variable *B*.
`if [ $A -gt $B ] ➥[ $A -lt $C ]`	Test if the variable *A* is greater than the variable *B* and if the variable *A* is less than the variable *C*.

Loops

do-while sh csh ksh

do-while

Loop a series of actions or commands until a specified condition is met.

sh Syntax

```
while condition ; do actions  ; done
```

csh Syntax

```
while (conditions)
actions
end
```

ksh Syntax

```
while condition ; do actions  ; done
```

Example

```
cat userlist.txt | while read USER
do
    mail $USER < mailmsg.txt
done
```

Read usernames from a text file and send the message stored in `mailmsg.txt` to each one.

exit sh csh ksh

exit

Terminate script and exit with the given exit status.

sh Syntax

```
exit n
```

csh Syntax

```
exit  (expression)
```

ksh Syntax

```
exit n
```

n is the exit status (optional). The C Shell can evaluate an expression to determine the number to return for the exit status.

foreach sh csh ksh

Repeat a set of actions once for every occurrence of the *key* in the *list*. foreach

sh Syntax

```
for key in list...  ; do actions ; done
```

csh Syntax

```
foreach key (list)
   ...
end

repeat count command
```

ksh Syntax

```
for key in list ...; do actions ; done
```

goto csh

Shell command to force scripts to process steps out of order. goto

Syntax

```
goto label
```

label is a label somewhere else in the script of the form `label:`.

3
Process Control

continues >>

>>continued

Starting Processes

at

```
/usr/bin/at [options] [arguments]
/usr/bin/batch [options] [arguments]
```


Queue commands to be run at a specific time in the future. The job will be run using a different instance of the user shell. Any output sent to standard out will be mailed to the user. Jobs are spooled to `/var/spool/cron/atjobs`.

After a job has been successfully queued, a status message similar to the following will be returned:

```
commands will be executed using /usr/sbin/tcsh
job 917486999.a at Wed Feb 27 20:29:59 1998
```

Option	Description
`-c`	Run command with `csh` (C shell).
`-f file`	Use *`file`* as the job rather than standard input.
`-k`	Run command with `ksh` (Korn shell).
`-l`	List all scheduled jobs.
`-m`	Notify the user by mail when the job has been run.
`-q queue`	Specify a queue to put the job in or to list with `-l`. The queues are named with single characters—letters a through z.
`-r id`	Remove the job with the job ID specified by *`id`*.
`-s`	Run command with `sh` (Bourne shell).
`-t time`	Run job at *`time`*.

Arguments

The following arguments can be used in conjunction with any of the previous options:

Argument	Description
`Job Id`	Job IDs are reported when jobs are originally scheduled by the at command.

continues >>

>>continued

Argument	Description
`Time`	Time values can be specified in 12-hour format (when used with `AM` or `PM` following the time) or in 24-hour format. The tokens `midnight`, `noon`, and `now` are also supported.

Example	Description

`at now + 1 hour`
`myscript.sh`
`<EOT>`
	Run a command one hour from now.

`at now tomorrow`
`myscript.sh`
`<EOT>`
	Run a command tomorrow.

▸ **See Also** `atq` (58), `atrm` (58), `crontab` (59)

atq

atq

`/usr/bin/atq`

List jobs queued using the `at` or `batch` command.

Option	Description
`-c`	List jobs in the order in which they were queued. (List by creation date/time.)
`-n`	Display the total number of queued jobs.

Example	Description
`atq -c`	Show all pending jobs, in the order in which they were queued.
`atq -n`	Check how many jobs are currently queued.

▸ **See Also** `at` (57), `atrm` (58), `crontab` (59)

atrm

atrm

`/usr/bin/atrm`

Remove jobs that were previously queued by `at` or `batch`.

Option	Description
-a	Remove all jobs from the queue.
-f	Force all informational messages to be suppressed.
-i	Interactively ask for confirmation for each job before it is removed.

▸ See Also at (57), atq (58), crontab (59)

crontab


```
/usr/bin/crontab [filename]
/usr/bin/ [options] [user]
```

Utility to manage a user's crontab file. The crontab file is used by the cron daemon to run jobs at scheduled times.

Option	Description
-e	Edit the current crontab file. The default editor is ed, but can be changed by setting the EDITOR environment variable to the path and name of the editor to use.
-l	List all entries in the crontab file.
-r	Remove all entries in the crontab file.

Date and Time Formats

[*minute*] [*hour*] [*day of month*] [*month*] [*day of week*]

Date or Time	Valid Values
minute	0 to 59
hour	0 to 23
day of month	1 to 31
month	1 to 12
day of week	0 to 6 (Sunday is 0, Monday is 1, and so on.)

An asterisk * in place of any of the date/time fields means "all." A list of dates or times can be given by separating the times with commas, such as in the examples that follow:

Example	Description
`0 2 * * 1-5 /home/➥home/mybackup.sh`	Perform a task every weekday at 2:00 AM (such as run a backup).
`0 12 1,15 * * /home/➥smithj/mytask`	Run a task on the first and fifteenth of each month at 12 noon.
`0,10,20,30,40,50 * * * * /➥home/smithj/checkbot`	Run a task every ten minutes, every hour, every day.
`0 0 7 2 * /home/mulligaj/➥bday.sh 2>&1 > /dev/null`	Run a task on February 7th and suppress any mail that might be sent to the user.
`0 17 * * * /home/smithj/➥mytask &| mail smithj`	Run a task each night at 5:00 PM and mail all output (including standard error) to the user.

▶ **See Also** `atq` (58), `atrm` (58), `ed` (11)

nice

nice

```
/usr/bin/nice [options] command
/usr/xpg4/bin/nice [options] command
```

Run a command with modified scheduling for better CPU usage. `/usr/bin/nice` uses `/usr/bin/sh` to execute commands. `/usr/xpg4/bin/nice` uses `/usr/bin/ksh` to execute commands.

Option	Description
-*n*	Set priority to *n* where *n* is `1...19` (`19` is low priority, `1` is high priority). Default is `10`.

Example	Description
`nice -n 1` *mycommand*	Run a command with a very high priority.
`nice -n 19` *mycommand*	Run a command with a very low priority.

▶ **See Also** `nice` (60), `ps` (67)

time

time

```
/usr/bin/time [options] command
```

Time a command in seconds. The following statistics are given: Elapsed time, User CPU time, System CPU time.

Option	Description
-p	Reformat the output of the time command to be one of the following: ■ `real` *realtime* ■ `user` *usertime* ■ `sys` *systime*

Example	Description
`time ls`	Time the `ls` command.
`time sh -c 'grep key ➥file|uniq -c|sort'`	Time a more complicated command.

▸ **See Also** `ps` (67), `timex` (60)

timex

`/usr/bin/timex [options] command`

Time a command. The following statistics are given: elapsed time, user time, system time, and process accounting data.

Option	Description
-o	If process accounting software is installed, give the number of blocks read/written during execution of the command.
-p	Process accounting. This command only works if process accounting software has been installed.
-f	Must be used with `-p`. Display exit status flags as well.
-h	Must be used with `-p`. Display the hog factor calculated as *(total CPU time)* ÷ *(elapsed time)*.
-k	Must be used with `-p`. Give kcore minutes.
-m	Must be used with `-p`. Display mean core size.
-r	Must be used with `-p`. Display *(user time)* ÷ *(system-time + user-time)*.
-t	Must be used with `-p`. Separate system and user times in the output.
-s	Return the total system time elapsed during the execution of the command.

▸ **See Also** `ps` (67), `time` (60)

Process Status

bg

bg

`bg [job-id]`

This is a built-in shell command used to control processes. Therefore, this command will behave slightly differently for each shell.

Shell	Function
sh	Resume a process that has previously been stopped. A job ID can be specified on the command line. If one is not given, the current job is used.
csh	Run the current or specified job in the background. When a suspended job ID is specified, it is the same as running the job followed by an ampersand (&).
ksh	Resume a suspended job and run it in the background.

Example	Description
bg 2	Run the process with a job ID of 2 in the background.
bg	Resume the current process, running it in the background.

▶ **See Also** fg (62), jobs (63)

fg

fg

`fg [job-id]`

This is a shell-specific command, and therefore it behaves slightly differently for each shell. The basic function is to run a process in the foreground.

Shell	Function
sh	Move a suspended or background job to the foreground.
csh	Move the current or specified job to the foreground.
ksh	Move the current or specified job to the foreground.

Example	Description
`fg 5`	Move the process with a job ID of `5` to the foreground.
`fg`	Move the current suspended job to the foreground.

▶ **See Also** `bg` (62), `jobs` (63)

history

`history`

Lists the last 16 commands.

jobs

`jobs [options] [job-id]`

Built-in shell job control. Options work slightly differently depending on which shell is used.

Options

Shell	Command	Description
`Sh`	`-l`	List the process group IDs and working directories of each job.
	`-p`	Same as `-l` but list only group IDs.
	`-x` *`command [options]`*	Replace each job ID found in command with the process group ID, and then run *`command`*.
`Csh`	`-l`	List the process IDs of each job.
`Ksh`	`-l`	List the job ID, current job, process group ID, state, and command that started the job, for each job.
	`-n`	Notify user of jobs that have exited since the last notification.
	`-p`	Similar to `-l`, but only list process IDs for leaders of jobs.

▶ **See Also** `at` (57), `bg` (62), `fg` (62), `stop` (74)

pgrep

pgrep `/usr/bin/pgrep [options] regexp`

Report process identification numbers (PIDs) matching a regular expression pattern. The pattern is matched against the executable name of the process unless the `-f` option is specified.

Option	Description
`-d delimiter`	Specifies the delimiter to be placed between PIDs. Default is the newline character.
`-f`	Match pattern against full process argument string rather than just the executable name.
`-g groups`	Only processes in the process groups specified by ***groups***.
`-G gids`	Only processes with real group IDs matching those in ***gids***.
`-l`	Verbose output. Prints more information including process name.
`-n`	Returns only the most recent process matching the pattern.
`-p ppids`	Only processes with the parent process IDs specified by *ppids*.
`-s sids`	Only processes with the specified session IDs are shown.
`-t terminals`	Only processes that are associated with the specified terminals are shown.
`-u euids`	Only processes with effective IDs matching those specified.
`-U uids`	Only processes with real user IDs matching those specified.
`-v`	Invert the pattern matching. Show only those not matching the pattern. Similar to using `grep -v`.
`-x`	Only processes with executable name exactly matching the one specified on the command line are reported.
`-signal`	Specify a signal to send to each process reported. Signals are given in Appendix F.

Example	Description
`pgrep sendmail`	Return the process identification number for the sendmail process.

continues >>

continued

Example	Description
`pgrep -x inetd -HUP`	Send a SIGHUP (hangup) signal to the process with an executable name exactly matching `inetd`.
`pgrep -t pts/0 ➥-KILL`	Send a SIGKILL (kill) signal to all processes associated with pseudoterminal 0. This would have the same effect as `pkill -t pts/0`.

▶ **See Also** `pkill` (73), `prstat` (65), `ps` (67)

prstat

`/usr/bin/prstat [options] [interval]`

prstat

This command reports statistics on the current active processes in a manner very similar to the `top` command. The default action of `prstat` is to display statistics on all processes, but the output can be limited by adding options to the command line. Unless the `-c` option is used, the statistics are updated in-place rather than scrolling the display. The statistical update period can be specified in seconds on the command line.

Option	Description
`-a`	Adds per-user statistics to the default output mode, including: number of processes, username, total virtual memory size, memory resident set size, percent usage, cumulative execution time, and percent CPU usage.
`-c`	New statistics are printed below the current screen of statistics rather than updating the current screen.
`-C list`	Report only those processes bound to the processor given in `list`, expressed as integers.
`-L`	Report light-weight-process (LWP) statistics.
`-m`	Report microstate process statistics.
`-n n1,n2`	Limit the number of output lines to the number of processes specified by *n1*, and (optionally) limit the output to the number of users specified by *n2*.
`-p pids`	Report only those process id numbers specified in `pids`.

continues >>

>>continued

Option	Description
`-P cpus`	Report only those processes that have recently been executed by the processor specified by `cpus`.
`-R`	Force `prstat` to run in real-time scheduling mode, giving it priority over other processes. (superuser only)
`-s` *`criterion`*	Sort output by the specified criterion in descending order (highest first). The sorting criterion can be one of the following: `cpu` - CPU usage (Default) `time` - Execution time `size` - Process image size `rss` - Resident set size `pri` - Process priority
`-S`	Same as `-s` but sorts in ascending order (lowest first).
`-t`	Show user statistics only. Output includes: number of processes, username, total virtual memory size, memory resident set size, percent usage, cumulative execution time, and percent CPU usage.This option can not be used with `-v`, `-m`, or `-a`.
`-u` *`euids`*	Report only those processes with effective user id numbers matching those specified in *`euids`*.
`-U` *`uids`*	Report only those processes with real user id numbers matching those specified in *`uids`*.
`-v`	Verbose output. Show all statistics for processes.

Heading	Description
`PID`	Process identification number
`USERNAME`	Real username
`SIZE`	Total virtual memory size
`STATE`	Process state: running on cpu, sleeping, runnable, zombie, or stopped
`PRI`	Priority
`NICE`	Nice value of process

Heading	Description
TIME	Cumulative execution time
CPU	Percent CPU usage
PROCESS	Process name (or name of the executed file)
LWPID	Light-weight process ID number
NLWP	Number of light-weight processes
USR	Percent time in user mode
SYS	Percent time in system mode
TRP	Percent time handling system traps
TFL	Percent time handling text page faults
DFL	Percent time handling data page faults
SLP	Percent time in sleep mode
VCX	Voluntary context switches
ICX	Involuntary context switches
SCL	System calls
SIG	Received signals

Example	Description
`prstat -t`	Show summary of process information for each user.
`prstat -n10 -scpu`	Show the top 10 processes by CPU usage.

▸ **See Also** `nice` (60), `pgrep` (64), `pkill` (73), `ps` (67), `renice` (71)

ps

`/usr/bin/ps [options]`

Display information about processes currently running.

Option	Description
-a	List all processes that are not group leaders.
-A	List all processes.
-c	Format output as described in `priocntl`.

continues >>

>>continued

Option	Description
`-d`	List all processes except session leaders.
`-e`	List all processes that are currently active.
`-f`	Format output as a full listing.
`-g` *`grouplist`*	List processes for listed group leaders.
`-G` *`gidlist`*	List processes that have a realgroup ID listed in *`gidlist`*.
`-j`	List processes, including session ID and group ID.
`-l`	Format output as a long listing.
`-o` *`format`*	Format output as specified by *`format`*.
`-p` *`proclist`*	List processes of those with process ID numbers specified in *`proclist`*.
`-s` *`sidlist`*	List processes for all session leaders listed in *`sidlist`*.
`-t` *`term`*	List all processes connected to the terminal specified by *`term`*.
`-u` *`uidlist`*	List all processes with the same effective UID as those given in *`uidlist`*.
`-U` *`uidlist`*	List all processes with the same real UID as those listed in *`uidlist`*.

Output Headings

Heading	Description
`F`	Flags
`S`	State ■ `O`: Running on CPU ■ `S`: Sleeping ■ `R`: Runnable ■ `Z`: Zombie ■ `T`: Stopped
`UID`	Effective user ID
`PID`	Process ID
`PPID`	Parent's process ID

continues >>

ntinued

Heading	Description
C	CPU usage for scheduling
CLS	Scheduling class
PRI	Priority
NI	nice value
ADDR	Memory address
SZ	Size of swappable image (given in pages)
WCHAN	The address of the process that the listed process is waiting for
STIME	Start time
TTY	Controlling terminal
TIME	Total active time for the process
CMD	Full command name
PGID	Process group leader PID
SID	Session leader PID

▸ **See Also** `at` (57), `atq` (58), `kill` (72)

ps (UCB version)

`/usr/ucb/ps [options]`

Show process information.

Option	Description
-a	List all processes, excluding process group leaders.
-c	List processes with more reliable command name information.
-g	List all processes including process group leaders.
-l	Format as a long listing: F, PPID, CP, PRI, NI, SZ, RSS, and WCHAN.
-n	Replace USER field with UID (numerical format).
-r	List on running processes.
-s	Display total CPU time for processes, including child times.

continues >>

>>continued

Option	Description
`-t` *`term`*	List processes controlled by the terminal specified by *`term`*.
`-u`	Format as user listing: `USER`, `SZ`, `RSS`, or `START`.
`-U`	Update `ps` database.
`-v`	Display virtual memory.
`-w`	Wide output format, using 132 characters (rather than 80).
`-x`	List processes that have no controlling terminal.
`-ww`	No limits on output width.

Output Headings

Heading	Description
`CP`	CPU usage factor (short-term)
`F`	Flags ■ `00`: Terminated ■ `01`: System process ■ `02`: Tracing parent ■ `04`: Parent is waiting ■ `08`: Process in main memory ■ `10`: Process locked in main memory
`NI`	Niceness
`PPID`	Parent PID
`PRI`	Priority
`RSS`	Resident memory size in KB
`SIZE/SZ`	Size in KB (*`stack + data`*)
`START`	Start time
`UID`	UID of process owner
`USER`	Username of process owner
`WCHAN`	Address of a process for which a sleeping process is waiting

▶ **See Also** `nice` (60), `ps` (67), `renice` (71)

renice

`/usr/bin/renice [options] ID`

Change the priority of a process that is already running.

Option	Description
`-g`	Treat all operands as unsigned decimal integer process GIDs.
`-n n`	Increment the priority of the process by *n*.
`-p`	Treat all operands as unsigned decimal integer PIDs.
`-u`	Treat all operands as users.

Example	Description
`renice -n 1 345`	Increase the priority of a running process (with PID of `345`).
`renice -n -1 345`	Decrease the priority of a running process.
`renice -n 19 345`	Maximize the priority of a running process.

▶ **See Also** `kill` (72), `nice` (60), `ps` (67)

w

`/usr/bin/w [options] [user]`

The `w` command displays information about the users currently logged into the local system.

Option	Description
`-h`	Do not print headers.
`-l`	Long output format. Display more information.
`-s`	Short output format. Do not display as much information.
`-u`	Show header line with `uptime` and system information.

▶ **See Also** `ps` (67), `uptime` (146), `rwho` (91), `whodo` (72)

whodo

whodo

```
/usr/bin/whodo [options] [user]
```

Show information about the users currently logged into the local system based on `utmpx`, `ps_data`, and `pid` files.

Option	Description
`-h`	Do not print headers.
`-l`	Long output format. Show more information about each user.

▶ **See Also** `ps` (69), `uptime` (146), `rwho` (91)

Stopping Processes

kill

kill

```
/usr/bin/kill -s signal pid-list
/usr/bin/kill -l [stat]
/usr/bin/kill [-signal] pid-list
```

Terminate (kill) processes or send special signals to processes. Use `ps` or `prstat` to obtain process ID numbers.

Option	Description
`-l`	List all signals, if no other arguments are given. If an exit status is specified by *`stat`*, the terminating signal of the process will be displayed.
`-s` *`signal`*	Specify the signal to send to the process.

Signals

The following is a list of signals for use with `kill` (generated from `kill -l`). For a full description of signals, see Appendix F, "Signals."

```
ABRT     ALRM     BUS      CLD      CONT     EMT      FPE
FREEZE   HUP      ILL      INT      KILL     LWP      PIPE
POLL     PROF     PWR      QUIT     RTMAX    RTMAX-1
RTMAX-2  RTMAX-3  RTMIN    RTMIN+1  RTMIN+2  RTMIN+3
SEGV     STOP     SYS      TERM     THAW     TRAP
TSTP     TTIN     TTOU     URG      USR1     USR2
VTALRM   WAITING  WINCH    XCPU     XFSZ
```

Example	Description
`kill -9 102`	Kill a process and all of its children.
`Kill -HUP 203`	Restart a process.
`Kill -HUP 'ps -ax	➥grep inetd	grep ➥-v grep	awk ➥'{print $1}''`	Restart `inetd`.
`ps -aux	grep inetd	➥grep -v grep	awk ' ➥{print $1}' |xargs ➥kill -9`	Kill all processes belonging to the user `smithj`.

▶ **See Also** `jobs` (63), `ps` (67)

pkill

`/usr/bin/pkill [options] *regexp*`

pkill

Kill processes matching the specified pattern. This command behaves similar to `pgrep`, except that it sends a SIGKILL signal to every process that matches the regular expression.

Option	Description
`-f`	Match pattern against full process argument string rather than just the executable name.
`-g` *`groups`*	Only processes in the process groups specified by *`groups`*.
`-G` *`gids`*	Only processes with real group Ids matching those in *`gids`*.
`-n`	Returns only the most recent process matching the pattern.
`-p` *`ppids`*	Only processes with the parent process Ids specified by *`ppids`*.
`-s` *`sids`*	Only processes with the specified session Ids are shown.
`-t` *`terminals`*	Only processes that are associated with the specified terminals are shown.
`-u` *`euids`*	Only processes with effective Ids matching those specified.
`-U` *`uids`*	Only processes with real user Ids matching those specified.

continues >>

>>continued

Option	Description
`-v`	Invert the pattern matching. Show only those not matching the pattern. Similar to using *grep -v*.
`-x`	Only processes with executable name exactly matching the one specified on the command line are reported.
`-signal`	Specify a signal to send to each process reported. Default signal is SIGKILL. Signals are given in Appendix F.

Example	Description
`pkill -U236`	Kill all processes belonging to the user with userid 236.
`Pkill -n1 -U595 -scpu`	Kill the process owned by userid 595 with the highest CPU usage.
`Pkill sendmail`	Kill all sendmail processes.

▶ **See Also** `pgrep` (64), `ps` (67), `prstat` (65)

stop

stop

`stop [job-id]`

Stop the job identified by *job-id*. If no ID is given, the background job is stopped.

▶ **See Also** `at` (57), `bg` (62), `fg` (62)

4
Network Clients and Utilities

Informational Utilities

finger

finger

```
/usr/bin/finger [options] [user]
/usr/bin/finger [options] [user@host]
/usr/bin/finger [options] [user@host@host@host.... etc.]
```

Retrieve information about users from the current host or remote servers. The remote server must be running a finger daemon (`in.fingerd`).

Option	Description
`-b`	Do not show home directories and shells in the information given.
`-f`	Do not print headers.
`-h`	Do not show `.project` files.
`-I`	Idle format. Output includes username, terminal, login time, and idle time.
`-l`	Long format. Output includes all information.
`-m`	Match *`user`* with username and not the full name of the user.
`-p`	Do not show `.plan` files.
`-q`	Quick format. Output includes username, terminal, and login time.
`-s`	Short format.
`-w`	Short format without printing full name.

Files

File	Description
`.project`	Text file that can optionally be kept in the user's home directory. If present, it is printed in the `Project:` field of the finger output.
`.plan`	Text file that can optionally be kept in the user's home directory. If present, it is printed at the end of the finger information for the user.

Finger Forwarding

Finger forwarding is when a `finger` request is sent to a remote host and then "forwarded" to another host, where it is processed and the resulting information is sent back to the original sender of the request. Consider the following example:

```
finger smithj@host1.com@host2.com@host3.com
```

The `finger` request will go from the local host to `host3.com`.

`host3.com` will forward the request to `host2.com`, `host2.com` will forward the request to `host1.com`, and `host1.com` will send the `finger` information (if available) back to the local host.

In each case, the request will be logged on the remote system as coming from the forwarding host. `host1.com` will log the request as being from the local host. It is for this reason that some system administrators disable finger forwarding on their servers. This is a recommended practice that can potentially make your entire network more secure. See `in.fingerd` for details.

Finger forwarding is not supported on all servers. The specifications for finger forwarding are defined in RFC 1288.

Example	Description
`finger`	To retrieve finger information for all users on the local host.
`finger` *`user`*	To retrieve finger information for a single user on the local system.
`finger` *`@remotehost.com`*	To retrieve finger information for all users currently logged into a remote host.
`finger` *`user@remotehost`*`.com`	To retrieve finger information for a single user on a remote host.

▸**See Also** `rwho` (91), `whois` (86)

netstat

`netstat [`*`options`*`] [`*`interval`*`]`

netstat

Show current network information for the local host. This command can be used to show all network connections to the local system, routing information, and network interface information.

Option	Description
[*interval*]	An interval can be specified, causing `netstat` to report the network status every *`interval`* seconds. This interval is optional. If omitted, `netstat` will run once.
`-a`	All socket and routing table states and entries are shown. If this option is omitted, daemon processes will not be shown and only limited routing table information will be given.
`-f` *fam*	Only show reports for those that are of the specified family. The family can be either of the following: ■ `inet`: AF_INET address family ■ `unix`: AF_UNIX address family
`-g`	Multicast group memberships for all interfaces are displayed.
`-I`	Display TCP/IP interface state.
`-I` *interface*	The current state of the network interface specified by *`interface`* is shown.
`-m`	Display statistics for `STREAMS`.
`-M`	Multicast routing tables are shown. Can be used with the `-s` option to give summary statistics using the multicast routing tables.
`-n`	Do not resolve addresses. This option will cause any hosts to be reported by IP address rather than by hostname. Using this usually greatly increases the speed of the `netstat` command.
`-p`	Display address resolution tables (ARP tables).
`-p` *protocol*	Only show network statistics for sockets using the protocol specified by *`protocol`*. This can be `tcp` or `udp`.
`-r`	Display routing tables.
`-s`	Give statistics sorted by protocol, such as `tcp` or `udp`. If used with `-M`, multicast routing statistics are used instead.
`-v`	Verbose. Reports are given in more detail.

TCP Socket States

State	Description
`CLOSED`	Closed. The socket has been closed and is not in use.
`CLOSE_WAIT`	Wait for close. The remote side has closed the connection and the local host is waiting for the socket to close.

continues >>

ontinued

State	Description
CLOSING	Closing. Socket has been closed and the remote connection has been shut down. The socket is waiting for acknowledgment.
ESTABLISHED	Connection established. A TCP/IP connection is established and working.
FIN_WAIT_1	Finish wait 1. The socket has been successfully closed and waiting to shut down the connection.
FIN_WAIT_2	Finish wait 2. Socket has been closed and is waiting for remote side to shut down connection.
LAST_ACK	Last acknowledgment. The remote side of the connection has been shut down and closed. Waiting for acknowledgment.
LISTEN	Listening. The socket is currently listening. Programs such as servers and daemons will usually spawn processes that open sockets to listen.
SYN_SENT	Synchronization sent. The socket is attempting to establish a connection with a remote host.
SYN_RECEIVED	Synchronization received. A response has been received after sending a synchronization request. The connection is being made.
TIME_WAIT	Wait after close. Socket has been closed, waiting for remote shutdown retransmission.

Example	Description
`netstat`	Check what remote hosts are connected to the local system.
`netstat -n`	Check what remote hosts are connected to the local system, but leave addresses as IP numbers (much faster).

▶**See Also** `rpcinfo` (82)

nslookup

`/usr/sbin/nslookup [options] [host] [DNS server]`

nslookup

Utility to query an Internet domain name server to resolve an IP address to a name or a name to an IP address. By default, `nslookup` uses the server in `/etc/resolv.conf` as the DNS server. It can be used in two general ways:

- Hostname specified on the command line.
- Run without hostname specified to use interactive mode.

Command-Line Options

Option	Description
`-option`	Set or change lookup state information. For example: `-retry=5` See the later section "State Keywords" for a list.
`DNSserver`	Specify a DNS server. If no DNS server is given, the one listed in `/etc/resolv.conf` is used.
`host`	Host can be either a domain name or an IP address. If a host is specified on the command line, the results are returned and interactive mode is not used.

Interactive Mode Commands

Command	Description
CTRL+D	Exit.
`exit`	Exit.
`finger[name]`	Finger the last host that was successfully looked up.
`help`	Show a command summary. Using `?` is the same as using `help`.
`host[server]`	Look up host using server as the DNS server. If *`server`* is not given, the DNS server listed in `/etc/resolv.conf` is used.
`ls [-ah]`	List all domain name service information for the domain: ■ `-a`: Show all aliases as well. ■ `-h`: Show host information including CPU and OS information.
`root`	Change the default server to `ns.nic.ddn.mil`.

`set`	Set a keyword value. Keyword definitions must be of one of the following forms:
	`set keyword`
	`set keyword = value`
	See the subsequent "State Keywords" section for a list of all keywords that can be set.

`server domain`	Change the default server to the domain specified by *`domain`*.
`view file`	Use more to view the given *`file`*.

State Keywords

Keyword	Description
`all`	Show all set keywords and their values.
`debug` or `nodebug`	Turn debugging on or off. The default is `nodebug`.
`defname` or `nodefname`	If `defname` is set, the default domain name is appended to every hostname that is looked up. The default is `nodefname`.
`domain = file`	Change the default domain to *`file`*. If no file is given, the domain given in `/etc/resolv.conf` is used.
`querytype = type`	Set query type (specified in RFC 833): ■ `A`: Host Internet address (default) ■ `CNAME`: Canonical name ■ `HINFO`: Host CPU and OS type ■ `MD`: Mail destination ■ `MX`: Mail exchanger ■ `MB`: Mailbox domain name ■ `MG`: Mail group member ■ `MINFO`: Mailbox or mail list information
`recurse` or `norecurse`	If `recurse` is set and the current server does not have the information, it will check other servers. The default is `recurse`.
`retry=n`	Retry the request *`n`* times if the initial request fails.
`root=host`	Change the root server (default is `ns.nic.ddn.mil`) to *`host`*.
`timeout=seconds`	Set the timeout for a query to the number of seconds specified by *`seconds`*.
`vc` or `novc`	Force the use of a virtual circuit. The default is `novc`.

▸**See Also** `whois` (86)

ping

`/usr/sbin/ping [options] [host] [timeout]`

ping

Uses the Internet Control Message Protocol (ICMP) to check whether a remote host is alive on the network.

Local host→ECHO_REQUEST→ Remote host

Local host←ECHO_RESPONSE← Remote host

Command	Description
`-I interface`	Use the interface specified by *interface* for outgoing packets.
`-I n`	Interval. Wait *n* seconds between pings.
`-l`	Loose source route. The packet will find a route to the destination host. Using this option, the reply packet will discover a route back to the originating host (not necessarily the same as the original route). This can be used to diagnose possible routing problems between two hosts on a network.
`-L`	No loopback of multicast packets. Do not copy multicast packets to members of the host group of the interface.
`-n`	Numerical addresses. Show IP numbers for hosts rather than DNS names.
`-r`	Skip routing tables. Packet is sent directly to host. This only works if the remote host is on the same network segment.
`-R`	Route recording. The route of the packet is stored in the IP header.
`-t livetime`	Time to live for packets is set to *livetime*. The default is one hop.
`-v`	Verbose output. List all ICMP packets received.

Example

Test connectivity as seen by NFS packets (using 8192 byte packets). Show degradation in passing through alternative packet-sized routing equipment.

```
ping -sv hostname 8192
```

►**See Also** whois (86)

rpcinfo

rpcinfo

`/usr/bin/rcpinfo [options] [host] [prog] [version]`

Use RPC calls to report RPC information. RPC information for both local and remote hosts can be reported. In general, `rpcinfo` can be used in three ways:

- List all registered RPC services on a host.
- List all `rpcbind` version 2 registered RPC services on a host.
- Make a call (procedure 0) to a specific program on a host.

Option	Description
`-a` *addr*	Use the address specified by *addr* as the universal address for the service. Used to `ping` a remote service.
`-b`	Broadcast procedure 0 of the service listed and report all responses from the network that are received.
`-d`	Delete a service registration for the specified program and version number.
`-l`	List entries matching the specified program and version number on a host.
`-m`	Show summary statistics for `rcpbind` on a remote host. Statistics for `rcpbind` versions 2, 3, and 4 are shown.
`-p`	Probe. The host is probed using version 2 of the `rpcbind` protocol. If a host is specified, that host is probed. If no host is specified, the local host is probed.
`-s`	Short list. Give a short list of all RPC programs registered on the specified remote host, or on the local host if no remote host is specified.
`-T` *transport*	Require the RPC service to be on the transport specified by *transport*. If this option is omitted, the transport in the environment variable `NETPATH` is used. If `NETPATH` is not set, the `netconfig` database is used to determine the transport.

Example	Description
`rpcinfo`	Check what RPC services are registered on the local host.
`rpcinfo` *remotehost*	Check what RPC services are registered on a remote host.
`rpcinfo -p` *remotehost*	Check what RPC services are registered on a remote host, showing only version 2 programs.

rup

`/usr/sbin/rup [`*options*`] [`*host*`]`

rup

Similar to the `uptime` command, but displays information for remote hosts. If no host is specified, the request is broadcast to all machines. Remote systems must be running the `rstatd` daemon to respond. Note that `ruptime` uses the `in.rwhod` daemon, whereas `rup` uses the `rstatd` daemon.

Option	Description
-h	Sort output by host name.
-l	Sort output by load average.
-t	Sort output by uptime.

▶See Also ruptime (84)

ruptime

ruptime

`/usr/bin/ruptime [options]`

Check information for a remote host. Information given is similar to that of uptime. Each machine on the local network is queried and a response must be received within five minutes. The remote server must be running the remote who daemon (in.rwhod). Note that ruptime uses the in.rwhod daemon, whereas rup uses the rstatd daemon.

Option	Description
-a	Include all users in the output. If omitted, any user idle for more than an hour will be excluded.
-l	Output sorted by load average.
-r	Output given in reverse order.
-t	Output sorted by uptime.
-u	Output sorted by number of users.

▶See Also rwho (91), rusers (84)

rusers

rusers

`/usr/bin/rusers [options] [host]`

A remote version of who to find out who is logged in to a remote host. More than one host can be specified on the command line. If no hosts are specified, rusers sends out a broadcast for rusersd protocol, version 3. This is followed by a broadcast of version 2. Hosts must be running the ruserd daemon in order to respond.

Option	Description
-a	Report machines even with no users logged in.
-h	Alphabetically list hosts.
-i	Reports are sorted by idle time.

Option	Description
-l	Long report format, giving more detail.
-u	Reports are sorted by the number of users logged in.

▸**See Also** rwall (97), rwho (91)

traceroute

/usr/sbin/traceroute [*options*] host [*len*]

Trace the route IP packets take from one Internet/intranet host to another host. This utility can use both IPv4 (time to live) and IPv6 (hop limit). The maximum hop limit is set to 30 by default but can be changed by using the -m option. traceroute traces the route from one host to another host at that moment. Given the dynamic nature of Internet routing today, results may vary from moment to moment.

Option	Description
-A addressfam	Specify the address family for the target host. Arguments can be inet for IPv4 and inet6 for IPv6.
-a	For multi-homed hosts, this option will probe all IP addresses.
-c class	Specify the probe packet traffic class as an integer from 0 to 255.
-d	Set the debugging socket option (SO_DEBUG).
-F	Set the no-fragment option.
-f firsthop	Override the default first-hop setting of 1, and set the starting time-to-live hop limit to *firsthop*.
-g gateway	Set up to eight additional gateways to use.
-I	Use ICMP ECHO rather than UDP datagrams.
-i interface	Specify source IP network interface (for IPv4) or the packet-transmitting interface (for IPv6). Can be an integer representing an interface index or an interface name (such as le0).
-L flow	Set the IPv6 flow label for the packets. Must be an integer between 0 and 1048575.
-l	Show the time-to-live for each packet received.
-m maxhop	Override the default, maximum time-to-live value of 30, and set it to *maxhop*.

continues >>

>>continued

Option	Description
`-n`	Do not perform DNS lookups on IP addresses.
`-P seconds`	Specify a pause (in seconds) between probe packets.
`-p port`	Specify the base UDP port to use when probing. Default value is 33434.
`-Q timeouts`	Stop the trace after the specified number of timeouts have been received.
`-q queries`	Specify the number of queries for probing. Default value is 3.
`-r`	Skip routing tables and send packets directly to host on network. Cannot be used with `-g`.
`-s sourceaddr`	Specify the source address when sending packets. The source address must match one of the machine's interfaces.
`-t servicetype`	Specify the type of service (ToS) for outgoing packets. Must be between 0 and 255. Default value is 0.
`-v`	Verbose. Show extra information when tracing, including packet size and destination.
`-w seconds`	Specify the time to wait for a response to a probe packet. Default value is 5.
`-x`	Skip checksums when using IPv4.

Example	Description
`traceroute www.microsoft.com`	Trace packet path from `localhost` to `www.microsoft.com`
`traceroute -vn helios`	Trace packet path from `localhost` to a machine called helios on your LAN and do not perform DNS lookups, showing verbose output.

▸**See Also** `netstat` (77), `ping` (81)

whois

whois

`/usr/bin/whois [options] [string]`

Check the InterNIC database for a domain record or records. If an exact match is found for the string, the domain record for the domain is printed. If the string matches multiple domains, summaries of the domains are shown. Other NICs can be checked by specifying the host using the `-h` option.

Example	Description
`whois` *`somedomain.com`*	Check if a domain is registered and/or find out contact and billing information for the domain.
`whois [`*`string`*`]`	Find all domains containing a certain string.

Option	Description
`-h`	Specify which host to use for lookups to find information at other NICs (optional).

▸**See Also** `finger` (76)

File Transfers

ftp

`/usr/bin/ftp [`*`options`*`] [`*`host`*`]`

File Transfer Protocol (FTP) client to upload and download files over the network. If no host is specified on the command line, an `ftp>` command prompt is given. The remote server must be running an FTP daemon (`in.ftpd`).

Option	Description
`-d`	Debugging mode.
`-g`	Do not use filename globbing.
`-i`	Do not ask for confirmation for each file of a multiple file transfer (non-interactive mode).
`-n`	Disable auto-login.
`-v`	Verbose. Show all diagnostics and give a summary of data transfer statistics.

Command	Description
`?` *`command`*	Same as `help`.
`!` *`command`*	Run *`command`* using the shell. If no command is given, the shell is used as the command interpreter until **`exit`** is typed.

continues >>

>>continued

Command	Description
`$ macro`	Run the macro specified by *macro*. See `macdef`, later in this table.
`account ➥password`	Provide an extra password to the remote system if necessary. If no password is given, the user is prompted for one.
`append ➥file1 file2`	Append the local file *file1* to the remote file, *file2*.
`ascii`	Set the transfer mode to ASCII (rather than binary).
`bell`	Toggle beeping after each file transfer.
`binary`	Set the transfer mode to binary (rather than ASCII).
`bye`	Close session and exit.
`case`	Toggle case mapping. Default is `off`. ■ `on`: All uppercase characters on the remote system are changed to lowercase. ■ `off`: No changes are made to upper- or lowercase characters.
`cd dir`	Change directories on the remote host to *dir*.
`cdup`	Change the current directory on the remote host to the parent directory.
`close`	Close FTP session.
`cr`	Toggle carriage-return (CR) stripping during ASCII mode.
`delete file`	Delete file on the remote host.
`debug`	Toggle debugging mode. Default is `off`.
`dir`	Give a directory listing of the current remote host working directory. Output is similar to that of `ls`.
`disconnect`	Same as `close`.
`get file ➥filename`	Download the file specified by *file* from the remote host to the local host. If *filename* is given, that name is used on the local host. If not, the remote name is used.
`glob`	Toggle globbing for use with `mdelete`, `mget`, and `mput`. Globbing is filename expansion, the same as done by `sh`.
`hash`	Toggle hash marks (#). If on, hash marks will usually be printed for every 8,192 bytes transferred. Some systems may use a different hash mark size, in which case it will be specified. Another common hash mark size is 2,048 bytes.

continues >>

continued

Command	Description
`help` *`command`*	Give help on *`command`*. If no command is specified, a list of commands is displayed.
`lcd` *`dir`*	Change local directory to *`dir`*.
`ls`	Similar to `dir`, but gives a briefer directory listing. If the `-a` option is given, all files are listed, including those that begin with a dot (`.`).
`macdef` *`macro`*	Define a macro by the name of *`macro`*. Input following `macdef` will be stored as the macro until a new line is given.
`mdelete` *`files`*	Multiple `delete`. Delete the file or files given by *`files`*.
`mdir` *`files`*	Multiple directory listing. List the files or directories specified.
`mget` *`files`*	Multiple `get`. Download all the files specified.
`mkdir` *`dir`*	Make directory. Create a directory on the remote system called *`dir`*.
`mls` *`files`*	Multiple `ls`. Same as `ls`, but more than one file or directory can be given.
`mput` *`files`*	Multiple `put`. Upload all of the files specified.
`open` *`host port`*	Open a connection with host on port. If no port is given, 21/tcp is used.
`prompt`	Toggle interactive prompting. If this is off, no prompt will be given between file transfers when using `mput` or `mget`.
`proxy` *`command`*	Run command on a secondary server. This can be used to transfer files between two remote servers.
`put file` ➥*`filename`*	Upload file to the remote host. If filename is given, it is renamed to filename on the remote host. If no filename is given, the original filename is used on the remote server.
`pwd`	Print the current working directory.
`quit`	Same as `bye`.
`quote` *`args`*	Send the specified file directly to the remote FTP server.
`recv` *`file`*	Same as `get`.
`remotehelp`	Same as `help`, but the remote server rather than the local server is used to obtain help.
`rename` *`old new`*	Rename the file specified by *`old`* from *`old`* to *`new`*.
`reset`	Clear the reply queue.

continues >>

>>continued

Command	Description
`rmdir` *`dir`*	Remove the directory on the remote server specified by *`dir`*.
`runique`	Toggle unique filenames. If it is on, and a duplicate filename is found, the new file will have a *`.n`* appended to it, where *`n`* is an integer that increments up starting at 1.
`send` *`file`*	Same as `put`.
`status`	Display current status.
`sunique`	Remote unique file naming. Refer to `runique`, earlier in this table.
`type` *`type`*	Set transfer type to *`type`*. Either binary (image) or ASCII (text).
`user` *`username`*	Give username to the remote system when logging in.
`verbose`	Toggle verbose mode. If verbose mode is on, all FTP server responses are shown.

FTP Autologin

A `.netrc` file can be placed in a user home directory to allow ftp file transfers to be automated to some extent. The file contains information about the connection including the hostname, login name, password, and other optional information.

The general format is as follows:

```
machine hostname login loginname password password
```

Consider the following example:

```
machine ftp.remotehost.com login anonymous password
➥user@localhost.com
```

It is very important that `.netrc` file permissions are set so that other users cannot access the file because it contains account names and passwords. Use the `chmod` command to set the `.netrc` file to mode 600.

▶**See Also** `rcp` (90)

rcp

rcp

`/usr/bin/rcp [`*`options`*`] [`*`files`*`]`

Copy files across a network. In order to use `rcp`, remote commands must be allowed by using `rsh`. This requires the use of a `.rhosts` file or `/etc/hosts.equiv`. See `rsh` for details.

Options	Description
-p	Attempt to preserve all the file properties of the original, giving the copy the same time, mode, and ACL if possible.
-r	Recursively copy the directory specified by the ***files*** argument.

Arguments

The arguments of `rcp` are specified as remote files or local files.

For local files:

```
path
```

For remote files:

```
host:path
user@host:path
```

> **rcp Warning**
>
> `rcp` cannot properly copy directories containing symbolic links. A possible alternative is to use `cpio` to pipe the directory to `rcp`.

Example	Description
rcp *remotehost:testfile testfile*	Copy a file from a remote machine to the local host.
rcp *remote1:report*.txt ➥*remote2:newreport*.txt	Copy a file between two remote machines (third-party copy).

▸**See Also** rsh (99), ftp (87)

rwho

/usr/bin/rwho [*options*]

List who is logged on to machines on the local network. Output is similar to that of `who`. The remote server must be running the `in.rwhod` daemon.

▸**See Also** finger (79), rusers (84), rwho (91)

Communications

mail

mail

`/usr/bin/mail [options] [recipient]`

Utility to read or send (using `sendmail`) electronic mail to users on the local system and over the Internet. If mail is run with no recipient given, it can be used to read and process mail. A question mark (`?`) will be given as a command prompt. If mail exits while a message is being composed, it will be saved to `dead.letter` in the current directory. Incoming mail is saved in `/var/mail/`*`username`* or at a location specified in the `$MAIL` variable, where *`username`* is the current login name of the user running mail.

Option	Description
`-e`	Mail is not printed. However, mail returns an error code: ■ `1` if there is no mail. ■ `0` if there is mail.
`-f file`	Use the file specified by *`file`* as the mailfile rather than the default.
`-h`	Show headers instead of latest message when starting.
`-m type`	Add a header to the message of the form: `Message-Type:` *`type`*
`-p`	Print all messages without checking dispositions.
`-P`	Print all headers when displaying messages.
`-q`	Quit and exit when an interrupt is received.
`-r`	Print messages in "first-in, first-out" order.
`-t`	Add a header to the message (for each recipient) of the form: `To:` *`recipient`*
`-w`	Do not wait for remote transfer program to exit before sending.
`-x` *`level`*	Set debugging level to *`level`* (creates a tracefile in `/tmp`).

Command	Description
?	Help. Displays all commands with their usages.
#	Print the current message number.
-	Previous message.
+ or newline	Next message.
!command	Use the shell to run command.
a	Display a message that arrived since mail was started.
d	■ d or dp: Delete the current message and display the next one. ■ d *n*: Delete message number *n*. ■ dq: Delete the current message and then quit.
h	■ h: Show headers for current message. ■ h *n*: Show headers for message number *n*. ■ h a: Show headers for all messages. ■ h d: Show headers for messages marked for deletion.
m *recipient*	Send the current message to *recipient*, and delete it.
number	Go to message number *n*.
p	Reprint the current message, ignoring non-printable characters.
P	Reprint current message showing all headers.
q or **CTRL+D**	Quit. Any messages that were marked for deletion are not deleted.
r *recipients*	Reply to sender. If *recipients* are specified, they are carbon-copied on the mail.
s *mailfile*	Save messages in the file specified by *mailfile*. Default file is mbox.
u *n*	Undelete message number *n*. If no number is given, the last message read is undeleted.
w *file*	Write the current message to *file*, suppressing any headers. If no file is given, mbox is used.
x	Save all messages and exit.
y *file*	Same as w.

►**See Also** write (98)

mail (UCB version)

mail (UCB version)

```
/usr/ucb/mail [options] users
/usr/ucb/mail
```

Use the UCB version of the mail utility to read or send (using `sendmail`) electronic mail to users on the local system and over the Internet. If mail is run with no recipient given, it can be used to read and process mail. A `?` will be given as a command prompt. If mail exits while a message is being composed, it will be saved to `dead.letter` in the current directory. Incoming mail is saved in `/var/mail/`*`username`* or at a location specified in the `$MAIL` variable in which *`username`* is the current login name of the user running mail.

Option	Description
`-B`	No buffer. Neither standard input nor standard output.
`-b` *`bcc`*	Blind carbon copy. Blind carbon copy the users in the list *`bcc`*. More than one recipient may be listed, but they must be enclosed in quotes.
`-c` *`cc`*	Carbon copy. Carbon copy the users in the list *`cc`*. More than one recipient may be listed, but they must be enclosed in quotes.
`-d`	Debug. Extra debugging information is given.
`-e`	Test for mail. No output is given. A return value is given indicating the presence of mail: ■ `0`: Mail ■ `1`: No mail
`-F`	The message is recorded in a file with the same name as the recipient.
`-f` *`msgfile`*	Read messages out of the file specified by *`msgfile`* rather than the default mailbox file.
`-H`	Header summary. Only message headers are shown.
`-h` *`num`*	Set the maximum number of "network hops" to *`num`*. Setting this option will prevent endless mail loops.
`-I`	Include newsgroup and article-id headers.
`-N`	No initial header summary.
`-n`	The system default rc files (`mailx.rc` and `Mail.rc`) are not read upon startup.
`-r` *`addr`*	Set the message return address to *`addr`*.

continues >>

...inued

Option	Description
-s *subject*	Set the message subject to *subject*. To be safe, the subject should be enclosed in quotes.
-T *file*	The message-id and article-id headers are saved to the file specified by *file*.
-t	Obtain To:, cc:, and bcc: fields from the message text rather than from the command line recipient list.
-u *user*	Use the mailbox of *user* rather than the current user mailbox.
-V	Display mail version number and exit.

Command	Description
!cmd	Execute the given shell command. If no command is given, a command shell is spawned—type **exit** to return to mail.
=	Display the current message number.
?	Display command summary.
alias *alias recip*	Make an alias for the specified mail recipient. Usually aliases are defined in the .mailrc file.
cd *dir*	Change directory to *dir*.
copy *file*	Same as the save command. However, the message is not marked as saved.
delete *msgs*	Delete the listed messages. If no messages are listed, the current message is deleted.
discard ➥*headers*	Discard specified headers when displaying messages.
ignore *headers*	Do not print the specified headers when displaying messages.
dp *msgs*	Delete-print. Delete the specified messages and then print the next message.
edit *msgs*	Edit the messages using the editor specified in the EDITOR environment variable.
exit	Exit mail.
field *header*	Display the contents of the header specified by *header*.
file *file*	Switch mailbox files to *file*. If no file is specified, the current filename is displayed.

continues >>

>>continued

Command	Description
`followup` *msg*	Reply to the author of the specified message.
`from` *msgs*	Print the header summary of *msgs*. If no messages are specified, print the header summary for the current message.
`hold` *msgs*	Hold the listed messages in the current mailbox.
`inc`	Incorporate new messages that arrive in the current mail list.
`load` *file*	Load the specified file as a mail message. The file must be in a standard single message format, with headers.
`mail` *recip*	Send a message to the specified recipient.
`Mail` *recip*	Send a message to the specified recipient and save a copy.
`more` *msgs*	Display the listed messages, pausing after each page.
`Unread` *msgs*	Mark the listed messages as unread.
`next`	Jump to the next message in the message list.
`pipe` *msgs* *command*	Pipe the listed messages through the specified command.
`print` *msgs*	Print the specified messages.
`put` *msgs* *file*	Write the specified messages to the specified file.
`quit`	Quit. Messages that were saved in a file are deleted; all others are saved.
`reply` *msgs*	Reply to each message specified. The subject line is taken from the first message in the list of messages.
`replyall` *msg*	Reply to the message, sending a copy to every recipient of the original message.
`Save`	Save the specified message, all addressing information is stripped.
`save`	Save the specified message to the mailbox file (usually `mbox`).
`source` *file*	Execute the commands in the specified file.
`shell`	Spawn a shell to run commands. Type **`exit`** to return to mail.
`top` *msgs*	Display only the first few lines (`top`) of the listed messages.
`unalias` ➥*aliases*	Remove an alias definition. Refer to `alias`, earlier in this table.
`undelete` *msgs*	Undelete the listed messages.
`unignore`	No longer ignore the specified headers. Refer to `ignore`, earlier in this table.
version	Display the current version of mail.
`visual`	Edit the message in visual mode. The editor given in the `VISUAL` environment variable is used. If this variable is not set, `vi` is used.

rwall

`/usr/sbin/rwall [options] [host]`

rwall

Broadcast a message to all users on a network. The message, when received, will be preceded by the following header:

```
Broadcast Message...
```

The remote server must be running the `walld` daemon.

Option	Description
`-n` *netgroup*	Broadcast the message to the network specified by *netgroup* rather than to a specific host.
`-h` *host*	Specify a single host to broadcast the message to. This option can be used in conjunction with the `-n` option.

▶**See Also** `rwho` (91), `rusers` (84)

talk

`/usr/bin/talk user [terminal]`

talk

Talk to other users using the UNIX talk protocol. It can be used to chat with another user on the same system or with other users across the Internet. The remote system must be running a talk daemon (`in.talkd`) listening on port 517/udp.

When connecting to a remote system, the other user will be prompted to talk with a message similar to the following:

```
Message from Talk_Daemon@remotehost at 8:55 ...
talk: connection requested by
mulligan@localhost.

talk: respond with: talk mulligan@localhost
```

After the other user responds, chatting can begin. The text is sent character by character.

Argument	Description
user	The login name of the user to talk to. It can either be a user-name (for the local system), or an Internet address of the form *user@remotehost* for Internet chatting.
terminal	Optional. If a user is logged in more than once, this specifies which terminal to talk to.

Command	Description
CTRL+L	Refresh the screen.
CTRL+D or **CTRL+C**	End the talk session and quit.

▶**See Also** `mail` (92), `write` (98)

`write`

write

`/usr/bin/write [`*`terminal`*`]`

Send a message to another user on the local system. Unlike `talk`, the text is sent line by line.

When used, `write` will send a message similar to the following to the other user:

```
Message from mulligan on host (pts/6) [ Tue Mar  4 09:11:22 ]
➥...
```

To stop sending messages, press **CTRL+D** or **CTRL+C**.

Argument	Description
`terminal`	Optional. If the other user is logged in more than once, this specifies which terminal to send the message to.

▶**See Also** `mail` (92), `talk` (97)

Remote Shells and Login

`rlogin`

rlogin

`/usr/bin/rlogin [`*`options`*`] [`*`host`*`]`

Description

Log in to a remote system using the remote login procedures rather than telnet. The user and/or host must be defined in a `.rhosts` or `hosts.equiv` file on the remote system. The remote server must be running the `in.rlogind` daemon. This is an unencrypted and relatively insecure method of remote login.

Option	Description
`-L`	Litout mode.
`-8`	Use 8-bit data instead of 7-bit.
`-e` *`char`*	Set escape character to *`char`*.
`-l` *`username`*	Use *`username`* as the username for remote login rather than the current one.

▶**See Also** `rcp` (90), `telnet` (100)

rsh

rsh

`/usr/bin/rsh [`*`options`*`] [`*`hostname`*`] [`*`command`*`]`

The remote shell executes commands on a remote system across the network. Alternatively, if no command is given, `rsh` behaves like `rlogin` and will log the user in to the remote system. This command uses the `.rhosts` or `/etc/hosts.equiv` file on the remote system to check if remote execution/login is allowed.

Option	Description
`-l` *`username`*	Use the username specified by *`username`* for logging in rather than the current username.
`-n`	Suppress standard output from `rsh`. Output is sent to `/dev/null`.

.rhosts and hosts.equiv

Two files are used to check authentication for the `rlogin`, `rsh`, and `rcp` programs: `.rhosts` and `hosts.equiv`. The `.rhosts` file is placed in a user home directory and lists the hosts and users that are allowed to log into the local account. The general form of the `.rhosts` file is as follows:

```
hostname username
```

If the username is omitted, then all users from the specified host are allowed. Optionally, a *`netgroup`* can be used in place of the username by specifying it as `+@`*`netgroup`*. The symbol + is used to represent "all." For example, the following allows remote logins from the user `smithj` from any host:

```
+ smithj
```

However, this leaves the account open to security exploits and should not be used.

continues >>

continued >>

The `/etc/hosts.equiv` file can be thought of as an `.rhosts` file for the entire system. If a remote user is allowed to log in based on the `host.equiv` file, she will be allowed to log in as any local user.

Note that the `.rhosts` and `/etc/hosts.equiv` files are two of the most common sources of security breaches. To be safe, follow these recommendations:

- Always use the *`hostname username`* form; never specify only a user or a host.
- Never use a `+` in an entry.
- Only list hosts that are completely trusted and very secure.
- Check `.rhost` and `host.equiv` files on a regular basis for signs that they have been altered or tampered with in any way.

Example

Display a text file that is located on a remote system:

```
rsh remotehost cat file.txt
```

▶**See Also** `rlogin` (98)

telnet

telnet

`/usr/bin/telnet [options] [host] [port]`

Interface to the `telnet` protocol to log in to a remote system. `telnet` can also be used to connect to an arbitrary port/service on a remote host.

Option	Description
`-8`	Use 8-bit data path.
`-E`	Suppress all escape characters.
`-L`	Use 8-bit data path on output.
`-c`	Do not read `.telnetrc` file.
`-d`	Toggle debugging mode `on`.
`-e` *`char`*	Set escape character to `char`.
`-l` *`user`*	Send the current username as the value of `user`.
`-n` *`file`*	Open *`file`* as a tracefile for the session.
`-r`	Force `telnet` to behave more like `rlogin`. Escape characters: `~`, `.\r`, and **CTRL+Z** can be used (see `rlogin`).

Command	Description
Ctrl-]	Drop back to a prompt. This is very useful when a connection is hung and needs to be terminated. Simply press **Ctrl+]** and then type **`quit`**.
`?` *`command`*	Help. Get help on *`command`*. If *`command`* is not specified, then a list of commands will be given.
`close`	Close the current session and exit.
`display` *`arg`*	Show values of parameters set by toggle.
`environ` *`args`*	Set variables that can be sent to the remote host through environment variables. Arguments include the following: ■ `define` *`variable value`* ■ `undefine` *`variable`* ■ `export` ■ `unexport` *`variable`* ■ `list` ■ `?`
`logout`	Same as `close`, if `logout` is supported on the remote side.
`open` *`host port`*	Open connection to host on port. If no port is given, 23/tcp is used. Optionally, `-l` user can be added to specify a username other than the current one.
`quit`	Same as `close`.
`send` *`args`*	Send *`args`* (including special characters) to the remote host. Arguments include the following: `escape`, `synch`, `brk`, `ip`, `abort`, `ao`, `ayt`, `ec`, `el`, `eof`, `eor`, `ga`, `getstatus`, `nop`, `susp`.
`set` or `unset` *`arg value`*	Set or unset any of the following arguments: ■ `echo`: Toggle local echoing. ■ `escape`: Set escape character to value. ■ `interrupt`: Set interrupt character to *`value`*. ■ `quit`: Set quit character. ■ `flushoutput`: Set flushoutput character. ■ `erase`: Set erase character. ■ `eof`: Set eof character.

continues >>

>>continued

Command	Description
	■ `ayt`: Set the Are You There character. ■ `lnext`: Set lnext character in the old line-by-line mode. ■ `reprint`: Set the reprint character. ■ `rlogin`: Set `rlogin` escape character. ■ `start`: Set start character. ■ `stop`: Set stop character. ■ `susp`: Set the suspend character. ■ `tracefile`: Set the trace file. ■ `worderase`: Set the worderase character.
`status`	Display status of `telnet`.
`toggle` *`args`*	Toggles on/off the following parameters: `autoflush`, `autosynch`, `binary`, `inbinary`, `outbinary`, `crlf`, `crmod`, `debug`, `localchars`, `netdata`, `options`, `prettydump`, `skiprc`, `termdata` Toggling `?` will show all available parameters.
`z`	Suspend `telnet`. Job control must be supported.

▸**See Also** `rlogin` (98)

II

Developer Reference

5
Compilers/Interpreters

Compiler

gcc

gcc

```
/usr/local/bin/gcc [options] [filename]
/usr/local/bin/g++ [options] [filename]
```

The GNU C compiler is an integrated C/C++ compiler. Source files for programs written in C are usually given a `.c` extension. Source code written in C++ is usually given a `.C`, `.cc`, `.cpp`, or `.cxx` extension. Calling the compiler as `gcc` will assume C style linking, and calling the compiler as `g++` will assume C++ style linking.

Option	Description
`-x lang`	Override the interpretation of the file extensions and specify which language to use. Valid languages include: `c`, `objective-c`, `c-header`, `c++`, `cpp-output`, `assembler`, and `assembler-with-cpp`.
`-c`	Compile only. Do not link object files after compilation.
`-S`	Stop after compilation and do not assemble. Output files will have the same name as the source files except that they will all have an `.s` extension.
`-E`	Preprocess only. Preprocessed source code is sent to standard out.
`-o file`	Set the output filename.
`-v`	Show all commands executed and compiler version number on standard error.
`-pipe`	Use pipes rather than temporary files.
`-ansi`	Use strict ANSI C, disabling the non-ANSI parts of GNU C.
`-fno-asm`	Do not use `asm`, `inline`, or `typeof` as keywords.
`-fno-builtin`	Only recognize built-in functions that begin with two leading underscores.
`-fhosted`	Set compilation for use in hosted environment.
`-ffreestanding`	Set compilation for use in a freestanding environment.

continues >>

ntinued

Option	Description
-fno-strict-➥prototype	Treat function declarations with no arguments in the C style rather than the C++ style.
-trigraphs	Include support for ANSI trigraphs.
-fdollars-in-➥identifiers	Allow $ symbols in identifiers in C++.
-fenum-int-➥equiv	Implicit conversion of integers into enumeration types is allowed (for C++).
-fexternal➥-templates	Creates smaller code by using only a single copy of each template function. Must use `#pragma` in the source code.
-fall-virtual	All member functions are treated as virtual functions.
-fcond-➥mismatch	All conditional type mismatches, making the value of the expression void.
-funsigned-➥char	Make char types unsigned.
-fsigned-char	Make char types signed.
-include *file*	Include and compile the contents of the specified file before the other source files.
-imacros *file*	Define macros that are defined in the specified file. All other output is discarded.
-idirafter ➥path	Set the secondary include directory to the specified path.
-nostdinc	Do not search for the standard include/header files.
-nostdincc++	Do not search for the standard C++ include/header files.
-undef	No nonstandard macros are predefined.
-E	Preprocess only. Output is sent to standard out.
-C	Do not discard comments when used with the `-E` option. Output is sent to standard out.
-P	Do not generate `#line` commands when used with the `-E` option. Output is sent to standard out.
-M	Generate a make rule for each object file.
-MM	Same as `-M` but only user (not system) header/include files are included.

continues >>

>>continued

Option	Description
`-Umacro`	Undefine the specified macro.
`-dM`	Display all defined macros at the end of preprocessing.
`-Wa,`*`option`*	Send the specified option to the assembler.
`-llibrary`	Use the specified library during linking.
`-lobjc`	Link an Objective C library.
`-nostartfiles`	Do not use the standard startup files.
`-nostdlib`	Do not use the standard libraries or startup files.
`-static`	Link the program statically (rather than dynamically).
`-shared`	Generate a shared object that can be used with other objects.
`-Wl,option`	Pass an option to the linker.
`-Ipath`	Add the specified path to the list of include directories.
`-Lpath`	Add the specified path to the list of directories to search for libraries.
`-Bpath`	Set the path to the compiler executables and libraries.
`-w`	Omit all warning messages.
`-pendantic`	Apply strict ANSI standard and output all warnings.
`-pendantic` ➥`-errors`	Apply strict ANSI standard (like `-pendantic`) and output all warnings as errors.
`-Wimplicit`	Warn when a variable declaration does not specify a type or a function is implicitly defined.
`-Wall`	Display all warnings when compiling. It is recommended that you use this option when compiling a program you have written to check for potential problems.
`-g`	Generate debugging output that can be used with either the system's native debugging system or with GDB.
`-ggdb`	Generate debugging output that includes the GDB extensions.
`-g`*`format`*	Generate debugging output in the specified format. Valid formats are: `stabs`, `stabs+`, `coff`, `xcoff`, `xcoff+`, `dwarf`, and `dwarf+`.

continues >>

continued

Option	Description
-save-temps	Preserve all temporary files and place them in the current working directory.
-Olevel	Optimize. The level argument is not required. If given, the -0 option specifies the level of optimization. Level 0 is no optimization. Level 3 is maximum optimization.
-finline ➥-functions	Put all simple functions into the program in an inline fashion.
-b machine	Set the compilation target machine as specified. Useful when cross-compiling.
-V version	Run the specified version of GCC if more than one is installed. If no argument is given, the current version information is printed.
-mtarget	Compile for the specified target machine. Valid arguments are: 68000, 6820, 68881, 68030, 68040, 68020-40, fpa, soft-float, short, nobitfield, rtd, unix, gnu, v8, sparclite, cypress, c1, c2, 29050, 29000, 88000, 88100, svr4, fp64, and fp32.

▸ **See Also** as (115), gdb (130), ld (117)

Interpreter

perl

`/usr/bin/perl [options] [script] [arguments]`

perl

Perl is an extremely versatile scripting language useful for countless tasks. Solaris 8 includes the Perl 5.005.3 package.

Option	Description
-0*n*	Set the input record separator, specified as an octal number.
-a	Enable autosplit mode if -n or -p are also specified.
-c	Check syntax of script only. The script is not actually executed.

continues >>

>>continued

Option	Description
`-d`	Run the script under the Perl debugger.
`-d:`*`module`*	Use the debugging or tracing module at `Devel::`*`module`*.
`-Dflags`	Sets the debugging flags. See the table in the following "Debugging Flags" section.
`-e` *`perl`*	Run a single line of Perl.
`-Fpattern`	If `-a` is in effect, split on the specified pattern.
`-Idir`	Specifies the directories in which to look for modules and include files.
`-l`	Enable automatic line ending processing.
`-M`*`module`*	Execute the specified module before executing the script.
`-n`	Iterate the script over filename arguments. Behavior is similar to that of *`sed`* `-n`.
`-P`	Run the C preprocessor before Perl compilation.
`-s`	Enable switch parsing on the command line after the script name.
`-S`	Use the PATH environment variable to look for the script to be executed.
`-T`	Force taint checks.
`-u`	Compile script and dump core.
`-U`	Allow unsafe operations such as the unlinking of directories while running as root.
`-v`	Display the current Perl version.
`-V`	Display Perl configuration.
`-V:config`	Display the value of the specified configuration variable.
`-w`	Provide comprehensive debugging information including warnings about variables that are used only once.
`-x`	Assume the Perl script is embedded in a text message. The parsing of the script will begin when a `#!` containing `perl` is encountered.

Debugging Flags

The debugging flag numbers given below are additive. For example, `-D3` is the same as `-Dps`.

Number	Letter	Description
1	p	Parsing and tokenizing
2	s	Stack snapshots
4	l	Loop stack processing
8	t	Trace execution
16	o	Overloading and method resolution
32	c	String/numeric conversions
64	p	Preprocessor commands
128	m	Memory allocation
256	f	Format processing
512	r	Regexp parsing and execution
1024	x	Syntax tree dump
2048	u	Tainting checks
4096	L	Memory leaks
8192	H	Hash dump
16384	X	Scratchpad allocation
32768	D	Cleanup
65536	S	Threads

▸ **See Also** `gcc` (106)

6
Programming Utilities

Programming Utilities

ar

ar

```
/usr/ccs/bin/ar [options] [position] [archive] [files]
```

The `ar` utility is used to create, update, and maintain library/archive files.

Compatibility with `ranlib`

In SunOS 4.x, the `ranlib` utility was used to convert archive libraries into random linkable libraries. The `ar` utility performs these tasks and more. Therefore, `ranlib` is no longer needed, although it has been included for compatibility with older software.

Option	Description
`-a`	New files in the archive are placed after the `position` operand.
`-b`	New files in the archive are placed before the `position` operand.
`-c`	Do not display diagnostic messages when archive is created.
`-d`	Delete the specified files from the archive.
`-m`	Move files in an archive. The specified files are moved to the position indicated by the `-a` or `-b` options. If neither `-a` or `-b` are given, the specified files are moved to the end of the archive.
`-p`	Print the contents of the archive.
`-q`	Append the specified files to the end of the archive.
`-r`	Replace or add files in the archive.
`-s`	Regenerate the archive symbol table.
`-t`	Print the table of contents for the archive.
`-T`	Truncate filenames of files in the archive that are longer than the operating system can support.
`-u`	Update old files. Only files with a modification time newer than the ones in the archive will be changed. This option is useful when used with `-r`.
`-V`	Display version information.

continues >>

continued

Option	Description
-v	Verbose.
-x	Extract the specified files out of the archive without altering the archive itself. Available in /usr/xpg4/bin/ar only.

▶ See Also gcc (106), ld (117), make (119)

as

/usr/ccs/bin/as [*options*] [*files*]

as

The assembler is used to read assembly language source code and generate object files. Temporary files are created in the /tmp directory unless the TMPDIR environment variable is set to something else.

Option	Description
-b	Generate extra symbol table information.
-K PIC	Generate position-independent code.
-L	Save symbols. All symbols, even those usually discarded, are saved in the ELF symbol space.
-m	Run the assembler input through the m4 macro processor.
-n	No warnings.
-o file	Specifies the output filename.
-p	Run all the input files through the C preprocessor (cpp).
-Dname=def	Defines C preprocessor options in the form of -Dname=definition.
-Qx	Option to include assembler version information in the comment section of the output file. x can be y (yes, include version information) or n (no, do not include version information).
-s	Put all stabs in the .stabs section rather than in the stabs.excl sections.
-T	Transition 4.x files to 5.x files.
-V	Display assembler version information.
-xF	Show performance information.
-q	Skip error checks and do a quick assembly.

continues >>

>>continued

Option	Description
`-xarch=`*`arch`*	Accept instructions from the specified architecture. Valid architectures include: v7 (SPARC version 7), v8 (SPARC version 8), v8a, v8plus, v9plusa, v9, and v9a.
`-S`*`x`*	Generate disassembled code to standard output. `x` can be: `a` (with address), `b` (with .bof), `c` (with comments), or `l` (with line numbers).

▶ **See Also** `ar` (114), `gcc` (106), `ld` (117)

dis

dis

`/usr/ccs/bin/dis [`*`options`*`] [`*`file`*`]`

Disassemble the given file and generate an assembly language listing.

Option	Description
`-C`	Show C++ symbol names in the disassembly.
`-d section`	Disassemble the specified section as data and print the actual address. The `-D` option has the same effect.
`-F function`	Disassemble the specified function.
`-l archive`	Disassemble the specified archive file. `-l foo` will disassemble `libfoo.a`.
`-L`	Look up C source labels in the symbol table and send to `stdout`.
`-o`	Display numbers in octal rather than the default of hexadecimal.
`-t section`	Disassemble the specified section as text.
`-V`	Display version information.

▶ **See Also** `ar` (114), `as` (115), `gcc` (106), `ld` (117)

error

error

`/usr/css/bin/error`

Insert error notations in source code at the appropriate lines. If any error messages cannot be categorized, they are not inserted into the source code.

Option	Description
-n	Do not alter any source code. Messages are sent to standard out.
-q	Prompt before touching a file.
-s	Display statistics concerning errors.
-v	Start vi upon completion.
-t suffixlist	Do not touch files with suffixes (file extensions) that are not in the suffixlist.

▶ **See Also** as (115), ld (117), vi (13)

help

`/usr/ccs/bin/help [SCCS command] [message number]`

help

The help utility provides information for SCCS commands related to error messages and warnings. Either a SCCS command or a message number enclosed in parentheses can be specified as an argument. Typing `help stuck` will show usage information for the help utility. This command does not support any options on the command line.

ld

`/usr/ccs/bin/ld [options] [filename]`

ld

The ld command resolves external symbols and acts as the link-editor for object files.

Option	Description
-a	Produce an executable object file if no undefined references exist in static mode.
-b	Do not perform special relocations when linking in dynamic mode.
-B mode	Set the linking mode, where *mode* is either static or dynamic. Other valid modes include: ■ eliminate: Eliminate any global symbols not assigned to a version definition. ■ group: Bind objects together as a group at runtime. ■ local: Reduce to local any global symbols not assigned to a version definition. ■ symbolic: Bind global symbol references to their definitions in dynamic mode.

continues >>

>>continued

Option	Description
`-c configfile`	Set the runtime configuration filename.
`-D tokens`	Show debugging information for each token (specified as a comma-delimited list).
`-e symbol`	Set the entry point address to the specified symbol.
`-G`	Allow undefined symbols and produce a shared object in dynamic mode.
`-h objectname`	Use the specified object name for the shared object rather than the regular system filename.
`-i`	Ignore the `LD_LIBRARY_PATH` environment variable.
`-I path`	Set the interpreter path when building an executable.
`-l libname`	Search for the libraries specified. For example, `-l socket` would search `libsocket.so` and `libsocket.a`.
`-L path`	Set the library search directory.
`-m`	Produce an input/output memory map.
`-M mapfile`	Set `ld` directives specified in the given map file. If a directory is specified, all of the files in the directory are read as map files.
`-N string`	Set the `DT_NEEDED` entry in the object to the specified string.
`-o outfile`	Set the object output filename.
`-p auditlib`	Set the audit library to be used at runtime.
`-P auditlib`	Set the audit library to be used at runtime to check dependencies.
`-r`	Produce a single relocatable file by combining relocatable objects.
`-R path`	Set the runtime linker library search directories (colon-delimited).
`-s`	Strip output file of symbolic information.
`-t`	Do not warn about multiply defined symbols that are not the same size.
`-V`	Print version information.
`-Z extractmode`	Set the extraction criteria to one of the following modes: `allextract`, `defaultextract`, or `weakextract`.

▸ **See Also** `ar` (114), `as` (115), `gcc` (106), `LD_LIBRARY_PATH` (45)

lex

`/usr/ccs/bin/lex [options] [files]`

Generate programs (in C) to perform lexical processing tasks and interfaces to yacc. Input files are specified on the command line. If no files are specified, standard input is used as input. The GNU program called flex has similar functionality and is included on the Solaris Software Companion CD (included with Solaris 8).

Option	Description
-e	Properly handle EUC characters. When this option is used, yytext[] is an unsigned char.
-n	Do not show summary statistics when finished.
-t	Send the generated program source to standard output.
-v	Show summary statistics when finished.
-w	Properly handle EUC characters. When this option is used, yytext[] is a wchar_t.
-V	Display lex version information.
-Qy	Send version information to the output file lex.yy.c.

▶ **See Also** yacc (123)

make

`/usr/ccs/bin/make [options] [target]`

Utility used to execute a series of shell commands to properly compile or update a program using a makefile. When using the make utility, a target can be specified on the command line. If none is specified, the first target defined in the makefile is used.

Option	Description
-d	Display reasons for rebuilding a target along with any new dependencies. MAKEFLAGS options are also displayed.
-dd	Verbose dependency check and process.
-D	Display the makefile on standard out as it is read in.
-DD	Display the makefile and all dependency reports on standard out.
-e	Makefile assignments are overruled by environment variables.

continues >>

>>continued

Option	Description
`-f makefile`	Specifies a makefile. If this option is not used, the makefile is assumed to be `./makefile`, `./Makefile`, or `s.makefile` (in that order of preference).
`-i`	Ignore error codes.
`-k`	Kill target (end all work) if a non-zero error status is returned by a rule.
`-K statefile`	Use the specified `statefile`. A specified `statefile` can be used to override the standard set of predefined rules and macros.
`-n`	No execution. Commands and output are printed as if they are being executed but no changes are actually made.
`-p`	Print complete macro definition and target description set.
`-P`	Do not build dependencies. They are reported.
`-q`	Question mode. Checks to see if the target file is up-to-date, returning a zero or nonzero status code.
`-r`	Do not read in `/usr/share/lib/make/make.rules` (the default makefile).
`-s`	Silent. Command lines are not printed when executed.
`-S`	Stop processing the makefile if a nonzero error code is returned by a command.
`-t`	Touch. The target files are brought up to date, but the rules are not performed.
`-V`	System V mode.

▶ **See Also** `ar` (114), `gcc` (106), `ld` (117)

nm

nm `/usr/ccs/bin/nm`

Display the name list for an ELF object file.

Option	Description
`-A`	Display the full object file path on each line.
`-C`	Fix C++ names before displaying them.
`-g`	Show only global symbol information.

continues >>

ntinued

Option	Description
`-h`	Suppress output-heading data.
`-l`	Append a * to the key letter for WEAK symbols.
`-n`	Sort symbols alphabetically by name before displaying them.
`-o`	Show sizes in octal.
`-p`	Terse output. (See the following table.)
`-P`	Display list in portable output format.
`-r`	Prepend the object filename to each line.
`-R`	Show the archive name, object filename, and symbol name.
`-s`	Show section name rather than index.
`-u`	Only show undefined symbols.

Terse Output Letter	Description
A	Absolute symbol
B	BSS symbol
D	Data object symbol
F	File symbol
N	No type
S	Section symbol
T	Text symbol
U	Undefined
LOCAL	Lowercase key letter
WEAK	Uppercase key letter

▶ **See Also** `ar` (114), `as` (115), `ld` (117)

size

`/usr/ccs/bin/size [file]`

size

Display size information for sections of ELF object files.

Option	Description
`-f`	Show sizes of allocatable sections.
`-F`	Show sizes of loadable segments.
`-n`	Show sizes of non-loadable segments and non-allocatable sections.

continues >>

>>continued

Option	Description
`-o`	Display numbers in octal format rather than decimal.
`-V`	Display version information.
`-x`	Display numbers in hexadecimal format rather than decimal.

▶ **See Also** `ar` (114), `as` (115), `gcc` (106), `ld` (117)

strings

strings

`/usr/bin/strings [options] [file]`

Search for and display any ASCII strings in a specified file or standard in. This utility can display strings stored in binary files such as executables, libraries, or any other file.

Option	Description
`-a`	Search for strings in entire file rather than just in initialized data space.
`-n len`	Specify the minimum string length. Default value is 4.
`-o`	Show strings with decimal offset.
`-t offset`	Display each string with its offset in the format specified. Valid arguments are `d` (decimal), `o` (octal), and `x` (hexadecimal).

Example	Description
`strings netscape`	Show all strings in the Netscape executable file.
`strings -a msdynlib.dll`	Show all strings in a `.dll` file, including the entire file.

tsort

tsort

`/usr/ccs/bin/tsort [file]`

Perform a topological sort of either standard input or the contents of a specified file. The sorting method is determined by the partial ordering of the items in the file on the stream. Duplicate items are ignored. This command does not support any options on the command line.

Example	Description
tsort << EOF	a
a b c d e h h g g	b
EOF	c
	d
	e
	f
	g
	h

unidef

`/usr/ccs/bin/unidef [options] [file]`

unidef

Resolve and replace `ifdef` statements in C source code.

Option	Description
`-c`	Retain all lines that would be removed or blanked in normal operation.
`-l`	Replaced removed lines with blank lines.
`-t`	Do not process comments, single quotes, and double quotes.
`-Dsymbol`	Resolve and remove lines with the defined symbol.
`-Usymbol`	Resolve and remove lines with the undefined symbol.
`-iDsymbol`	Print and then ignore any lines with the specified symbol.
`-iUsymbol`	Print and then ignore any lines with the undefined symbol.

▶ **See Also** `gcc` (106)

yacc

`/usr/ccs/bin/yacc`

yacc

The `yacc` utility is "*yet another compiler-compiler*" that acts as a general tool to describe the input to a program. The GNU utility called `bison` has similar functionality and is included on the GNU Companion CD-ROM (included with Solaris 8).

continues >>

>>continued

Option	Description
`-b prefix`	Set the prefix of the output files to `prefix`, rather than the default of `y`.
`-d`	Associate `yacc` token codes with token names using `#define` statements.
`-l`	Resulting code will not contain any `#line` constructs.
`-P parser`	Use the specified parser rather than `/usr/ccs/bin/yaccpar`.
`-p prefix`	Use the specified prefix rather than the default prefix of `yy` for external `yacc` names.
`-Qx`	Set version information display. If `x` is `y`, version information is placed in `y.tab.c`. If `x` is `n`, the version stamping is suppressed.
`-t`	Compile runtime debugging code.
`-V`	Display version information.
`-v`	Report grammar ambiguity conflicts to a file called `y.output`.

▶ **See Also** `lex` (119)

7
Debugging

Proc Tools—Tools for Manipulating the /proc Filesystem

pcred

pcred

`/usr/bin/pcred [pid]`

Show the effective and real credentials of each given process. A core dump may be specified instead of a process ID.

pfiles

pfiles

`/usr/bin/pfiles [options] [pid]`

Show all `fstat()` and `fcntl()` information for the given process.

Option	Description
`-F`	Force. Take the given processes even if another process currently has control.

pflags

pflags

`/usr/bin/pflags [options] [pid]`

Display `/proc` tracing flags for the specified process identification number. Alternatively, a core may be specified.

Option	Description
`-r`	Show the registers of the process.

pldd

pldd

`/usr/bin/pldd [options] [pid]`

Show a list of dynamically linked libraries for each process. A core dump may be specified instead of a process ID.

Option	Description
-F	Force. Take the given processes even if another process currently has control.

pmap

`/usr/bin/pmap [options] [pid]`

pmap

Show the memory map for each process. A core dump may be specified instead of a process ID.

Option	Description
-r	Show reserved addresses.
-x	Show mapping details including resident/shared/private.
-l	Show unresolved dynamic linker map names.
-F	Force. Take the given processes even if another process currently has control.

prun

`/usr/bin/prun pid`

prun

Run each process. This has the opposite effect of `pstop`.

psig

`/usr/bin/psig [options] [pid]`

psig

Show all signal actions for a given process.

pstack

`/usr/bin/pstack [options] [pid]`

pstack

Display a stack trace for each lightweight process (lwp) in each given process. Displayed as a hex/symbolic trace. A core dump may be specified instead of a process ID.

Option	Description
`-F`	Force. Take the given processes even if another process currently has control.

`pstop`

pstop

`/usr/bin/pstop pid`

Stop each specified process. This has the opposite effect of `prun`.

`ptime command [`*`arguments`*`]`

ptime command

`/usr/bin/ptime`

Time the given process excluding children. This is more accurate than using the `time` command.

`ptree [`*`options`*`] [`*`pid`*`]`

ptree

`/usr/bin/ptree`

Display a process tree for the given process identification numbers. This will use indenting to show child processes.

Option	Description
`-a`	Include all the children of process zero in the process tree.

`pwait`

pwait

`/usr/bin/pwait`

Wait until all the given processes have been terminated.

Option	Description
`-v`	Verbose.
`-F`	Force. Take the given processes even if another process currently has control.

pwdx

`/usr/bin/pwdx [options] [pid]`

pwdx

Show the current working directory (cwd) of each process.

Option	Description
`-F`	Force. Take the given processes even if another process currently has control.

Debugging Tools

Application Debugging (apptrace)

`/usr/bin/apptrace [options] command`

apptrace

The application tracing utility (`apptrace`) will trace all function calls of the given command to the Solaris shared libraries. The output can be formatted using the `-v` function. Objects and function calls can be excluded by prefixing the object/call with `!` when using the `-F`, `-T`, `-f`, and `-t` options.

Option	Description
`-F list`	Set a comma-delimited list of shared objects to trace. Calls from these objects are shown.
`-T list`	Set a comma-delimited list of shared objects to trace. Calls to these objects are shown.
`-o outfile`	Send output to the specified file.
`-f`	Set the trace to follow all processes spawned by `fork()`.
`-t calls`	Trace specific function calls.
`-v calls`	Display output in a verbose "formatted" style of the given function calls.

dumpadm

`/usr/sbin/dumpadm [options]`

dumpadm

Management utility for the Solaris crash dump facility.

Option	Description
`-c type`	Set the dump content type. Valid arguments are kernel (kernel memory pages only) and all (all memory pages).
`-d device`	Set the dump device for when a crash dump is written. Usually on the local filesystem.
`-m minspace`	Maintain the specified minimum amount of space when saving a crash dump. Can be specified as: kilobytes (k), megabytes (m), percent free (%).
`-r root`	Set the root directory so that the save directory is relative to the specified root. If this option is not given, / is used as the root directory.
`-s savedir`	Set the save directory for crash dumps.
`-u`	Force the kernel to update the dump configuration.
`-y`	Automatically run `savecore` on reboot.

Example	Description
`dumpadm d/dev/dsk/ ➥-c0t2d0s2`	Set dump device to the local disk.
`dumpadm -y`	Enable `savecore` on reboot.

▶ **See Also** `gdb` (130), `truss` (131)

GNU Debugger (gdb)

gdb

`gdb [options] [program] [pid]`

The GNU Debugger (GDB) allows developers to trace the execution of a program even to the exact point where the program crashes. It can also be used to cause a program to stop on a specific condition.

Option	Description
`-help`	Display all possible options with descriptions. Same as `-h`.
`-s file`	Read a symbol table from the specified file.
`-e file`	Use the specified file as the executable file.
`-c coredump`	Examine the specified coredump file.
`-x file`	Execute the GDB commands in the specified file.

>>continued

Option	Description
-d dir	Add the specified directory to the source file search path.
-n	Do not execute any .gdbinit file commands.
-q	Quiet. The copyright and introduction messages are suppressed.
-batch	Run in batch mode.
-cd=dir	Use the specified directory as the GDB working directory.
-f	Output the filename and line number each time a stack frame is displayed.
-b bps	Set the serial line speed, in bits per second, of any serial interface used by GDB.
-tty=device	Use the specified device for program I/O.

▶ **See Also** apptrace (129), dumpadm (129), gdb (130)

truss

/usr/bin/truss [*options*] command

Trace the system calls and signals of the specified command. Alternatively a process identification number (pid) can be provided instead of a command by using the -p *pid* option.

Option	Description
-p	Use a pid rather than a command. A list of pids to trace can be provided.
-f	Follow all fork() and vfork() calls.
-c	Provide a count of traced system calls, faults, and signals. The line-by-line trace is omitted.
-a	Show all argument strings passed in any exec() system calls.
-e	Show all environment strings that are passed in any exec() system calls.
-i	Do not report open() and read() function calls.
-d	Include timestamps when tracing.
-D	Show delta times when tracing.

>>continued

continues >>

Option	Description
-t syscalls	Trace only the specified system calls. System calls can also be excluded by prefixing a ! to the system call.
-T syscalls	Stop the trace when the specified system call is encountered.
-v syscalls	Verbose. Show all structures and information for the specified system calls.
-s signals	Trace only the specified signals. Signals can also be excluded by prefixing a ! to the signal.
-S signals	Stop the trace when the specified signals is encountered.
-m faults	Trace only the specified machine faults. Faults can also be excluded by prefixing a ! to the faults.
-M fault	Stop the trace when the specified machine fault is encountered.
-r filedescriptor	Show the I/O buffer contents for any read on the specified file descriptors.
-w filedescriptor	Show the I/O buffer contents for any write on the specified file descriptors.
-o outfile	Send output to the specified file.

Example	Description
truss ls	Trace the ls command.
truss -c ls	Trace the ls command, only show system call counts and other totals.
truss -t open ls	Trace all open() calls of the ls command.

▶ See Also dumpadm (129), gdb (130)

Administration and Maintenance Task Reference

8
Startup and Shutdown

Power Management

Configuring the Power Management System (pmconfig)

pmconfig

`/usr./sbin/pmconfig [options]`

The power management system is configured at boot time using the `pmconfig` command. There is no need to run this command manually; it is run automatically when the system starts up. It works by reading the `/etc/power.conf` to determine the proper configuration and then sends the appropriate commands to the Power Management daemon.

Option	Description
-r	Restore all power management configuration options to original settings.

▸**See Also** powerd (139), /etc/power.conf (136)

Power Management Configuration File (/etc/power.conf)

/etc/power.conf

`/etc/power.conf`

The `/etc/power.conf` file is the configuration file for the Solaris power management system. It is a plain text file and can be manually edited. This file is read by the `pmconfig` utility and sets the properties for the power management daemon (`powerd`). The file contains only two types of entries: *device entries* and *system entries*.

Device Entry Format

device threshold dependents

Field	Required?	Description
device	Required	The name of the device to configure. Although full SCSI names can be used, it is usually easiest to use the relative path name such as `/dev/fb1` instead. If the relative path begins with `/devices`, the `/devices` part can be omitted.

continues >>

inued

Field	Required?	Description
threshold	Required	This field specifies the number of seconds of idle time that must pass before a specific component under power management shuts down. If a value of -1 is used, power management for the specified device is disabled.
dependents	Optional	Optional devices that can be specified. Dependent devices must be idle and shut off before the power-managed device can be shut off. Usually these devices are not physically connected to a power-managed device (such as a keyboard).

System Entry Format

keyword threshold time-of-day

Field	Description
keyword	One of the special keywords given in the following table.
threshold	Idle time, in seconds, required.
time-of-day	Period of the day during which the action is allowed. Times are specified as a pair of *hh:mm* times. To have a time-of-day from 8:00 AM to 11:00 AM would be specified as follows: 8:00 11:00

List of Keywords

Keywords	Description
shutdown	Shut down the system after the idle threshold has been exceeded. The current time must also be within the *time-of-day* time span.
noshutdown	Disable automatic shutdowns.
autowakeup	Shut down the system after the idle threshold has been exceeded and the current time is within the *time-of-day* time span. Restart the system when the current time is equal to the end time of the time span. Not all hardware has the capability to do this.

continues >>

>>continued

Keywords	Description
`default`	Allow the system to assume its default behavior. This behavior depends on the hardware. Consult the manuals that came with the hardware.
`unconfigured`	Disable automatic shutdowns. This keyword is only set before the system has been rebooted for the first time.

Other keywords are also supported by the power management system. The format of configuration lines using these keywords is given here.

Special Keywords	Description
`ttychars` ➥*`maxchar`*	Specify a maximum number of tty characters that can be read before the system is considered non-idle. The default value of *`maxchar`* is `0`.
`loadaverage` ➥*`maxload`*	Specify a maximum load average that can be achieved before the system is considered non-idle. The default value of *`maxload`* is `0.04`.
`diskreads` ➥*`maxdr`*	Specify a maximum number of disk reads that can be performed before the system is considered non-idle. The default value of *`maxdr`* is `0`.
`nfsreqs` ➥*`maxnfsrq`*	Specify the maximum number of NFS requests that can be sent or received before the system is considered non-idle. The default value of *`maxnfsrq`* is `0`. Null requests are not counted toward the total.
`idlecheck` ➥*`pathname`*	Specify a pathname to a program that is run to check if the system is idle or not. The return code of the program should be the system idle time given in minutes. By default, the `idlecheck` parameter is not set.

U.S. EPA EnergyStar Compliance and Sun Desktops

Starting with Sun desktop systems manufactured after September 1995, the U.S. Environmental Protection Agency (EPA) mandated that all desktops be set (by default) to power down after a certain amount of idle time to conserve energy. Sun systems will shut down after 30 minutes of idle time, unless this option is changed during installation or by editing the `/etc/power.conf` file.

The following lines are in the `/etc/power.conf` on a freshly installed Solaris system.

```
/dev/kbd                1800
/dev/mouse              1800
/dev/fb                 0 0             /dev/kbd /dev/mouse
autoshutdown            30              9:00 9:00
default
```

Power Management Daemon (powerd)

`/usr/lib/power/powerd [options]`

powerd

Two types of shutdowns utilize the Solaris Power Management daemon (`powerd`). These are automatic shutdowns and low-power shutdowns.

Automatic shutdowns can occur if the current time is within the time limits specified under `autoshutdown` in the `/etc/power.conf` file and if the system has been idle for at least as long as specified in the same line in the `configuration` file.

Low-power shutdowns are used by battery-operated systems and are not an issue for most Solaris systems. If the daemon detects that the battery charge is too low, the system will perform an orderly shutdown before the battery gives out. In all cases, a warning message is sent to the `syslog` facility before shutting down.

The daemon is configured using the `/etc/power.conf` file and the `pmconfig` utility. The daemon can be forced to reload this configuration file by sending a HUP signal to the `powerd` process (`kill -HUP` *`powerd-pid`*).

Never place a piece of hardware under power management that is not designed for it.

Option	Description
`-n`	Do not send a warning message to the `syslog` facility when shutting down.

▸**See Also** `etc/power.conf` (136), `pmconfig` (136)

PROM Level Booting

Boot Configuration Parameters (eeprom)

eeprom

`/usr/sbin/eeprom [options] [param=value]`

The `eeprom` command can be used to set or display boot configuration parameters stored in the `NVRAM`. `eeprom` will also detect and report any corrupted EEPROM settings. If no value is given, the current value of the parameter is displayed. If a value is specified, the parameter is set to the new value.

Option	Description
`-`	Read the parameters and values from standard input, one line at a time.
`-f device`	The EEPROM device is the device specified by *device*.

Boot Configuration Parameters

Parameter	Description	Default Value
`auto-boot?`	Automatically boot after a reset or when the power is turned on.	`true`
`ansi-terminal?`	Interpret ANSI escape sequences.	`true`
`boot-command`	Auto-boot command.	`boot`
`boot-device`	Define the default boot device.	`disk net`
`boot-file`	File to boot.	`empty-string`
`boot-from`	Where to boot from, including the device and file.	`vmunix`
`boot-from-diag`	Define the diagnostic boot device.	`le() unix`
`diag-device`	Define the diagnostic boot source.	`net`
`diag-file`	Define the diagnostic boot file.	`empty-string`

continues >>

ntinued

Parameter	Description	Default Value
diag-level	Diagnostic level (off, min, max, and menus).	platform-dependent
diag-switch?	Specify if the system is to run in diagnostic mode.	true
fcode-debug	Include Fcodes plug-in parameters.	false
input-device	Default input device to use upon booting (keyboard, ttya, and ttyb).	keyboard
keyboard-click?	Enable keyboard clicks for key presses.	false
load-base	Define the client program load address.	16384
local-mac-address?	Use network device drivers rather than the system MAC address.	false
mfg-mode	POST mode (off or chamber).	off
mfg-switch?	Continuously repeat system diagnostics until **STOP+A** is pressed.	false
nvramrc	NVRAMRC contents.	empty-string
oem-banner	Define the custom OEM banner (if oem-banner? is set to true).	emtpy-string
oem-banner?	Use custom OEM banner.	false
oem-logo	Define the custom OEM logo if oem-logo? is set to true. Must be a byte array in hexadecimal.	no-value
oem-logo?	Use custom OEM logo.	false
output-device	Output device to use upon boot (screen, ttya, or ttyb).	screen
sbus-probe-list	Probe order for the SBus slots.	0123
screen-#columns	Screen width (characters per line).	80
screen-#rows	Screen height.	34
scsi-initiator-id	Host adapter SCSI bus address (0 through 7).	7

continues >>

>>*continued*

Parameter	Description	Default Value
security-mode	Set the system security level (none, command, full). If the mode is set to full, a PROM password is required to logon.	none
security-password	Define the firmware password if security-mode is set to full.	no-value
selftest-#megs	Define the amount of RAM to test at boot-time (in MB).	1
sunmon-compat	Use the Sun restricted monitor prompt.	false
tpe-link-test?	Enable 10BaseT link test.	true
ttya-mode	Set the mode for TTYA by defining five fields: *baud rate*, *data bits*, *parity*, *top bits*, and *handshake* (-,h,s). Example: 9600,8,n,1,s	9600,8,n,1,-
ttyb-mode	Set the mode for TTYB by defining five fields: *baud rate*, *data bits*, *parity*, *stop bits*, and *handshake* (-,h,s). Example: 9600,8,n,1,s	9600,8,n,1,-
ttya-ignore-cd	Ignore carrier detect.	true
ttyb-ignore-cd	Ignore carrier detect.	true
ttya-rts-dtr-off	Do not use DTR and RTS.	false
ttyb-rts-dtr-off	Do not use DTR and RTS.	false
use-nvramrc?	Run NVRAMRC commands on boot.	true
version2?	PROM starts in Version 2 mode if possible.	true
watchdog-reboot?	Reboot after watchdog reset.	false

Example	Description
`eeprom input-device`	Show the input device to use when the system boots.
`eeprom input-device=ttya`	Set the boot-time input device to `TTYA`.
`eeprom diag-switch?=true`	Set the diag-switch parameter to `true`.

Shutdowns and Rebooting

Halting the Kernel (halt)

`/usr/sbin/halt [options]`

halt

The `halt` command is used to halt the system. Any information that is waiting to be written to the disks is written and the processor is stopped. The `halt` is logged using the `syslog` facility, unless the `-n` or `-q` option is used. If possible, use the `shutdown` command instead of `halt` because `halt` does not run the `rc0 stop` scripts as `shutdown` does.

Option	Description
`-l`	Do not log the username of the user who performed the halt.
`-n`	Do not sync the disks before halting.
`-q`	Quick halt. This option quickly halts the system without attempting an orderly shutdown process and writes out pending data.
`-y`	Allow halts from a dialup connection.

Example	Description
`halt -l`	Halt the system and do not log the username of the user executing the command.
`halt -qy`	Quick halt from a dial-up terminal.

last

`/usr/bin/last [options] [name]`

last

Print `wtmpx` file information about all logins and logouts performed on the local system. This utility can be used to quickly determine the dates of recent reboots.

Option	Description
`-a`	Print hostname in last column of output.
`-f file`	Use the specified file rather than `/var/adm/wtmpx`.
`-n`	Limit output to the number of entries specified by *n*.

▸**See Also** `uptime` (146), `w` (71), `whodo` (72)

Reboot or Shutdown (shutdown)

shutdown

`/usr/sbin/shutdown [options] [message]`

The `/usr/sbin/shutdown` command is used to both reboot and shut down the system. Its function is to change the `init` state of the system.

Special Keywords	Description
`-g time`	Grace period. Wait the time specified by *`time`* (in seconds) before shutting down.
`-i state`	`init` state. For a complete listing of `init`/run states, see "Run States" (p. 146).
`-y`	Automatically respond `YES` to confirm the shutdown when prompted. If this is excluded, the root user must confirm the shutdown after the command has been issued; otherwise, the shutdown will be aborted.
`message`	An optional message can be specified that will be shown to all users logged into the system before shutting down.

There are two versions of shutdown available on Solaris systems:

System	Shutdown	Description
System V version	`/usr/sbin/shutdown`	Slower than the UCB version because it takes time to run all the stop scripts in `rc0.d/`. This version will kill all processes before shutting down. This is the recommended version to use.

continues >>

ntinued

System	Shutdown	Description
UCB version	/usr/ucb/shutdown	Faster than the System V version. It does not run the scripts in rc0.d and only kills all non-single-user processes.

Example	Description
#/usr/sbin/shutdown -i5 -g0 -y	Reboot immediately. No grace period. No confirmation required.
#/usr/sbin/shutdown -iS -g0	Reboot to single-user mode. Must confirm shutdown when prompted.
#/usr/sbin/shutdown -i5-g60 -y "SYSTEM GOING DOWN FOR REPAIRS"	Shut down and remove power when done, if possible. Wait one minute (60 seconds) before doing so. Do not ask for confirmation. Display warning message.

Restarting the Operating System (reboot)

/usr/sbin/reboot [*options*]

reboot

The reboot command is used to restart the system kernel in the normal multiuser run state. It is recommended that shutdown be used instead to warn users of the reboot. The reboot is logged by the syslog facility.

Option	Description
-d	Dump core before rebooting.
-l	Do not log the reboot to syslog.
-n	Do not sync the filesystems before the reboot. The failure to sync the filesystems can potentially corrupt data and is not recommended.
-q	Quick reboot. Processes are not shut down before the reboot.

Example	Description
`reboot`	Perform a normal orderly reboot.
`reboot -ql`	Perform a quick, unlogged reboot of the system.

uptime

uptime

`/usr/bin/uptime`

Display the time since last shutdown or reboot, current time, current system load, and number of active users.

Example	Description
`uptime`	Show system uptime.

▶**See Also** `last` (143), `w` (71)

Run States

Run State	Description
0	■ Stop system services, including servers and daemons. ■ Terminate all running processes. ■ Unmount all filesystems. ■ Stop operating system. ■ Safe to remove power.
1	■ Single-user state, only console is active. ■ Stop system services, including servers and daemons. ■ Terminate all running processes, although not all user processes may be terminated. ■ Unmount all filesystems.
2	■ Set the `TIMEZONE` variable. ■ Mount the `/usr` filesystem. ■ Remove all files in `/tmp` and `/var/tmp`, as well as UUCP temp files. ■ Initialize network interface. ■ Start the `cron` daemon.

continues >>

ntinued

Run State	Description
	■ Start `sendmail` and printer (`lp`) services.
	■ No NFS in this run state.
	■ Network as a client—server functions not started.
3	■ Set the `TIMEZONE` variable.
	■ Mount the `/usr` filesystem.
	■ Remove all files in `/tmp` and `/var/tmp`, as well as UUCP temp files.
	■ Initialize network interface.
	■ Start the `cron` daemon.
	■ Start `sendmail` and printer (`lp`) services.
	■ NFS services are started.
4	■ Not used. (Available for your use.)
5	■ Stop system services, including servers and daemons.
	■ Terminate all running processes.
	■ Unmount all filesystems.
	■ Stop operating system.
	■ Remove power if possible (this feature depends on what hardware is used).
	■ Safe to remove power.
6	■ Reboot.
	■ Terminate all running processes.
	■ Unmount all filesystems.
	■ Reboot to initdefault entry in `/etc/inittab`.
S,s	■ Single-user state, only console is active.
	■ Terminate all user processes.
	■ Filesystems required for multiuser logins are not mounted.

Automatically Starting Services When Booting

Write the start/stop script using this basic format:

1. Copy the script to `/etc/init.d/`*`servicename`*.
2. Link the service start/stop script into the correct run state directory.

```
ln /etc/init.d/servicename /etc/rcrunstate.d/SNNservicename
```

3. Link the service start/stop script into the correct run state directory. K scripts are used to kill processes and S scripts are used to start processes when entering the run state. Also note that K scripts are executed before the S scripts.

   `ln /etc/init.d/servicename /etc/rcrunstate.d/KNNservicename`

Field	Description
`servicename`	The name of the service or command to run (for example, `webserver`, `snmp`, and so on).
`runstate`	The run state that this service will be started in. This is usually `2` or `3`. See "Run States" (p. 146).
`NN`	A number specifying the order in which to run multiple scripts. Use `99` if this is to be the last service started. Multiple services may be numbered the same.

> ***`rc.local`* Replaced**
>
> Starting with Solaris 2, `/etc/rc` and `/etc/rc.local` are no longer used. They have been replaced with start/stop scripts in `/etc/init.d`.

Basic Format of Start/Stop Scripts

```
#!/bin/sh
#Solaris startup script
#

case "$1" in
start)
            #Commands to start service
            ;;
stop)
            #Commands to stop service
            ;;
esac
```

inittab

inittab

Solaris uses a program called `init` to start up processes at boot time, usually servers and daemons. This program is controlled by a file called `/etc/inittab`. The file is a plain text file and can be manually edited.

Each line of the file consists of four fields:

`identifier   run state   action   process`

identifier

A two-character identifier that is unique to the process to be started. For example, the console control process (`ttymon`) can be identified by `co`. Both numbers and letters are allowed.

run state

Specifies the run states in which to spawn the process. The run state can be an integer between `0` and `6`, or `S` (for single-user mode), corresponding to the Solaris run states (see "Run States," p. 146). More than one state can be specified. For processes that should be started under normal, multiuser conditions, the run state should be set to `3`. For a process that is to be started under all run states, leave this field blank.

If the run state is changed, as in the case of a reboot rather than a shutdown, all processes in the `inittab` that do not have the new run state listed will be sent a `SIGTERM` signal. The process is then allowed five seconds to terminate. If, after this time, the process has not terminated, a `SIGKILL` signal is sent.

action

The *action* field specifies how to handle the process to be started. The action can be one of 11 defined keywords.

Keyword	Description
`respawn`	Start the process if it is not already running. If the process dies it is restarted.
`wait`	Start the process and wait for it to finish. Commands with the `wait` action are only executed once per run state.
`once`	Start the process and do not wait for it to finish.
`boot`	Run the process only at boot-time. Do not wait and do not restart it if it dies.
`bootwait`	The process is run when the system switches from single to multiuser states. Once the process is started, it waits for its termination.
`powerfail`	The process is started when `init` receives a `SIGPWR` signal (power failure).
`powerwait`	The process is started when `init` receives a `SIGPWR` signal (power failure). `init` will then wait for the process to finish.

continues >>

>>continued

Keyword	Description
off	If the process is running, it is killed. This is done by sending a SIGTERM, waiting five seconds, and then sending a SIGKILL.
ondemand	Same as respawn.
initdefault	This process is started when and only when the inittab is initially read. Note that if the run-state field is blank or 0123456, it will cause the system to continuously boot and become unusable.
sysinit	The process is started before the console is activated (displaying the login: prompt).

process

The *process* field represents the actual command to be run. This command can be any valid Solaris command line. The command line is actually passed to the Bourne Shell (sh) via an sh -c exec call. An example of an inittab file follows:

```
ap::sysinit:/sbin/autopush -f /etc/iu.ap
fs::sysinit:/sbin/rcS                    >/dev/console 2>&1
➥</dev/console
is:3:initdefault:
p3:s1234:powerfail:/usr/sbin/shutdown -y -i5 -g0  >/dev/
➥console 2>&1
s0:0:wait:/sbin/rc0                      >/dev/console 2>&1
➥</dev/console
s1:1:wait:/usr/sbin/shutdown -y -iS -g0    >/dev/console 2>&1
➥</dev/console
s2:23:wait:/sbin/rc2                     >/dev/console 2>&1
➥</dev/console
s3:3:wait:/sbin/rc3                      >/dev/console 2>&1
➥</dev/console
s5:5:wait:/sbin/rc5                      >/dev/console 2>&1
➥</dev/console
s6:6:wait:/sbin/rc6                      >/dev/console 2>&1
➥</dev/console
fw:0:wait:/sbin/uadmin 2 0               >/dev/console 2>&1
➥</dev/console
of:5:wait:/sbin/uadmin 2 6               >/dev/console 2>&1
➥</dev/console
rb:6:wait:/sbin/uadmin 2 1               >/dev/console 2>&1
➥</dev/console
sc:234:respawn:/usr/lib/saf/sac -t 300
co:234:respawn:/usr/lib/saf/ttymon -g -h -p "`uname -n`
➥console login: " -T sun -d /dev/console -l console -m
➥ldterm,ttcompat
```

9

User Management

Basic User Management Tasks

Adding a User (useradd)

useradd

1. Create a new account for a user:

   `useradd [options] username`

2. Set the password for the new user:

   `passwd username`

The `/usr/sbin/useradd` command is used to add new users to the system. The command edits the `/etc/passwd`, `/etc/shadow`, and `/etc/group` files to include the new user. It is possible to add a new user by manually editing these files—however, it is not recommended. The `useradd` command should be used to add new accounts whenever possible. The `useradd` command does not set a password for the account. The `passwd` command should be run after adding the account. Also, by default, the new account is set to use the `/sbin/sh` shell. Most users prefer the `csh` or `ksh` shells. If the user shell is changed (using the `-s` option), be sure that any files in the `/etc/skel` directory are meant to use the new shell. The options given in the following section explain all of the different parameters that can be set when creating a new user. Alternatively, the `admintool` utility can be used to create and manage user accounts using a graphical user interface.

Option	Description
`-b basedir`	Set the base directory of the system to `basedir`. Subsequent `useradd` commands will set the user's home directory to `basedir/login` if the `-d` option is not specified.
`-c comment`	Set the comment field to the string specified by `comment`. It is recommended to enclose the comment in quotes, but it is not necessary. The comment is usually the full name of the user or description of the account. This is the information that is shown by the `finger` command.
`-D`	Display the default values for `useradd`. By default these values are as follows: ■ `group = other,1` ■ `base_dir = /home`

continues >>

ontinued

	■ `skel = /etc/skel` ■ `shell = /sbin/sh` ■ `invalid = 0` (for use with the `-f` option) ■ `expire = (not set)` The `-D` option can also be used to set new default values, such as `useradd -D -s/sbin/csh`.
`-d` *`homedir`*	Set the home directory of the new user to the directory specified by *`homedir`*. If omitted, the default home directory is *`basedir/login`*, where *`basedir`* is the system base directory and *`login`* is the new user login name.
`-e` *`expiration ➥date`*	Expire the account (lock the account) on the specified date. The date can be specified in the following formats: ■ `2/7/99` ■ `"February 7, 1999"` Expiration dates are used to create temporary accounts for users.
`-f` *`days`*	Lock (invalidate) the account if it has not been used in the number of days, specified by *`days`*. Setting this option can increase the security of the system by locking inactive and possibly vulnerable accounts. However, if the number of days is set too low, it can be a nuisance.
`-g` *`group`*	Set the group membership of the new account. By default the group is set to `other`. Either the name (a string) or number (an integer) can be used to specify the group.
`-G` *`other_group`*	Set the supplementary group of a new account. Users can belong to more than one group, and this option sets the secondary group membership (*`other_group`*). Either the name (a string) or number (an integer) can be used to specify the group.
`-k` *`skeldir`*	Specify a skeleton directory. The skeleton directory contains files (such as `.cshrc`, `.profile`, and so on) that are copied to the new user's home directory. Any files that are in the skeleton directory are copied to all new accounts.
`-m`	Make the new directory. If the new user's home directory does not already exist, it is created and skeleton files (refer to `-k` *`skeldir`*, earlier in this table) are copied.

continues >>

>>continued

`-o`	Duplicate a user account, using the same UID number.
`-s` *`shell`*	Set the user shell to *`shell`*. The shell must be specified by a fully qualified path name (such as `/sbin/csh`). By default the shell is set to `/sbin/sh`.
`-u` *`UID`*	Set the user ID number to *`UID`*. By default a new UID is assigned that is one greater than the highest UID already assigned. New UIDs must be less than `MAXUID` as defined in `/sys/param.h`.

Third-Party Shells and the `/etc/shells` File

If a new user account is created and the user can log in via telnet, but cannot FTP to the system, check the `/etc/shells` file. All user shells must be listed in `/etc/shells` for FTP access to work. If a non-standard shell is set as a user's shell (such as `tcsh` or `zsh`), be sure to add the shell to `/etc/shells`. This file does not exist on a newly installed system—therefore, it must be manually created.

Example	Description
`useradd -c ➥"John Smith" smithj`	Add a new user account for the user John Smith with the login name `smithj`.
`useradd -c "Guest" ➥-e 1/1/99 guest`	Create a temporary guest account that expires on January 1, 1999.
`useradd -c ➥"John Smith" -m -d/ ➥home2/smithj smithj`	Add a new user account for John Smith with a new home directory at `/home2/smithj`.

Broadcasting a Message to All Users (wall)

wall

`/usr/sbin/wall [`*`options`*`] [`*`file`*`]`

Broadcast a message to all users on the local system, in a manner similar to `write`. All users will see a message similar to the following:

```
Broadcast Message from mulligan (pts/8) on ns1 Wed Apr 12
➥20:24:52...
```

If a file is specified, the contents of the file will be written as the message. If no file is specified, a message can be typed, line by line, until a **CTRL+D** is sent.

The other user on the system must have writeable terminals in order for the `wall` command to work. Therefore, only the root user can usually use this command to broadcast messages to all the users on a system. To make `wall` usable by all users, make it `setuid root` using the following command as root:

```
chmod 4755 /usr/sbin/wall
```

This should only be done on a system on which all of the users are trusted not to abuse the `wall` utility.

Option	Description
`-a`	Broadcast message to all terminals—console and pseudo-terminals.
`-g` *`group`*	Broadcast only to the group specified by *`group`*.

▶ **See Also** `rwall` (97), `write` (98)

Deleting an Existing User Account (userdel)

userdel

1. Lock the user account (this step and step 2 are not necessary, but are recommended):

   ```
   passwd -l username
   ```

2. Wait until the next backup is performed.
3. Delete the user account:

   ```
   userdel [options] username
   ```

Accounts are deleted using the `userdel` command. This command removes the account entries from the `/etc/passwd` and `/etc/shadow` files. Optionally `userdel` can also remove the user's home directory and all files contained in it. The `/etc/passwd` and `/etc/shadow` files can be manually edited to remove accounts in a similar manner—however, this is not recommended. One alternative to immediately deleting unwanted accounts is to lock the account for a while and then delete it. This will render the account unusable—and yet, if for some reason something needs to be recovered from the account, it will be available. It is recommended to lock the account until the next backup is performed and only then delete the account. The `admintool` utility can be used to delete user accounts using a graphical user interface.

Option	Description
`-r`	Remove the user's home directory when the account is deleted. The user's home directory and all contents will be permanently deleted and will not be able to be recovered (unless a backup exists).

Remove Quotas Before Deleting the Account

Using `userdel` to delete a user does not remove a user's quota limits if set. Before deleting a user, remove their quota limits using `edquota`. Then update with `quotacheck`, and then use `userdel` to delete the account. Although this is not necessary, it will keep excess information from building up in `filesystem` quota files.

Example	Description
`userdel smithj`	Delete the user `smithj` but do not delete the home directory.
`userdel -r smithj`	Delete the user `smithj` and remove the associated home directory.

▶ **See Also** "Locking an Existing User Account" (161)

Modifying an Existing User Account (usermod)

usermod

1. Make sure that the user is not currently logged in:

```
finger
last username
```

2. Modify the user account:

```
usermod username
```

After an account has been created using the `useradd` command, it can be modified using the `usermod` command. The `usermod` options are very similar to `useradd` and can modify any of the parameters set by the `useradd` command. As with `useradd`, the command changes the `/etc/passwd` and `/etc/shadow` files, which can also be done by manually editing the files. However, manual editing is not recommended. The `admintool` utility can be used to modify user accounts using a graphical user interface.

Option	Description
-b *basedir*	Set the base directory of the system to *basedir*. Subsequent useradd commands will set the user's home directory to *basedir/login* if the -d option is not specified.
-c *comment*	Set the comment field to the string specified by comment. It is recommended to enclose the comment in quotes, but this is not necessary. The comment is usually the full name of the user or description of the account.
-d *homedir*	Set the home directory of the new user to the directory specified by *homedir*. If omitted, the default home directory is *basedir/login*, where *basedir* is the system base directory and *login* is the new user login name.
-e *expiration_date*	Expire the account (lock the account) on the specified date. The date can be specified in the following formats: ■ 2/7/99 ■ "February 7, 1999" Expiration dates are used to create temporary accounts for users.
-f *days*	Lock (invalidate) the account if it has not been used in the number of days specified by *days*. Setting this option can increase the security of the system by locking inactive and possibly vulnerable accounts. However, if the number of days is set too low, it can be a nuisance.
-g *group*	Set the group membership of the new account. By default, the group is set to other. Either the name (a string) or number (an integer) can be used to specify the group.
-G *other_group*	Set the supplementary group of a new account. Users can belong to more than one group, and this option sets the secondary group membership (*other_group*). Either the name (a string) or number (an integer) can be used to specify the group.
-l *login*	Change the login name to *login*.
-m	Move the home directory, creating the new directory if it does not exist. The home directory is created and skeleton files (see the preceding table's useradd options) are copied.

continues >>

>>continued

-s *shell*	Set the user shell to *shell*. The shell must be specified by a fully qualified path name (such as /sbin/csh). By default the shell is set to /sbin/sh.
-u *UID*	Set the user ID number to UID. By default a new UID is assigned that is one greater than the highest UID already assigned. New UIDs must be less than MAXUID as defined in /sys/param.h.

Modifying Active Accounts

When modifying a user account, the user cannot be logged in during the changes. If the user is logged in, usermod will return an error (error code 6).

Example	Description
usermod -l jsmith ➥smithj	Change a user's login name from smithj to jsmith.
usermod -c ➥"system op" ➥manager	Modify the comment field of the user account manager from "system admin" to "system op".
usermod -d/home2/ ➥smithj -m smithj	Move a user's home directory from /home/smithj to /home2/smithj.

Ancillary User Management Tasks

Changing an Existing User Password (passwd)

passwd *username*

passwd

Users commonly forget their passwords, in which cases the passwords must be changed. Also, after a new account is created using the useradd command, the passwd command must be used to set the password. This is done using the passwd command as root.

This is the same procedure that is used to unlock an account after it has been locked using the passwd -l command. Note that only the first eight characters of the password are significant.

Prior to Solaris 2.5, the passwd command changed only the user's password in the file /etc/shadow on the local host. If NIS was running, the yppasswd command was used to change the user's password in the NIS database, and if NIS+ was running, the nispasswd command was used to change the password in the NIS+ database. However, in Solaris 2.5 and later, the passwd command by default changes the user's password in the first password source listed in the file /etc/nsswitch.conf. The commands yppasswd and nispasswd still exist for backward compatibility, but their use is discouraged. They are, in fact, just links to the passwd command.

For more information, please refer to Chapter 12 "Security."

Example	Description
passwd smithj	Change the password for the account smithj.
passwd -r *files*	Change the password on the local host.
passwd -r nis	Change the password in the NIS database.
passwd -r nisplus	Change the password in the NIS+ database.

Checking the Group File for Errors (grpchk)

grpchk

grpchk

The grpchk utility checks the group file (/etc/group) for errors. The group file has the following format:

groupname:*blank*:*GID*:*members*

Parameter	Description
Number of fields	Each entry must have four fields.
Groupname	All group names must be valid.
GroupID (*GID*)	All group IDs must be valid.
Number of groups	No user can belong to more groups than is specified in NGROUPS_MAX as defined in sys/param.h
Login names	All login names must appear in the password file (/etc/passwd).

Example

The following is an example listing of a group file (/etc/group).

```
root: :0:root
other: :1:
bin: :2:root,bin,daemon
sys: :3:root,bin,sys,adm
adm: :4:root,adm,daemon
uucp: :5:root,uucp
mail: :6:root
tty: :7:root,tty,adm
lp: :8:root,lp,adm
nuucp: :9:root,nuucp
staff: :10:
student: :30:
faculty: :40:
gcg: :500:
www: :600:
daemon: :12:root,daemon
sysadmin: :14:
nobody: :60001:
noaccess: :60002:
```

Checking the Password File for Errors (pwck)

pwck

pwck

If the password file (/etc/passwd) is never manually edited, there is little chance that it will be corrupted when adding, deleting, or modifying users. Occasionally, however, slight problems may arise with the file. The pwck utility can be used to check the password file for common problems. Not all of the problems that pwck reports are serious, and each error reported should be taken on a case-by-case basis. For example, long usernames are not necessarily a problem, but should be avoided.

The password file has the following format:

username:x:*UID*:*GUID*:*comment*:*home_directory*:*shell*

Parameter	Description
Number of fields	Each entry must have seven fields delimited by a :.
Login name	Login names must be eight or fewer characters.
User ID (*UID*)	All user IDs (UIDs) must be less than MAXUID as defined in sys/param.h.
Group ID (*GUID*)	Group IDs must be valid as listed in /etc/group.

continues >>

continued

Home directory	The home directory must exist.
Shell	The shell must exist. This does not check if the shell is in /etc/shells.

Example

```
root: x:0:1:Super-User:/:/sbin/sh
daemon: x:1:1::/:
bin: x:2:2::/usr/bin:
sys: x:3:3::/:
adm: x:4:4:Admin:/var/adm:
lp: x:71:8:Line Printer Admin:/usr/spool/lp:
smtp: x:0:0:Mail Daemon User:/:
uucp: x:5:5:uucp Admin:/usr/lib/uucp:
nuucp: x:9:9:uucp Admin:/var/spool/uucppublic:
➥/usr/lib/uucp/uucico
listen: x:37:4:Network Admin:/usr/net/nls:
nobody: x:60001:60001:Nobody:/:
noaccess: x:60002:60002:No Access User:/:
mulligan: x:100:10:John Mulligan:/home/ouser/
➥mulligan:/bin/tcsh
```

Locking an Existing User Account (passwd -l)

`passwd -l` *`username`*

passwd-1

It may be necessary in some situations to temporarily disable a user account. This can be done by setting the account entry in /etc/shadow to show that the account is locked (*LK* in the password field). This is done by using the passwd command. Note that when an account is locked, the current password is lost. Therefore, a new password must be set to unlock an account.

If an account is suspected of being used for malicious purposes or some form of cracking, the account should be locked as soon as possible. The ability to lock accounts is also useful when an account is to be deleted. In this case, the account can be locked for a while until it is absolutely certain that nothing in the account is of any value, at which point it is deleted.

Example	Description
passwd -l smithj	Lock the account smithj.
passwd smithj	Unlock the account smithj, and reset the passwd.

▸ **See Also** "Deleting an Existing User Account" (155)

Switching Users and Changing to the Root User (su)

su

1. Use the `su` command to switch to a new user:

   `su [options] [username]`

2. Enter password when prompted.

The `su` command is used to switch users, changing the effective user ID number of the user. By default, if no login name is specified, the `su` command attempts to change the user to the root `user`.

If the user invoking the `su` command is already root (`uid=0`), then the user is immediately switched to the other user. Otherwise, the user is prompted for the password of the other user account.

Uses of the `su` command are logged to `/var/adm/sulog`.

Option	Description
-	If a dash is given on the command line before the username, the other user's environment is used. This simulates logging in as the other user.

Example	Description
`su`	Switch to root.
`su smithj`	Switch to the user `smithj`.
`su - smithj`	Switch to the user `smithj` and use the environment variables (including path) of `smithj`.

Quotas

Checking a Single User's Disk Quota (quota)

quota

`quota -v username`

The `quota` command can be used to check a user's `ufs` disk quota including disk usage and quota limits. Non-root users can use the `quota` command to check their own quotas and disk usage, but only the root user can specify a username on the command line to check other users. When used without any options, `quota` will only report any exceeded quotas.

Quotas are set using the `edquota` utility.

Option	Description
-v	Display all available information.

Output from quota -v is similar to the following:

```
Disk quotas for mulligan (uid 252):

Filesystem         usage  quota  limit
/home/www/student    500  10000  10000

➥timeleft  files  quota  limit    timeleft
              0      0      0
```

The fields displayed are as follows:

Field	Description
Filesystem	The filesystem on which the quota is set.
Usage	The disk space used, in kilobytes.
Quota	The soft quota limit. If this limit is exceeded for longer than the time limit, the soft limit becomes the hard limit. Given in kilobytes.
Limit	The hard quota limit. At no point may this disk usage amount be exceeded. Given in kilobytes.
Timeleft	The time left before the soft limit becomes the hard limit.
Files	The number of files on the filesystem owned by the user.
Quota	The soft limit for the number of files allowed on the filesystem. If this limit is exceeded for longer than the time limit, the soft limit becomes the hard limit.
Limit	The hard limit for the number of files allowed on the filesystem. At no time may this number of files be exceeded.
Timeleft	The time left before the soft file limit becomes the hard limit.

Example	Description
quota	Check if the quota of the user invoking quota has been exceeded (non-root).
quota -v	Check the status of the quota if the user invoking quota has been exceeded (non-root).

continues >>

>>continued

`quota smithj`	Check if another user has exceeded his quota (root only).
`quota -v smithj`	Display all information about another user's quota (root only).

Editing User Quotas (edquota)

edquota

`edquota username`

The `edquota` command is used to edit quotas of individual users. By default, `edquota` invokes the `vi` editor to edit the quota limits, but this can be changed by setting the `EDITOR` environment variable to the desired editor. Only the root user may edit quotas.

When invoked, the `edquota` utility will create a temporary file that can be edited to set the quota. The quota will only be updated after the editor exits. The temporary file will have the following form:

```
fs mountpoint blocks (soft = slimit, hard =hlimit) inodes
➥(soft =slimit, hard = hlimit)
```

`mountpoint` is the mount point for the filesystem. The `blocks` section sets the soft and hard limits for the disk usage (given in 1,024 byte blocks). The `inodes` section sets the soft and hard limits for the number of files allowed on the filesystem that are owned by the user. Hard limits cannot be exceeded under any circumstances. Soft limits can be exceeded for a specified time limit before the soft limit becomes a hard limit.

Option	Description
`-p`	Use prototype user. Copy the quota of the specified user and apply the quota to the user whose quota is being edited.
`-t`	Change the soft limit time for the filesystem. If set to `0`, the default time is used as defined in `/usr/include/sys/fs/` ➥`ufs_quota.h`.

Setting New Quotas

If quotas are being set for the first time for a user, the `quotacheck` utility must be run for the quotas to take effect.

Example	Description
`edquota smithj`	Edit the quota for the user `smithj`.

Enabling/Disabling Quotas on a Filesystem (quotaon)

`quotaon [options]`

quotaon

Before quotas can be used on ufs filesystems, the quota system must be enabled. This is done by using the quotaon command. Similarly, to disable quotas on a filesystem, the quotaoff command is used. Although quotas are turned on for filesystems as a whole, each user's quota limits are individually set.

The quotaon and quotaoff commands modify the /etc/mnttab file. When quotas are enabled, the filesystem entry will be marked quota under the mntopts. If the quotas are disabled using quotaoff, the entry will be marked quotaoff. This can be done manually, without using quotaon and quotaoff, but it is not recommended.

At boot time, quotas are enabled on any filesystems with "rq" in the mntopts field of /etc/vfstab.

Option	Description
-a (quotaon)	Enable all quotas on any filesystems with "rq" in the mntopts field of /etc/vfstab.
-v (quotaon)	Verbose. Report status after each filesystem quota is enabled
-a (quotaoff)	Shut off quotas for all filesystems in /etc/mnttab.
-v (quotaoff)	Verbose. Report status after each filesystem quota is disabled.

Example	Description
quotaon -a	Turn on all quotas.
quotaoff -a	Turn off all quotas.
quotaon -av	Turn on all quotas, reporting which ones were enabled.

Reporting Filesystem Quotas (repquota)

`/usr/sbin/repquota [options]`

repquota

The repquota utility is used to report quota information for multiple users at a time. For displaying quota information for one user at a time, the quota command can be used. A filesystem, to be reported, must be specified unless the -a option is given, in which case all filesystems with quotas are reported.

Keeping Quotas Private

By default, Solaris allows all users of the system to use the `repquota` command. The `repquota` in `/usr/sbin` is actually a link to another file:

```
lrwxrwxrwx   1 root           22 Oct 21  1996
/usr/sbin/repquota -> ../lib/fs/ufs/repquota
```

The linked file is as follows:

```
-r-xr-xr-x   1 bin          8616 May  2  1996
../lib/fs/ufs/repquota
```

This file is executable by all. This means that all users on the system will be able to use the `repquota` utility.

In most cases this is not a problem, but if for some reason quota limits and disk usages are to be kept private, change the execute permission of `/usr/lib/fs/repquota` as follows (as root):

```
chmod 550 /usr/lib/fs/repquota
```

Option	Description
`-a`	Report all filesystems with quotas enabled. Filesystems with quotas enabled will have a `rq` in the `mntopts` field of `/etc/vfstab`.
`-v`	Report quota summaries for all users regardless of disk usage.

The output from `repquota` is similar to the following:

```
Block limits                                 File limits
User      used   soft   hard  timeleft  used  soft   hard timeleft
smithj —    19  10000  10000               4     0      0
jonesb - 3121  10000  10000              77     0      0
smithk -    39  10000  10000               7     0      0
jonesw - 6393  10000  10000             175     0      0
smithr - 4271  10000  10000             135     0      0
```

Reporting Quotas over the Web

In some cases it may be desirable to allow users to check their quota usage over the Web. There are many ways to do this. The following CGI script is just one example of the way this can be done. It assumes that the username has been taken from an HTML form and passed to the `$FORM_uname` variable. It also assumes that `$HOME` is the base directory of the HTML files in the account, and that `$WWW` is the base of the URL (such as `http://www.`*`somedomain`*`.com`). It also uses two GIF images that are scaled using the `WIDTH` option in the `<IMG>` tags to display a bar graph representation of the quota usage. It should be noted that this script can be used by any user to check any other user's quota. If quotas are to be kept very private, this script should be modified.

CGI Security Issues

Never run CGI scripts as root or other privileged users on the system. The script included in this section should probably be run as user `nobody`.

```
if [ -z "$FORM_uname" ];then
FORM_uname="none"
fi

DATE=`date`
WWW=http://www.somedomain.com
QUOTA=`/usr/sbin/repquota -a| grep $FORM_uname |head -1| awk
➥'{print $4}'`

cat << EOM
<TITLE>Quota for $FORM_uname</TITLE>
<BODY BGCOLOR="#FFFFFF" TEXT="#000000">
<CENTER>
<TABLE BORDER=0 CELLPADDING=4 CELLSPACING=0 WIDTH=500>
<TR><TD BGCOLOR="#666699">
EOM

#check if there is no quota set for user
if [ -n "$QUOTA" ]; then
QUOTA=`/usr/sbin/repquota -a| grep $FORM_uname|head -1 | awk
➥'{print $5}'`
USED=`/usr/sbin/repquota -a| grep $FORM_uname |head -1 | awk
➥'{print $3}'`
PUSED=`expr  $USED \* 100 / $QUOTA`
PFREE=`expr 100 - $PUSED`
NAME=`grep $FORM_uname /etc/passwd|head -1|awk '{FS=":";print
➥$5}'`

if [ $PFREE -lt 0 ];then
PFREE=1
fi

if [ -z "$NAME" ];then
NAME=`/usr/sbin/repquota -a| grep $FORM_uname|head -1 | awk
➥'{print $1}'`
fi
cat << EOM
<FONT FACE="Arial, Helvetica" SIZE=5 COLOR="#FFCC00">Quota for
$NAME</FONT>
```

```
<CENTER>
<TR><TD BGCOLOR="#FFFFCC">
EOM

if [ $PUSED -gt 100 ]; then
cat << EOM
<FONT FACE="Arial,Helvetica" COLOR="#FF0000" SIZE=4>
YOU ARE OVER YOUR QUOTA LIMIT</FONT>
<P>
<FONT FACE="Arial,Helvetica">Immediately remove unwanted
➥files from your account in order to decrease your disk
➥usage.</FONT><P>
EOM
fi

cat << EOM
<FONT FACE="Arial, Helvetica">You are currently using $USED KB
➥of disk space in your web account.  That means you are using
➥$PUSED% of your quota limit.<P><BR>
<FONT FACE="Arial Black, Arial, Helvetica"  SIZE=6><CENTER>
➥$PUSED% FULL</FONT>
<BR CLEAR=both>
<IMG BORDER=0 WIDTH=$PUSED HEIGHT=20 HSPACE=0 ALT="$PUSED%
➥used"
SRC="$WWW/images/blue_button.gif">
<IMG BORDER=0 WIDTH=$PFREE HEIGHT=20 HSPACE=0 ALT="$PFREE%
➥free"
SRC="$WWW/images/blank_button.gif"><P><BR>
EOM
else
cat << EOM
<FONT FACE="Arial" COLOR="#FFCC00" SIZE=5>NO QUOTA</FONT>
<TR><TD BGCOLOR="#FFFFCC">
<FONT FACE="Arial, Helvetica">
No quota set for $FORM_uname. Perhaps you typed the user name
➥incorrectly.
Please resubmit your query.
<BR CLEAR=both><P><BR>
<A HREF="$WWW/quota.html">Try again.</A>
EOM
fi
echo "</TABLE><PRE></CENTER>"
echo "$DATE: $REMOTE_HOST checked $FORM_uname" >>
➥$HOME/log/quota.log
```

The accompanying HTML that includes a form to use is given here:

```
<FORM METHOD=GET ACTION="/cgi-bin/quotacheck">
<FONT FACE="Arial, Helvetica">
Enter your username: </FONT>
<INPUT NAME="uname" SIZE=15><P>
```

```
<CENTER>
<FONT FACE="Arial, Helvetica" SIZE=3>
<INPUT TYPE=RESET VALUE="Reset form">
<INPUT TYPE=SUBMIT VALUE="Press to Check"></FONT>
</FORM>
```

Updating Quotas (quotacheck)

quotacheck [*options*]

quotacheck

The quotacheck utility performs the following tasks on the specified filesystem (or all filesystems, if -a is used):

1. Examine each mounted ufs file system.
2. Build a table of current disk usage.
3. Compare disk usage against established quota limits.
4. Update the quota file, fixing any discrepancies.

It is necessary to run quotacheck after a quota has been set (using edquota) for each new user. It is also a good idea to run quotacheck once in a while to keep the quota files up to date and free from problems.

Safely Updating Quotas

Filesystems should not be very active while quotacheck is being run. Although it is not necessary to reboot into single-user mode, the less activity there is, the less chance there is for problems.

It is recommended that, as root, the wall command is used to urge users to save their work and log out before quotacheck is run.

Option	Description
-a	All filesystems. All filesystems that have rq in mntopts in the /etc/vfstab file, have a quota file, and are listed as ufs filesystems in /etc/mnttab are checked and updated.
-p	Update quota files in parallel.
-v	Verbose. Show quota information for all users. If omitted, quotacheck will report user information only if a change was made.

> **Largefile Safe**
>
> It should be noted that all the quota commands are largefile safe. They are safe for systems using file sizes greater than 2GB.

Example	Description
`quotacheck -ap`	Check all filesystems in parallel.
`quotacheck /home`	Check the `/home` filesystem.
`quotacheck -v /` ➥`home/student`	Check the `/home/student` filesystem, showing disk usage for all users.

10 Network Administration

continues >>

Daemons and Servers

Boot Parameter Server (rpc.bootparamd)

`/usr/sbin/rpc.bootparamd [options]`

The Boot Parameter server (also known as a BOOTP server), `rpc.bootparamd`, is used to pass boot parameters to diskless clients on the network. The daemon must be running on the same IP subnet as the diskless client. Boot parameters are defined in the `/etc/nsswitch.conf` and `/etc/bootparams` files.

Option	Description
`-d`	Show debugging information.

The `/etc/bootparams` file has the following format:

hostname id

The first field (*hostname*) is the hostname of the diskless client. This field can be a specific hostname of a client, or a wildcard (*) can be used to represent all clients. If the wildcard is specified and individual clients are specified, the client-specific lines override the wildcard lines. As in the case of most Solaris configuration files, long lines can be split using a backslash (\) to break the line.

The second field (*id*) is the identification field. It can be of either the following forms:

File-specific: *id=host:path*

Non-file-specific: *id=domain*

File-specific configuration IDs instruct the diskless client to use the exported file or filesystem on the named host. The host and the pathname to the file or filesystem must be separated by a colon. The non-file-specific configuration ID assigns a domain name to the client. If a domain name is specified after the equal sign, it is used. If none is specified, the server's domain name is used. The only IDs that can be used for SPARC diskless clients are `root`, `swap`, and `dump`.

The final type of entry is the name service configuration line. It has the following format:

`ns=[nameserver]:[nameservice]:[(netmask)]`

The name server is specified in the first field, *nameserver*. The second field can be one of three name service types: `nis`, `nisplus`, or `none`. The last field is the netmask for the client. Netmasks are used to specify which part of an IP address is a network address and which part is the host address. For an IP address of `192.168.0.4` with a netmask of `255.255.255.0`, the `4` in the IP is the host address.

By default, NIS+ is used as the naming service if a NIS+ server is found. Otherwise, a NIS server is used if found. If no name service is found, an interactive screen is displayed on the client asking for which name service to use. The following is an example of an `/etc/bootparams` file.

```
*     root=fs1:/export/cslab/root
ice9 root=fs1:/export/ice9/root
     swap=fs1:/export/ice9/swap
     domain=cslab.somecollege.edu
     ns=mach:nis(255.255.255.0)
```

Domain Name Server (in.named)

in.named

`/usr/sbin/in.named [options]`

The Domain Name server provides domain name service (DNS) to clients on the network. By default, the daemon uses the file `/etc/named.boot` to gather initial DNS information. A separate utility called `named-xfer` is used by the daemon to perform zone transfers. This utility should not be manually run at any time. The daemon can be forced to reread the `named.boot` file by sending a `SIGHUP` (`kill -HUP` *daemonpid*) to the daemon.

Getting DNS to Work

By default, Solaris systems are set to use only local files for DNS lookups. To allow Internet lookups using a DNS server, the `/etc/nsswitch.conf` file must be edited. Locate the following line in the file:

```
hosts: files
```

Edit it to read as follows:

```
hosts: files dns
```

This causes lookups to be first attempted using the `/etc/hosts` file and then by using the DNS nameserver specified in the `/etc/resolv.conf` file.

Option	Description
`-b` *`file`*	Rather than using `/etc/named.boot`, use the file specified by *`file`*.
`-d` *`level`*	Debug. Extra information is printed for debugging purposes. The higher the level, the more detail is given.
`-p` *`port`*	Specify a port to listen on.

The configuration file `/etc/named.boot` supports the following types of entries:

Entry	Description
`domain` *`domain`*	The DNS domain. No leading dot is needed.
`primary` *`domain file`*	Specifies that the domain information for *`domain`* is located in the file *`file`*. The file is usually `named.db`.
`secondary` *`domain`* ➥*`server1 server2`* `....`	Specifies one or more secondary servers to gather DNS information about *`domain`*.
`cache` *`file`*	Specifies what database file is to be placed in the cache.

The `/etc/resolv.conf` file is used to configure how hostnames are resolved on the local host. The file is plain text and can be manually edited. The file can contain the following types of entries:

Entry	Description
`nameserver` *`addr`*	Specifies the nameserver (DNS server) that the system should use to look up Internet names. More than one nameserver can be specified by adding additional `nameserver` *`addr`* lines. This way, backup servers can be listed.
`domain` *`name`*	Default domain name to append to hostnames if no domain name is given.

File Transfer Protocol Daemon (in.ftpd)

`/usr/sbin/in.ftpd [`*`options`*`]`

in.ftpd

The File Transfer Protocol (FTP) daemon (`ftpd`) handles file transfer requests sent by FTP clients. The daemon is run via the `inetd` service. By default, only users with accounts on the system (valid usernames and passwords) can FTP to the system. If the user's username is listed in /etc/ftpusers, access is denied. However, it is possible to set up "anonymous FTP" that allows any user with access to the system to perform file transfers in restricted directories.

User Shells Must Be in /etc/shells

One common problem that exists on Solaris systems is that if a user is using a nonstandard command shell (such as tcsh or zsh), he cannot FTP to the host. To fix this problem, add the user's shell to the /etc/shells file. The full path must be specified.

If the /etc/shells file does not exist, the default shells that are allowed are as follows:

```
/bin/csh          /bin/jsh          /bin/ksh
/bin/sh           /sbin/jsh         /sbin/sh
/usr/bin/csh      /usr/bin/jsh      /usr/bin/ksh
/usr/bin/sh
```

Options	Description
-d	Debug. Extra information is logged using the syslog facility.
-l	Log each access of the FTP daemon to the syslog facility. This is highly recommended as a security precaution.
-t *timeout*	Specify the amount of inactivity (in seconds) before the daemon disconnects.

Supported Operations

Operation	Description
ABOR	Abort.
ACCT	Set account.
ALLO	Allocate storage.
APPE	Append to file.
CDUP	Change the current working directory to the parent directory.
CWD	Change working directory.
DELE	Delete.
HELP	Print command summary.
LIST	List files (same as ls -gl).

continues >>

tinued

Operation	Description
MKD	Make directory.
MODE	Set mode of transfer.
NLST	List files and directories (same as `ls`).
NOOP	No operation (do nothing).
PASS	Password.
PASV	Passive mode.
PORT	Set port.
PWD	Print working directory.
QUIT	Exit.
RETR	Get a file.
RMD	Delete a directory.
RNFR	Rename from.
RNTO	Rename to.
STOR	Store.
STOU	Store (unique name).
STRU	Structure.
TYPE	Type of data transfer.
USER	Username.
XCUP	Change current working directory to the parent of the current directory.
XCWD	Change working directory.
XMKD	Make directory.
XPWD	Print working directory.
XRMD	Remove directory.

Internet Daemon (inetd)

`inetd [options] [config file]`

inetd

The Internet daemon controls Internet services hosted by the system. By default, `inetd` is started when the system is booted in any networked run state. The daemon reads the configuration file at `/etc/inetd.conf` when it is started. The Internet daemon is not usually manually started; however, if it is, options can be used.

Option	Description
`-d`	Do not send `inetd` to background. The daemon is run in the foreground to provide debugging information.
`-r n interval`	Detect broken servers. If any service managed by `inetd` is started more than *n* times per *interval* seconds, it is considered broken and shut down for 10 minutes. After 10 minutes, the service is restarted. By default, `inetd` uses a behavior similar to `-r40 60`.
`-s`	Standalone. The daemon will not contact the service access controller (SAC) as it usually does.
`-t`	Trace all TCP service accesses using the `syslog` facility (`daemon.notice priority`). UDP services cannot be traced using this option.

UDP Services and `nowait`

Never set a UDP service to run as `nowait`. This will cause problems between `inetd` and the UDP service, resulting in the spawning of multiple UDP servers. Eventually, the performance of the entire system will be adversely affected.

The `inetd` daemon is configured using the `/etc/inet/inetd.conf` file. There is a symbolic link to `/etc/inetd.conf` that has been provided for BSD compatibility. The file is plain text and can be manually edited. Send a `HUP` signal to the `inetd` process with the `kill` command.

To disable a service, it can be commented out by placing a `#` as the first character of the line and restarting the `inetd` process. By default, Solaris starts many network daemons. For security reasons, you should disable all the services you do not need. A third-party tool such as TCP Wrappers can also aid in increasing `inetd` security.

The file has the following format:

```
service socket protocol wait-status uid program arguments
```

Field	Description
service	The name of the service as listed in the `/etc/services` file.
socket	Specify the type of socket: ■ `stream`: Stream ■ `dgram`: Datagram

continues >>

- `raw`: Raw
- `seqpacket`: Sequenced packet
- `tli`: Any transport layer interface endpoint

`protocol` The protocol used for the service. It must be a protocol listed in the `/etc/inet/protocols` file. For RPC services, the protocol can be specified as `rpc/*`.

`wait-status` Either `wait` or `nowait`. Most services use `nowait` except for datagram (UDP) services.

`uid` Specify which user the daemon will run as. Most run as `root`.

`program` Full path to the actual daemon program file.

`arguments` Any arguments that are added to the program file command line. Only five arguments can be specified.

Kernel Statistics Daemon (rstatd)

`/usr/lib/netsvc/rstat/rpc.rstatd`

rstatd

The Kernel Statistics daemon (`rstatd`) responds to requests sent by the `rup` utility. The statistics are pulled from the kernel and sent out over the network. Unless a specific need for this daemon can be determined, it should be disabled for security reasons.

Name Service Cache Daemon (nscd)

`/usr/sbin/nscd [`*`options`*`]`

nscd

The Name Service Cache daemon (`nscd`) maintains an internal database of the most commonly used DNS lookups. This daemon is used to cache information from the `passwd`, `group`, and `hosts` files. It takes up to ten seconds for the `nscd` to update its records after one of these files has been modified. Note that unlike these files, the `/etc/nsswitch.conf` file is not re-read after modification by `nscd`. If edited, `ncsd` must be restarted or the system must be rebooted. Commands can be passed to `nscd` by running it again on the command line. Any new options are passed to the currently running instance.

Restarting nscd

When the /etc/nsswitch.conf or /etc/nscd.conf files are modified, the Name Service Cache daemon (nscd) must be restarted. This can be done by issuing the two following commands as the root user:

```
/etc/init.d/nscd stop
/etc/init.d/nscd start
```

Wait a few seconds for the nscd to properly exit before running the start command.

It should also be noted that the Name Service Cache daemon continues to make network requests to refresh its internal database. This may cause problems when using asynchronous PPP (aspppd). To prevent this from occurring, set keep-hot-count to 0 in /etc/nscd.conf.

Option	Description
-e *cache*,*yesno*	Enable or disable the cache specified by *cache*. If *yesno* is yes, the cache is enabled. If it is no, the cache is disabled.
-f *configfile*	Use a configuration file other than the default. The configuration file is specified by *configfile*.
-g	Show current configuration.
-i *cache*	Invalidate the specified *cache*.

The Name Service Cache daemon is configured by editing the /etc/nscd.conf file. The file is parsed line by line. Comment lines begin with a # and are ignored. Valid cache names include hosts, passwd, and groups.

Configuration Attributes

Attribute	Description
check-files ➥*cachename* ➥*yesno*	Specify if the named cache should check its related files (such as the host file) for changes every ten seconds. If the value of *yesno* is yes, it is enabled. If it is set to no, file checking is disabled.
debug-level ➥*level*	Set the level and detail of debugging information provided. 0 provides the least detail, and 10 provides the most. Setting this to a non-zero value causes nscd to run in the foreground rather than in the background.

continues >>

tinued

Attribute	Description
enable-cache ➥*cachename* ➥*yesno*	Specify if the named cache should be enabled. The value of *yesno* is either yes (enable) or no (disable).
keep-hot-count ➥*cachename n*	Set the number of entries (*n*) to keep in the cache.
logfile *file*	Send debugging information to the specified file. The file can also be a special device such as /dev/tty (to send output to the console).
negative- ➥time-to-live ➥*cachename n*	Specify the time to live for unsuccessful queries. The time is specified by *n*, in seconds.
positive- ➥time-to-live ➥*cachename n*	Specify the time to live for successful queries. The time is specified by *n*, in seconds.
suggested-size ➥*cachename* ➥*size*	Sets the internal hash table size. The size should be a prime number.

Network Finger Daemon (in.fingerd)

/usr/sbin/in.fingerd

in.fingerd

The Network Finger daemon handles requests for finger information on port 79/tcp. Finger requests sent to the Finger daemon are actually passed to the finger command on the server host to generate a reply. Note that, by default, finger requests are not logged and can give out information to potential system intruders. The Finger daemon should be run only if truly necessary, as it is a security concern. To disable the Finger daemon, comment out the appropriate line in the /etc/inetd.conf file. It is highly recommended that the finger daemon be disabled.

▸**See Also** Internet Daemon (inetd) (177).

Network Listen Daemon (listen)

/usr/lib/saf/listen [*options*]

listen

The Listen daemon (listen) is part of the Service Access Facility (SAF). It listens on the network for requests for servers. After a request has been detected, the daemon invokes a new instance of the appropriate server for each valid connection.

Options

Option	Description
`-m` *`prefix`*	Use *`prefix`* as the prefix of the pathname.

Network Lock Daemon (lockd)

lockd

`/usr/lib/nfs/lockd [`*`options`*`]`

The Network Lock daemon (`lockd`) is part of the NFS system. The daemon controls network file locking operations using the `fcntl()` and `lockf()` function calls. Any `fcntl()` calls that are received are forwarded to the lock manager on the appropriate NFS server. If the `lockd` daemon is killed while running state, information can be lost.

Option	Description
`-g` *`graceperiod`*	If the server is rebooted, the clients have *`graceperiod`* seconds to reclaim locks.
`-t` *`timeout`*	Specify the time to wait (*`timeout`*, in seconds) before resending a lock request to an NFS server.

Network Router Discovery Daemon (in.rdisc)

in.rdisc

`/usr/sbin/in.rdisc`

The Network Router Discovery daemon (`in.rdisc`) populates the network routing tables when the system is booted by using the UCMP router discovery protocol. If the host is a non-routing host, `in.rdisc` listens on the `ALL_HOSTS` multicast address (`224.0.0.1`) for other routers. Routers of the highest priority (as set in their advertise messages) are accepted unless `-a` is specified on the command line. If the host is a routing host, the daemon also alerts other systems to the router present, sending out messages to the `ALL_HOSTS` multicast address every 600 seconds.

Option	Description
`-a`	Accept. Accept all routers that are discovered while listening on the `ALL_HOSTS` multicast address.
`-f`	Forever. Force the daemon to keep running even if no routers are discovered.

continues >>

ntinued

Option	Description
`-p pref`	When sending out messages to find routers, this option sets the preference (*pref*). By default, the value of *pref* is `0`.
`-r`	Route. The daemon behaves as if it is running on a router rather than on a host.
`-s`	Send out three messages to attempt to find other routers. If none are found, the daemon exits unless the `-f` option has been also specified.
`-T time`	Set the time between successive advertise messages. The default value is 600 seconds.

Network Routing Daemon (in.routed)

`/usr/sbin/in.routed [options]`

The Network Routing daemon controls the system routing tables for network activity, listening on 520/udp for routing packets. If the host is a routing-host, the daemon also provides copies of the routing tables to other hosts. As soon as the daemon is started, it looks for configured network interfaces. If two interfaces are found, it assumes that packets are to be forwarded between the two interfaces (between the two networks). Network routing tables are updated as necessary. Unused entries are deleted about every four minutes. The files `/etc/gateways` and `/etc/networks` are used for configuration purposes.

Option	Description
`-g`	Gateway. Used on hosts acting as routers to provide a default route.
`-q`	Do not supply routing information.
`-s`	Supply routing information. This information is supplied whether or not the host is a router.
`-S`	Enter only default routes for internetwork routing (if acting as an internetwork router).
`-t`	Trace. Print all packets received on standard output.

Network Spray Daemon (sprayd)

sprayd `/usr/lib/netsvc/spray/rpc.sprayd`

The Network Spray daemon (`sprayd` daemon) responds to packets sent by the spray utility. The service works similarly to pinging a system to find a response time and number of dropped packets. However, the Spray daemon can be unreliable at times, causing packets to be incorrectly reported as dropped.

Network Status Daemon (statd)

statd `/usr/lib/nfs/statd`

The Network Status daemon is used by the NFS facility, along with the Lock daemon, to prevent and recover from crashes. The Status daemon does this by alerting other systems that the host has been successfully rebooted after a crash. After the other systems have been alerted, an attempt can be made to reclaim any locks and continue operation.

Files

File	Description
`/var/` ➥`statmon/sm`	File containing hosts that should be contacted after a crash and reboot.
`/var/statmon/` ➥`sm.bak`	A list generated by the daemon of hosts that could not be contacted after the last crash.
`/var/statmon` ➥`/state`	A file containing a single number that denotes the system status.

Network Time Protocol Daemon (xntpd)

xntpd `/usr/lib/inet/xntpd [`*`options`*`]`

A complete network time server as specified by RFC 1305 (compatible with RFC 1059 and RFC 1119). This daemon sets and maintains UNIX system time. The default configuration file for the daemon is `/etc/inet/ntp.conf`. The default locations of the drift file, key file, and server configuration files are `/etc/inet/ntp.drift`, `/etc/inet/ntp.keys`, and `/etc/inet/ntp.server`, respectively.

Option	Description
-a	Authentication mode.
-A	Unauthenticated mode.
-b	Watch for broadcasted NTP packets and synchronize to them if found.
-c configfile	Set an alternate configuration file. Default value is /etc/inet/ntp.conf.
-d	Run in debug mode.
-e delay	Specify an authentication delay in seconds. This is the time required to compute the encryption field.
-f driftfile	Set the location of the drift file.
-k keyfile	Set the location of the key file required for authentication.
-l logfile	Set the location of the log file. Default value is syslog.
-m	Watch for multicast messages and synchronize to them.
-p pidfile	Set the file that stores the daemon process ID.
-r delay	Specify delay in seconds to use to compensate for network delay.
-s statdir	Set the directory to store statistical files.
-t trustkey	Add a trusted key number.
-v	Add a variable.

Example	Description
xntpd -a	Runs daemon in authentication mode.
xntpd -A -c /etc/xntpd.➥conf.new	Runs daemon in non-authenticated mode, using a different configuration file.

Network Username Daemon (rusersd)

/usr/lib/netsvc/rusers/rpc.rusersd

rusersd

The Network Username daemon (ruser daemon) responds to requests from the rusers command. The daemon is started when either the Listen daemon or inetd receive a request that was broadcast on the network.

Network Wall Daemon (rwalld)

rwalld `/usr/lib/netsvc/rwall/rpc.walld`

The Network Wall daemon (`rwalld`) processes requests from the `rwall` command (see `rwall`). The daemon takes the request and passes it to the `wall` command on all network machines. This daemon is not necessary, and disabling it should be considered. It keeps users from broadcasting unnecessary messages to every machine on the network. To disable it, comment out the `walld` line in `/etc/inetd.conf` and restart the `inetd` process.

►**See Also** `rwall` (97)

NFS Daemon (nfsd)

nfsd `/usr/lib/nfs/nfsd [`*`options`*`] [`*`maxthreads`*`]`

The NFS daemon controls requests for network filesystems via the NFS service. When `nfsd` is started automatically (in networked run states), it is run with the `-a` option, causing it to be started on both UDP and TCP transports. Optionally, an argument can be specified on the command line to limit the number of simultaneous connections (number of threads) to *`maxthreads`*.

Option	Description
`-a`	Start `nfsd` on both UDP and TCP transports.
`-c` *`max`*	Set the maximum number of connections (*`max`*) allowed to connect to the NFS server. By default, no limit is set.
`-p` *`protocol`*	Start the daemon only on the specified *`protocol`* (`UDP` or `TCP`).
`-t` *`dev`*	Run `nfsd` using the same transport as the specified device.

Remote Login Daemon (in.rlogind)

in.rlogind `/usr/sbin/in.rlogind`

The Remote Login daemon (called the `rlogin` daemon) handles remote login requests from the `rlogin` program. The daemon listens on port 514/tcp. Authentication and access is based on a hostname/username-based system. This system uses `.rhosts` files as well as `/etc/hosts.equiv`. If the Kerberos system is used, these files are not necessary, and authentication is based on Kerberos tickets. Also, the client's source port must be in the range of 0–1023 or it is denied access to the system. If all security checks are passed, a pseudo-terminal is created, and the user is allowed to log in.

continues >>

ntinued

The `rlogin` and `rsh` systems are not very secure. The `rlogind` and `rshd` daemons should be used only on very trusted networks. It is recommended that they not be used at all unless absolutely necessary.

Remote Shell Daemon (in.rshd)

`/usr/sbin/in.rshd`

in.rshd

The Remote Shell daemon (`rshd`) handles command execution requests from the `rsh` command. Access depends on the `/etc/hosts.equiv` and user `.rhosts` files. This system uses a host/username-based authentication system. However, if Kerberos is used, there is no need to use the `.rhosts` files, providing higher degree of security.

▸**See Also** Kerberos (275), `rlogin` (98), `rsh` (99)

RPC Remote Execution Daemon (rpc.rexd)

`/usr/sbin/rpc.rexd [`*`options`*`]`

rpc.rexd

The Remote Execution daemon (`rpc.rexd`) handles remote program execution requests from the network. Non-interactive programs run via remote execution are run in a manner similar to `rsh`. Interactive programs have a pseudo-terminal assigned so that the session behaves similarly to an `rlogin` session. This daemon can be a security hazard and should only be run if absolutely necessary. Diagnostic messages from the daemon are usually sent to the console.

Option	Description
`-s`	Secure. Any remote execution request must have valid DES encryption credentials to be processed. Authentication is set using the `chkey` command.

System Status Daemon (in.rwhod)

`/usr/sbin/in.rwhod [`*`options`*`]`

in.rwhod

The System Status daemon (sometimes called the `rwho` daemon), `in.rwhod`, handles requests from the `rwho` and `ruptime` client programs. The daemon gathers information about the local system and sends it out as a broadcast/multicast for other `rwho` daemons to pick up off the network. Also, it listens for information coming from other daemons, recording it in the `/var/spool/rwho` directory.

Daemon Can Cause Excessive Network Traffic

Each System Status daemon on the network constantly sends out system information to other `rwho` daemons. If only a few hosts are running these daemons on a network, this is not a problem. However, if a large number of hosts are running these daemons, the daemon activity can substantially increase the amount of network traffic, causing possible slowing of the network. For this reason, and for security reasons, this daemon should only be used if absolutely necessary.

Option	Description
`-m`	Use the multicast address (`224.0.1.3`) when sending out system information to other `rwho` daemons. The daemon multicasts on all interfaces but is not forwarded by multicast routers.

Talk Daemon (in.talkd)

in.talkd

`/usr/sbin/in.talkd`

The Talk daemon (`in.talkd`) is used to communicate using the talk program, listening for requests on port 514/udp. Although `talkd` listens on a UDP port, after the connection has been established, the chatting via the talk programs is accomplished via the TCP protocol.

▸**See Also** `talk` (97)

TCP Network Access Control Daemon (netacl)

netacl

`netacl [-`*`version`*`] [-`*`daemon port`*`]` *`service`*

Although the Internet Services daemon (`inetd`) provides the framework for configuring network services, it provides no means of controlling access to these services. `inetd` only provides individual services to *everyone* or to *no one*. In cases in which it is desirable to allow or deny access to individual network services to specific hosts, the TCP Network Access Control daemon (`netacl`) can be used. `netacl` is one component of the *TIS Firewall Toolkit* (`fwtk`), a collection of programs for enhancing the security of UNIX systems, written by Trusted Information Systems, Inc., and made available free of charge to anyone for non-commercial use (`http://www.tis.com/research/software/fwtk`). `netacl` is invoked by `inetd` for each service for which access control is desired. `netacl` consults a configuration file (`/usr/local/etc/netperm-table`) to determine if the requested service is to be permitted to the requesting host, and if so, invokes the program configured to provide the service.

Option	Description
-version	Print netacl version information to the standard output (stdout) and exit.
-daemon *port*	Indicate that the netacl program should act as a daemon, listening for connection requests on the specified port, rather than being invoked by inetd. Port can be specified by name or number.
service	The mandatory service argument specifies a name by which an instance of netacl will identify its configuration file entries from those intended for other instances of netacl. This is customarily the same name as the program that netacl is to invoke to provide the service.

The configuration file /usr/local/etc/netperm-table is shared by all components of the TIS Firewall Toolkit. Configuration entries for netacl have the following format:

```
netacl-service: permit-hosts host-pattern [options args] -exec
➥program [args]
```

```
netacl-service: deny-hosts host-pattern
```

host-pattern is a hostname or IP address specification, which may include an asterisk (*) as a wildcard character. Additional configuration item options include the following:

Option	Description
-user *UID*	Specify a user ID under which netacl should invoke the specified program.
-group *GID*	Specify a group ID under which netacl should invoke the specified program.
-chroot *path*	Specify a path to which netacl should perform a chroot(2) before invoking the specified program.

Example

The /etc/inetd.conf entry

```
login stream tcp nowait root /usr/local/bin/netacl rlogind
```

accompanied by the /etc/inetd.conf entries

```
netacl-rlogind: permit-hosts 1.2.3.* -exec /usr/sbin/
➥in.rlogind
netacl-rlogind: deny-hosts *
```

results in the `rlogin` service being permitted to all hosts with IP addresses of the form `1.2.3.*` and being denied (and the attempt logged) for all others.

Telnet Daemon (in.telnetd)

in.telnetd

`/usr/sbin/in.telnetd`

The Telnet daemon (`in.telnetd`) allows remote users to log in to the system and work via a pseudo-terminal. The daemon listens on port 23/tcp for connections. Environment variables can be passed via the Telnet daemon during the initial terminal negotiation. This capability is commonly used to pass a `DISPLAY` variable to use OpenWindows.

Anonymous FTP

Setting Up Anonymous FTP

Anonymous FTP can be set up under Solaris by performing the following steps. Remember, however, that Anonymous FTP opens up your system to allow anonymous users to perform file transfers. In general, Anonymous FTP should be considered a security concern and should be enabled only if it is absolutely necessary. Also, to allow FTP to work properly in a `chroot` environment, make sure that the file system containing the FTP home directory is not mounted as `nosuid`.

1. Create the FTP home directory structure:

```
mkdir /export/ftp/pub
mkdir /export/ftp/bin
mkdir /export/ftp/dev
mkdir /export/ftp/etc
mkdir /export/ftp/usr
mkdir /export/ftp/usr/lib
```

2. Add the `ls` command to the FTP bin directory:

```
cp /usr/bin/ls /export/ftp/bin
chmod 111 /export/ftp/bin/ls
```

3. Copy the necessary libraries into the FTP directory structure:

```
cp /usr/lib/ld.so* /export/ftp/usr/lib
cp /usr/lib/libc.so.1 /usr/lib/libdl.so.1
/export/ftp/usr/lib
cp /usr/lib/libintl.so.1 /usr/lib/libw.so.1 /export/ftp/
➥usr /lib
cp /etc/passwd /etc/group /etc/netconfig /export/ftp/etc
```

4. Copy the necessary files into the FTP directory structure to resolve NIS names:

```
cp /usr/lib/nss*.so.1 /export/ftp/usr/lib
cp /usr/lib/libnsl.so.1 /export/ftp/usr/lib
cp /usr/lib/straddr.so /export/ftp/usr/lib
cp /etc/nsswitch.conf /export/ftp/etc
```

5. Set the permissions for the `/export/ftp/usr/lib` and `/export/ftp/etc` directories:

```
chmod 555 /export/ftp/usr/lib/*
chmod 444 /export/ftp/etc/*
```

6. Set the permissions of all of the created directories:

```
chmod 555 /export/ftp/usr/lib
chmod 555 /export/ftp/usr
chmod 555 /export/ftp/bin
chmod 555 /export/ftp/dev
chmod 555 /export/ftp/etc
chmod 755 /export/ftp/pub
chmod 555 /export/ftp
```

7. Add the following line to the `/etc/passwd` file:

```
ftp:x:30000:30000:Anonymous FTP:/export/ftp:/bin/false
```

8. Add the following line to the `/etc/shadow` file:

```
ftp:NP:6445::::
```

9. Make sure that everything is owned by root and not by FTP:

```
chown -R root /export/ftp
```

Wuarchive-FTP (wu-ftp)

`/usr/sbin/in.ftpd [options]`

wu-ftp

`Wuarchive-FTP` (a.k.a. `wu-ftp`) is an FTP daemon that was developed at Washington University (`www.wustl.edu`). It is currently the most popular anonymous FTP daemon in use today. `Wuarchive-FTP` is not installed by default on a new Solaris system. It is included on the software companion CD and must be manually installed.

Option	Description
`-V`	Print out copyright and version information.
`-d`	Enable debugging. Informational messages are written to `syslog`.

continues >>

>>continued

Option	Description
`-l`	Log every FTP session in `syslog`.
`-t` *`seconds`*	Set the anonymous FTP timeout for an inactive session. The default value is 15 seconds.
`-a`	Use the `ftpaccess` file for configuration.
`-A`	Do not use the `ftpaccess` file for configuration. By default, the `ftpaccess` is not used.
`-L`	Log all commands sent to the FTP daemon.
`-i`	Log all received files to `xferlog`.
`-I`	Disable ident (RFC931) lookups of usernames on the client.
`-o`	Log all sent files to `xferlog`.
`-u` *`umask`*	Set the default umask to the one specified.
`-W`	Do not log user logins in the `wtmp` file.
`-S`	Run the FTP daemon in the background.
`-s`	Run the FTP daemon in the foreground.
`-p` *`portnum`*	Set the FTP control port to the specified port number.
`-P` *`portnum`*	Set the FTP data port to the specified port number.
`-q`	Use PID files.
`-Q`	Do not use PID files.
`-r`	Force the daemon to `chroot` to the specified directory when it loads.

Example	Description
`in.ftpd -p 37337 -o -i`	Run the FTP daemon on port 37337 and log all file transfers.

▶**See Also** `in.ftpd` (175)

PPP

aspppd

This is the link manager for the asynchronous data link protocol (`aspppd`) as defined in RFC1331. Using this utility, users can dial into an ISP and establish a PPP link to the Internet. Configuration is done through the `/etc/asppp.cf` file. The configuration is provided by a series of tokens (one per line), followed by a space or tab, and then the setting. Configuration tokens are given below. Log messages are kept at `/etc/log/aspppd.log`.

aspppd

Option	Description
`-d` *`level`*	Sets the debugging level. Valid levels are 0 (less information) to 9 (more information).

Token	Description
`chap_name` ➥`string`	A series of octets identifying the local host.
`debug_level` *`n`*	Sets the debugging level. Valid levels are integers between 0 (less messages) and 9 (most messages).
`default_route`	Sets the peer IP address as the default route when active.
`ifconfig` ➥`options`	All options specified with this token are executed by the `ifconfig` command.
`inactivity-` ➥*`timeout`* ➥*`seconds`*	Sets the timeout period to the specified number of seconds.
`interface` ➥*`interface`*	Forms an association between the point-to-point interface specified (where *`n`* is an integer, or a `*` for dynamic) with the current path. Valid interfaces include: `ipd`*`n`*, `ipdptp`*`n`*, and `ipdptp*`.
`ipcp_` ➥`compression` *`x`*	Enable IP compression, where *`x`* is `vj` for the Van Jacobson compression algorithm or off for no compression.
`lcp_` ➥`compression` *`x`*	Enable PPP address, control, and protocol field compres sion, where `x` is either on or off.
`lcp_mru` *`n`*	Sets the maximum-receive unit packet size expressed in octets.
`negotiate_` ➥`address` *`x`*	Negotiate a dynamic IP address, where `x` is either on or off.

continues >>

>>continued

Token	Description
`pap_id name`	Sets the name of the host sent to the authenticator, expressed as octets.
`pap_password ➥passwd`	Sets the password (expressed as octets) that will be sent to the host.
`pap_peer_ ➥id name`	Sets the name of the peer to be authenticated.
`pap_peer_ ➥password ➥passwd`	Sets the password (expressed as octets) of the peer that will be authenticated.
`path`	All tokens following the path token are grouped together. This token is required.
`peer_ip_ ➥address ➥ipaddr`	Associated the given IP address with the current path.
`require_ ➥authentication ➥type`	If the local host is the authenticator, this token sets the required authentication type. Valid types are: off (no authentication), pap, or chap.
`version` *n*	Sets the version to use when parsing the configuration file.

▶**See Also** `asppls` (194)

asppls

`/usr/sbin/asppls`

asppls

The `asppls` command is the asynchronous data link protocol manager. The manager will connect a peer to `aspppd` and establish a connection. The `asppls` is usually started by the serial port monitor when someone tries to log into a PPP account (usually via a modem). The configuration of this command is done by editing the `/etc/asppp.cf` file. It uses the same maintenance tokens that `aspppd` uses. See the `aspppd` section for full details.

▶**See Also** `aspppd` (193)

PPP

PPP

The Point-to-Point Protocol (PPP) as defined in RFC 1331 is implemented in Solaris through the following STREAMS modules: `ppp`, `ppp_diag`, `ipd`, `ipdptp`, and `ipdcm`. The IP layer of the protocol is formed by using pseudo device drivers. Actual connections are established and disabled by the link manager (`aspppd` and `asppls`).

Pseudo Device	Description
/dev/ipd	Point-to-point interface pseudo device driver.
/dev/ipdptp	Point-to-multipoint interface pseudo device driver.
/dev/ipdcm	Link manager, ipd, and ipdptp interface pseudo device driver.

►See Also asppd (193), asppdls (194)

DHCP

dhcpagent

/sbin/dhcpagent [*options*]

dhcpagent

Configures the local machine's network parameters using the Dynamic Host Configuration Protocol (DHCP). The DHCP agent runs as a daemon on the local machine and is configured by using the ifconfig command. This daemon can be started manually; otherwise, it is started automatically by ifconfig when required. The use of DHCP requires that a DHCP server (or BOOTP server) be present on the network. Errors are sent to syslog for logging. The interface configuration is set in /etc/dhcp/*interface*.dhc, where *interface* is the interface name.

Option	Description
-a	For use in boot scripts for diskless clients, this option adopts a configured network interface.
-d *level*	Set the debug level to either 1 or 2.
-f	Run in the foreground as a regular process rather than as a daemon. Errors are sent to standard error.
-v	Verbose output.

►See Also dhcpinfo (197)

dhcpconfig

/usr/sbin/dhcpconfig

dhcpconfig

The DHCP configuration tool is a shell script used to configure the DHCP/BOOTP services and agents. The user is presented with four options upon running the script: Configure DHCP Service, Configure BOOTP Replay Agent, Unconfigure DHCP or Relay Service, or Exit. The dhcpmgr utility is provided as a graphical interface to configure and manage the DHCP service on a host. It has the same functionality as using

continues >>

>>continued

dhcpconfig, dhtadm, and pntadm from the command line. The DHCP host configuration file is located at /var/dhcp/dhcptab. The default location for the DHCP configuration file is /etc/default/dhcp. The DHCP service also uses the hosts file located at /etc/inet/hosts.

Menu Option	Description
Configure DHCP Service	This allows the items such as startup options, dhcptab rescan interval, and BOOTP compatibility mode to be set. If BOOTP clients are to be served, BOOTP compatibility must be turned on in this menu option.
Configure BOOTP Relay Agent	This simply accepts a list of BOOTP/DHCP servers to which requests are to be forwarded.
Unconfigure DHCP or Relay Service	These options uninitialize the DHCP/BOOTP service and remove all DHCP tables. Be sure that no other hosts are using the DHCP tables or information before unconfiguring the service.

▸**See Also** dhcpconfig (195), dhcpinfo (197), dhtadm (198), pntadm (198)

DHCP daemon (in.dhcp)

in.dhcp

/usr/lib/inet/in.dhcp [*options*]

The DHCP daemon handles requests from DHCP clients for configuration information. The daemon hands out IP addresses and other network configuration information. The daemon can optionally handle BOOTP requests as well. The daemon gets its information from the DHCP service table, dhcptab. The proper way to start and stop the daemon is to use /etc/init.d/dhcp start and /etc/init.d/dhcp stop. These commands should always be used when momentarily restarting the daemon. The DHCP daemon reloads the dhcptab file when it is started or restarted.

Option	Description
-b *mode*	Set the BOOTP compatibility mode. Can be either automatic or manual.
-d	Debug mode. DHCP transactions are logged to the console.
-h *maxhops*	Set the maximum hops between relay agents allowed for DHCP/BOOTP packets.

continues >>

tinued

Option	Description
-i interface	Specify which network interface should be monitored for DHCP/BOOTP requests.
-l syslog-➥facility	If the -l option is given, DHCP logging is turned on and logged via syslog using the specified syslog facility number. The number can be between 0 and 7.
-n	No duplicate IP address detection. If this option is not given, the daemon pings an address to make sure it is not in use before leasing it to another DHCP client.
-o *cachetime*	Amount of time, in seconds, that the daemon should cache responses to clients. Default value is 10 seconds.
-r *host*	Enable BOOTP relay mode and specify a list of relay agents (comma-delimited list of IP addresses or hostnames).
-t *rescantime*	Amount of time, in seconds, between consecutive scans of the dhcptab information.
-v	Verbose mode.

▶**See Also** dhtadm (198)

dhcpinfo

/sbin/dhcpinfo [*options*] parameter

dhcpinfo

This command displays the value of the specified DHCP parameter on standard out. It is useful for debugging DHCP problems or errors. The parameter can be specified by either its numerical value or its identifier name.

Option	Description
-c	Canonical format output.
-i *interface*	Get the DHCP values for the specified network interface.
-n *limit*	Set the maximum number of lines to be displayed when retrieving DHCP parameter values.

▶**See Also** dhcpagent (195)

dhtadm

dhtadm

`/usr/sbin/dhtadm [options]`

Administrative utility for configuring the DHCP service table (`dhcptab`).

Option	Description
`-A`	Add a macro or symbol to `dhcptab`. The `-d`, `-m`, or `-s` options must be used in conjunction with this option.
`-d` *`definition`*	Set a macro or symbol definition.
`-m` *`macro`*	Set a macro name.
`-s` *`symbol`*	Set a symbol name.
`-C`	Create the DHCP configuration table file (`dhcptab`).
`-D`	Delete a macro or symbol from `dhcptab`. The `-d`, `-e`, `-n`, `-m`, or `-s` options must be used in conjunction with this option.
`-e`	Specify a symbol/value pair (given as symbol=value).
`-n`	Specify a new macro name.
`-p` *`pathname`*	Define the resource path and set it to pathname. Default value is `/etc/default/dhcp`.
`-P`	Print the DHCP resource table, `dhcptab`.
`-r` *`resource`*	Specify a resource type other than that specified in `/etc/default/dhcp`. Values can be files or nisplus.
`-R`	Remove and delete the DHCP resource table, `dhcptab`.

pntadm

pntadm

`/usr/sbin/pntadm [options] network`

DHCP network client table management utility. This utility only updates the DHCP tables in `/var/dhcp` and not the netmasks file. If new subnets are added to the DHCP service, the netmasks table must be updated as well.

Option	Description
`-A` *`host`*	Add a host, specified by hostname or IP address, to the DHCP network table. Can be used with `-c`, `-e`, `-f`, `-h`, `-i`, `-m`, or `-s`.
`-c` *`text`*	Specify a comment.

continues >>

ntinued

Option	Description
`-e` *date*	Specify an absolute lease date (mm/dd/yyyy format).
`-f` *keywords*	Specify a flag value.
`-h` *host*	Specify a client hostname.
`-i` *cid*	Specify a client identifier.
`-s` *host*	Specify a server by IP address or hostname.
`-C`	Create the DHCP network table.
`-D` *host*	Delete a host, specified by hostname or IP address, from the DHCP network table. When `-y` is specified with this option, the related hosts table entry is deleted as well.
`-L`	List configured DHCP tables.
`-M` *host*	Modify the specified host entry, given by either hostname or IP address. Can be used with `-c`, `-e`, `-f`, `-h`, `-i`, `-m`, `-n`, or `-s`.
`-n` *ipaddr*	Specify a new IP address.
`-P`	Print the DHCP network table.
`-v`	Verbose output.
`-p` *pathname*	Specify a path to the DHCP resource path. Default value is `/etc/default/dhcp`.
`-R`	Remove and delete the DHCP network table.
`-r` *resource*	Set the resource type. Can be either files or nisplus. Default value is given in `/etc/default/dhcp`.

▶See Also `dhtadm` (198), `in.dhcpd` (196)

LDAP

ldapadd

`/usr/bin/ldapadd [options]`

ldapadd

Use this command to add an LDAP entry. This command is actually a link to `ldapmodify -a`. Therefore, the options are exactly the same. See `ldapmodify` for details.

▶See Also `ldapclient` (200), `ldapmodify` (203)

ldap_cachemgr

ldap_cachemgr

`/usr/lib/ldap/ldap_cachemgr [options]`

The LDAP cache manager is started at boot time for LDAP systems. Usually, this process does not need to be manually started or controlled. In fact, LDAP still works if it is not running. However, running the cache manager greatly increases performance of LDAP services. This service may not be included in future releases of the operating system.

Option	Description
`-g`	Display current configuration on stdout. LDAP cache statistics are also shown.
`-l log`	Set the log file for the cache manager. Default value is `/var/ldap/cachemgr.log`.
`-r delay`	Set the delay time in between cache refreshes. Default value is 600 seconds.

▸**See Also** `ldapclient` (200)

ldapclient

ldapclient

`/usr/sbin/bin/ldapclient [options] serveraddr`

This utility initializes machines as LDAP clients and/or shows the LDAP client cache. The simplest method to provide all the correct LDAP settings is to use the `-p` option to specify a profile name stored on another server. The LDAP server address is specified as host, an IP address with an optional port number (for example, `192.168.12.1:389`). If no port number is specified, 389 is used.

Option	Description
`-a authtype`	Specify the type of authentication to be used. Valid types of authentication include `none`, `simple`, and `cram_md5`.
`-b baseDN`	Specify the base distinguished name for the server.
`-B altDN`	Specify an alternate base distinguished name for the server.
`-d name`	Specify the default domain for the LDAP client.
`-D BindDN`	Specify the Bind distinguished name.
`-e ttl`	Specify the client time to live (ttl) if using a client profile. Valid times to live are written like the following: `0` (no expiration), `1d` (one day), `3h` (3 hours), `10m` (10 minutes), `45s` (45 seconds), and so on.

continues >>

ntinued

Option	Description
`-i`	Initialize as LDAP client.
`-l`	Display the LDAP client cache in a readable format. By default, this information is sent to standard out.
`-m`	Modify configuration files.
`-o` *timeout*	Set the LDAP timeout. Default value is 3 minutes.
`-O`	Only connect to servers on the preferred list.
`-p` ➥`preferredlist`	Specify the preferred LDAP servers as a comma-delimited list of IP addresses. To unset the preferred list, use `-p ""`.
`-P` *profile*	Automatically configure LDAP using an existing profile.
`-r` *ref*	Set the type of search referral. Valid arguments are `followref` and `noref`. Default value is `followref`.
`-u`	If `ldapclient` was used to initialize the client, this option undoes the initialization.
`-v`	Verbose mode.
`-w` *passwd*	Set the client password when using an authentication scheme other than none (such as `simple` or `cram_md5`).

▸**See Also** `ldap_cachemgr` (200)

ldapdelete

`/usr/bin/ldapdelete [`*options*`] [`*names*`]`

Delete an LDAP entry. Distinguished names can be specified on the command line to delete their entries.

Option	Description
`-n`	Preview only. Preview the changes, showing output, but no records are actually deleted.
`-v`	Verbose mode.
`-c`	Continuous operation. Errors are ignored, and records are deleted.
`-d` *level*	Debug mode. Acceptable values are `1` (trace), `2` (packets), `4` (arguments), `32` (filters), and `128` (access control). Modes are additive. To show packets and arguments, the value would be `6` (as in 2+4).

continues >>

>>continued

Option	Description
`-f` *`file`*	Read deletion information from a file. Normally, the information is made from stdin.
`-w` *`passwd`*	Specify the password when using CRAM-MD5 authentication.
`-h` *`host`*	Set an alternate LDAP server host.
`-M` *`authtype`*	Set the authentication method. Can be set to CRAM-MD5.
`-p` *`portnum`*	Set the LDAP port number to use. Default value is 389.

▸**See Also** `ldapadd` (199), `ldapmodify` (203), `ldapsearch` (204)

ldap_gen_profile

ldap_gen_profile

`/usr/sbin/ldap_gen_profile -P profilename [`*`options`*`]`

Creates an LDAP client profile. This profile can then be used to automatically configure other clients with `ldapclient`. This command is similar to `ldapclient` in how the options are used; however, `-P profilename` is required.

Option	Description
`-a` *`authtype`*	Specify the type of authentication to be used. Valid types of authentication include `none`, `simple`, and `cram_md5`.
`-b` *`baseDN`*	Specify the base distinguished name for the server.
`-B` *`altDN`*	Specify an alternate base distinguished name for the server.
`-d` *`name`*	Specify the default domain for the LDAP client.
`-D` *`BindDN`*	Specify the Bind distinguished name.
`-e` *`ttl`*	Specify the client time to live (ttl) if using a client profile. Valid times to live are written like the following: `0` (no expiration), `1d` (one day), `3h` (3 hours), `10m` (10 minutes), `45s` (45 seconds), and so on.
`-i`	Initialize as LDAP client
`-l`	Display the LDAP client cache in a readable format. By default, this information is sent to standard out.
`-o` *`timeout`*	Set the LDAP timeout. Default value is 3 minutes.
`-O`	Only connect to servers on the preferred list.

continues >>

continued

Option	Description
-p ➥preferredlist	Specify the preferred LDAP servers as a comma-delimited list of IP addresses. To unset the preferred list, use `-p ""`.
-r *ref*	Set the type of search referral. Valid arguments are `followref` and `noref`. Default value is `followref`.
-u	If `ldapclient` was used to initialize the client, this option undoes the initialization.
-w *passwd*	Set the client password when using an authentication scheme other than `none` (such as `simple` or `cram_md5`).

►**See Also** `ldap_cachemgr` (200)

ldaplist

`/usr/bin/ldaplist [options] [database]`

ldaplist

This command searches for naming information from the LDAP service and displays it on standard out, relying on the protocol outlined in RFC 2307.

Option	Description
-d	List all attributes, rather than entries, for the database specified on the command line.
-h	Print database mapping.
-l	Print attributes that match the given search criteria.
-v	Verbose output. This option displays the LDAP search criterion used, prefixed by +++.

Example	Description
`ldaplist passwd mulligan`	Finds user mulligan in password database.

ldapmodify

`/usr/bin/ldapmodify [options]`

ldapmodify

This command is used to modify LDAP entries on an LDAP server. The `ldapadd` command is a hardlink to this command and is the same as running `ldapmodify -a`.

Option	Description
`-a`	Add an entry to the LDAP server. The same as running `ldapadd`.
`-b`	Binary format handling. When used, all values that begin with a slash are interpreted as a pathname to a file containing the attribute name.
`-c`	Continuous. Do not exit when an error is encountered. Errors are reported but the modifications are performed anyway.
`-n`	Preview only. This option previews the changes to check for errors but does not actually make the changes.
`-v`	Verbose mode.
`-F`	Force application of all changes.
`-d`	Debug mode. Acceptable values are 1 (trace), 2 (packets), 4 (arguments), 32 (filters), 128 (access control). Modes are additive. To show packets and arguments, the value would be 6 (as in 2+4).
`-f` *`file`*	Use modification specified in the given file rather than by stdin.
`-w` *`passwd`*	Specify the password when using CRAM-MD5 authentication.
`-h` *`host`*	Set an alternate LDAP server host.
`-M` *`authtype`*	Set the authentication method. Can be set to CRAM-MD5.
`-p` *`portnum`*	Set the LDAP port number to use. Default value is 389.
`-l` *`num`*	Set the number of simultaneous connections that `ldapmodify` will use to make the necessary changes.

▸**See Also** `ldapclient` (200), `ldap_gen_profile` (202)

ldapsearch

ldapsearch

`/usr/sbin/ldapsearch [`*`options`*`] filter [`*`attributes`*`]`

Perform a search on an LDAP server using the specified filter. Matching entries are printed on standard out.

Option	Description
`-n`	Preview only. Show what search would be performed but do not actually perform the search.
`-u`	User-friendly distinguished name format.
`-v`	Verbose mode.
`-t`	Use temporary files for storing retrieved values.
`-A`	Check for the presence of a particular attribute but do not retrieve the values.
`-B`	Display all values, even non-ASCII ones.
`-L`	Alternate display format. Also forces all values, even non-ASCII ones, to be displayed.
`-R`	Do not follow referrals.
`-F` *`delim`*	Set the delimiter that separates fields.
`-S` *`attribute`*	Sort entries by the specified attribute.
`-d` *`level`*	Debug mode. Acceptable values are 1 (trace), 2 (packets), 4 (arguments), 32 (filters), 128 (access control). Modes are additive. To show packets and arguments, the value would be 6 (as in 2+4).
`-w` *`passwd`*	Specify the password when using CRAM-MD5 authentication.
`-h` *`host`*	Set an alternate LDAP server host.
`-M` *`authtype`*	Set the authentication method. Can be set to CRAM-MD5.
`-p` *`portnum`*	Set the LDAP port number to use. Default value is 389.
`-b` *`base`*	Set the search base.
`-s` *`scope`*	Set the search scope. Valid scopes are `base`, `one`, and `sub`.
`-l` *`timeout`*	Set the search timeout in seconds.
`-z` *`limit`*	Set the maximum number of entries to return.

►**See Also** `ldapadd` (199), `ldapdelete` (201), `ldapmodify` (203)

Network File System (NFS)

Display NFS Statistics

Display NFS Statistics

`/usr/bin/nfsstat [options]`

Statistical information concerning the NFS system can be retrieved using the `nfsstat` utility. The utility directly pulls information from the kernel of the local host. If used with the `-z` option by the root user, statistics can be reset with this command as well. The default behavior (no options) is the same as `nfsstat -cnrs`.

Option	Description
`-c`	Client information. Client-side NFS and RPC information is summarized and displayed.
`-m`	Show extra information for each mounted filesystem, including the following: ■ Mount flags ■ Read/write sizes ■ Resend count ■ Round trip time ■ Server address ■ Server name ■ Timers
`-n`	NFS client and server information. Both client and server information for NFS is summarized and printed.
`-r`	Display only RPC information.
`-s`	Display only server information.
`-z`	Zero stats. Reset all statistics back to zero and start over. This option can be used only by the root user.

Display Fields

Field	Description
badcalls	Number of calls rejected
badlen	Number of calls that were too short
badverfs	Number of bad verifiers
badxids	Number of bad received calls
calls	Number of calls (NFS or RPC, depending on options) received
cantconn	Number of times a connection could not be made to the server
clgets	Number of received client handles
cltoomany	Number of times cache had no unused entries
dupchecks	Number of duplicate request cache lookups
dupreqs	Number of duplicates found
interrupts	Number of interrupts received
newcreds	Number of authentication refreshes
nomem	Number of times a call failed due to lack of memory
nullrecv	Number of times an unavailable call was reported as received
retrans	Number of times a call was resent
timeouts	Number of timed-out calls
timers	Number of inconsistent timeout values
xdrcall	Number of calls with bad XDR headers

Example

To print only server NFS information, use the following utility and options:

```
nfsstat -ns
```

Mounted Filesystem Table

Mounted Filesystem Table

`/etc/mnttab`

The mounted filesystem table (called the mount-tab file), `/etc/mnttab`, contains information of all mounted filesystems. The `mount` command adds entries to this file (unless the `-m` option is used). The `umount` command removes entries from this file. The file has the following format:

`special mount_point fstype options time`

NFS mounted filesystem resource names are in *`host`*`:`*`resource`* format and are marked `nfs` in the *`fstype`* field.

Field	Description
special	Resource name.
mount_point	Resource mount point.
fstype	Filesystem type.
options	Mount options.
time	Mount time.

Example

The following is an example of a working `/etc/mnttab` file. Both UFS and NFS filesystems are shown. In this example, NFS filesystems have been mounted on `host11` and `host22`.

```
/dev/dsk/c0t3d0s0       /      ufs      rw,suid,
➥dev=800018   905203176
/dev/dsk/c0t2d0s6       /usr   ufs      rw,suid,
➥dev=800016   905203176
/proc    /proc    proc     rw,suid,dev=2700000  905203176
fd       /dev/fd fd        rw,suid,dev=2780000  905203176
/dev/dsk/c0t3d0s3       /var   ufs      rw,suid,
➥dev=80001b   905203176
/dev/dsk/c0t2d0s5       /tmp   ufs      suid,rw,
➥dev=800015   905203178
/dev/dsk/c0t2d0s7       /var/tmp        ufs   suid,rw,
➥dev=800017   905203179
/dev/dsk/c1t2d0s1       /var/spool/news ufs   suid,rw,
➥dev=800089   905203179
/dev/dsk/c1t1d0s6       /home  ufs      suid,rw,
➥dev=800086   905203178
/dev/dsk/c1t1d0s7       /home/ouser     ufs   suid,rw,
➥dev=800087   905203179
/dev/dsk/c0t0d0s6       /home/suser     ufs   suid,rw,quota,
➥dev=800006   905203179
```

continues >>

```
/dev/dsk/c0t0d0s7       /home/host22    ufs   suid,rw,
➥dev=800007    905203179
-hosts   /net     autofs  ignore,indirect,nosuid,
➥dev=2880001  905203222
-xfn     /xfn     autofs  ignore,indirect,dev=2880002  905203222
host11:vold(pid209)     /vol    nfs      ignore,noquota,
➥dev=2840001 905203244
host22:/usr/local       /usr/local      nfs   soft,d
➥ev=2840002      905203257
host22:/opt      /opt    nfs    soft,dev=2840003       905203257
host22:/usr/share/man   /usr/share/man  nfs   soft,
➥dev=2840004      905203257
host22:/usr/X11R6.1     /usr/X11R6.1    nfs   soft,
➥dev=2840005      905203257
```

Mounting and Unmounting NFS Filesystems

The `mount` and `umount` commands are used to mount and unmount filesystems, respectively. Mounting a filesystem attaches it to the existing filesystem hierarchy so that it can be used. A table of mounted filesystems is kept in the `mnttab` (pronounced mount-tab) file at `/etc/mnttab`.

Options Used with All Filesystem Types

Option	Description
`-a`	Mount all filesystems specified in `/etc/vfstab` as "mount at boot" in parallel if possible. If the `umount` command is being used, all filesystems listed in `/etc/mnttab` are unmounted.
`-a` *`mountpoints`*	If the `umount` command is being used, only the mount points listed are unmounted.
`-F` *`type`*	Specify the type of filesystem to mount.
`-m`	Mount filesystem without adding an entry to `/etc/mnttab`.
`-o`	Specify filesystem-specific mount options. Options should be separated by commas.
`-O`	Overlay. The filesystem is mounted over a currently mounted mount point. The underlying filesystem will not be usable after this operation.
`-p`	Print the filesystems in `/etc/vfstab`. No other options can be used with this option.
`-r`	Mount the filesystem as read-only.

continues >>

>>continued

Option	Description
`-v`	Print the filesystems in `/etc/vfstab` showing all information (verbose). No other options can be used with this option.
`-V`	Print the command line, but do not execute anything.

Options Used with NFS Filesystems

Option	Description
`acdirmax=`*n*	Do not cache attributes for more than *n* seconds after update.
`acdirmin=`*n*	Cache attributes for at least *n* seconds after directory update.
`acregmax=`*n*	Do not cache attributes for more than *n* seconds after file modification.
`acregmin=`*n*	Cache attributes after file modification for at least *n* seconds.
`actimeo=`*n*	Set both min and max times for files and directories. The times are set to *n*, in seconds.
`bg`	Background mount if first mount attempt is not successful.
`fg`	Foreground mount.
`grpid`	Set newly created directory group ownerships to that of the parent directory.
`hard`	Continue to retry even if server does not respond initially.
`intr`	Allow keyboard interrupts to halt processes that are hung due to NFS.
`kerberos`	Require Kerberos authentication.
`noac`	Do not cache data or attributes.
`nointr`	Do not allow keyboard interrupts to halt processes that are hung due to NFS. The default is to allow interrupts.
`noquota`	Disable quotas.
`nosuid`	`setuid` execution is not allowed.
`port=n`	Set the NFS server port number.
`posix`	Use POSIX.1 semantics.
`proto=`*netid*	Set the protocol transport by network ID from `/etc/netconfig`.
`quota`	Enable quotas.

continues >>

continued

Option	Description
`remount`	Remount filesystem from `ro` to `rw`.
`retrans=n`	Set number of retransmissions.
`retry=n`	Number of times to retry on failure.
`ro`	Read-only access allowed.
`rsize=n`	Set buffer size to *n* bytes. The default value is 32,768 bytes.
`rw`	Read-write access allowed.
`secure`	NFS requires the use of DES authentication.
`soft`	Return an error if the server does not respond.
`suid`	`setuid` execution allowed.
`timeo=n`	Set timeout to *n* in tenths of a second. Default is 11.
`vers=n`	Set the NFS version number.
`wsize=n`	Set write buffer size to *n* bytes.

Examples

Mount a filesystem on `nserv1` on the local machine as `/usr/foo`:

```
mount nserv1:/usr/export/foo /usr/foo
```

Mount the same filesystem, but as read-only:

```
mount -ro nserv1:/usr/export/foo /usr/foo
```

Manually mount the remote ufs filesystem `/data` from host `tokyo` to the directory `/data` on the local system:

```
mkdir -p /data
mount -F nfs tokyo:/data /data
```

Or, to have the filesystem automatically mounted each time the system is rebooted, add the following line to the file `/etc/vfstab`:

```
tokyo:/data - /data nfs - yes -
```

Then type the following:

```
mkdir -p /data
mountall
```

Manually mount the remote `hsfs` filesystem `/cdrom` from host `tokyo`, read-only, to the directory `/net/tokyo/cdrom` on the local system:

```
mkdir -p /net/tokyo/cdrom
mount -F nfs -r tokyo:/cdrom /net/tokyo/cdrom
```

Or, to have the filesystem automatically mounted each time the system is rebooted, add the following line to the file /etc/vfstab:

```
tokyo:/cdrom - /net/tokyo/cdrom nfs - yes ro
```

Then type the following:

```
mkdir -p /net/tokyo/cdrom
mountall
```

Use the automounter to automatically mount the remote filesystem /usr/man from any of the hosts tokyo, boston, or rio to the directory /usr/man on the local system, each time an attempt is made to access the /usr/man directory.

Add the following line to the file /etc/auto_master:

```
/- auto_direct
```

Add the following line to the file /etc/auto_direct:

```
/usr/man tokyo,boston,rio:/usr/man
```

Then type the following:

```
mkdir -p /usr/man
automount
```

Sharing/Exporting NFS Resources

Sharing/
Exporting NFS
Resources

/usr/bin/share [*options*] [*pathname*]

The share command is used to export NFS filesystems to other computers. If no *pathname* to export is specified, the command displays all filesystems that are currently exported.

Option	Description
-F *type*	Specify the filesystem type. If this option is not used, the first type listed in ./etc/dfs/fstypes is used.
-o *options*	Specify filesystem-specific options that can be used. Options should be in the form of a comma-delimited list.
-d *descrip*	Add a description of the shared resource. The description is set to the string *descrip*.

Options for Sharing NFS Filesystems

Option	Description
`aclok`	If this option is specified, every user accessing the shared resource has the rights of the most unrestricted user. This severely decreases the amount of security provided. Care should be taken when using this option.
`anon=`*`uid`*	Set the effective UID of unauthenticated users to that specified by *`uid`*. If *`uid`* is set to `-1`, all unauthenticated users are denied access. Default behavior is to set the effective `uid` to that of the "nobody" user.
`kerberos`	Only Kerberos is accepted as a valid method of authentication. Unauthenticated users are treated as specified by the `anon` option.
`nosub`	No subdirectories may be mounted in shared directories. This option increases the security of the shared filesystems.
`nosuid`	If this option is set, users are not allowed to create `setuid` or `setgid` files.
`ro`	Read-only.
`ro=`*`host`*`:` ➥*`host2`*`:` ➥*`host3`*`.....`	Set access to read-only for specified clients. Hosts are listed in a colon-delimited list after the equal sign (=).
`root=`*`host`*`:` *`host2`*`:` *`host3`*`.....`	Root access can only be achieved from the listed hostnames. Hosts are listed in a colon-delimited list after the equal sign (=).
`rw`	Read-write access.
`rw=`*`host`*`:` ➥*`host2`*`:` ➥`host3....`	Set access to read-write for the listed hosts. Hosts are listed in a colon-delimited list after the equals sign (=).
`secure`	Secure mode. All clients must use DES authentication. Unauthenticated users are treated as defined by the `anon` option.

File	Description
`/etc/dfs/` ➥`dfstab`	Commands to be executed when the system is booted.
`/etc/dfs/` ➥`fstypes`	Identify the default filesystem type (NFS), as well as all other filesystem types.
`/etc/dfs/` ➥`sharetab`	Table of all shared resources.

Unshare an NFS Resource

Unshare an NFS Resource

`/usr/bin/unshare [options] [pathname]`
`/usr/bin/unshareall`

Remove a shared resource from `/etc/sharetab` so that it is no longer exported as an NFS filesystem. To get a list of what filesystems are shared, use the `share` command with no options. The `unshareall` command unshares all currently shared filesystems.

Option	Description
`-F type`	Specify a filesystem type. By default, NFS is used. Other valid types are listed in the `./etc/dfs/fstypes` file.
`-o`	Specify other filesystem-specific options.

Mail

sendmail

sendmail

`/usr/lib/sendmail [options] [address]`

The `sendmail` daemon routes email for both the local host as well as Internet email. In most cases, `sendmail` is not used manually and is instead called by other programs. However, `sendmail` can be used from the command line to send mail. If no options are specified, the daemon reads data from standard input until an EOF or a line with a single dot is reached. If the address given is a single username, it is assumed to be a user on the local system. If the address is of the format *`user@host.com`*, it is assumed to be Internet email and is routed accordingly. Undeliverable mail is sent back to the sender (known as "bouncing the message"). More information is available at `www.sendmail.org`.

Option	Description
`-B type`	Body type: `7BIT` or `8BITMIIME`.
`-ba`	ARPANET mode. All lines of input must be terminated with a return-linefeed. Both the `From:` and `Sender:` fields are checked for the address of the sender.
`-bd`	Run as a daemon.
`-bi`	Initialize the aliases database.

continues >>

continued

Option	Description
`-bm`	Default method of mail delivery.
`-bp`	Print mail queue summary.
`-bt`	Test mode. Parsing steps for addresses are shown.
`-bv`	Do not deliver the message—verify only.
`-C` *`file`*	Specify a configuration file other than the default.
`-d` *`n`*	Set debugging level to *`n`*.
`-F` *`fullname`*	Set the sender's full name.
`-f` *`name`*	Set the `From:` field of the mail. Only trusted users can use this option.
`-h` *`n`*	Set hop count to *`n`* hops. Mail will be bounced after *`n`* hops.
`-M` *`id`*	Mail the message with mail-id of *`id`*.
`-n`	No aliases.
`-o` *`a value`*	Processing option. *`a`* is the option and *`value`* is the value. For a list of common options, see the next section, "`sendmail` Configuration."
`-p` *`protocol`*	Define the protocol for sending mail.
`-q`	Process the mail queue. If a time is specified, the mail queue is processed on a regular basis. The time is specified as a number and units. Valid units are as follows: ■ `s`: Seconds ■ `m`: Minutes ■ `h`: Hours ■ `d`: Days ■ `w`: Weeks
`-R` *`string`*	Attempt to send any queued mail with a recipient matching the specified string.
`-t`	Scan messages for `To:`, `Cc:`, and `Bcc:` fields to determine recipients.
`-v`	Verbose. Extra information will be given, including alias expansions.
`-X` *`log`*	Log all `sendmail` uses in the specified log file.

sendmail Configuration

sendmail Configuration

`/usr/lib/sendmail.cf`

The `sendmail` daemon can be configured by editing the `sendmail.cf` file. A full reference for the administration of `sendmail` is beyond the scope of this text. Some of the basic configuration options have been listed below. Individual options can also be specified on the `sendmail` command line using the `-o` option.

Basic Configuration Options

Option	Description
`7`	Force input to be stripped to `7-BIT` to comply with old systems.
`A` *`file`*	Specify an alias file.
`a` *`n`*	Wait *`n`* minutes for an `@:@` entry in the mail aliases database before starting.
`B` *`c`*	Set black substitution character to *`c`*.
`b` *`n/m w`*	Only send mail if at least *`n`* blocks are free on the mail queue filesystem. A maximum mail size can also be set by adding the `/m`, where *`w`* is the size.
`C` *`n`*	Checkpoint large mail queues every *`n`* addresses. The default value is 10.
`D`	Rebuild the aliases database.
`d` *`mode`*	Delivery mode: ■ `i`: Interactive ■ `b`: Background ■ `q`: Queue and do not send
`E` *`/file`*	Preface all mailed error messages with the file containing a message.
`e` *`mode`*	Handle errors in mode: ■ `p`: Print errors ■ `q`: Quiet, no messages ■ `m`: Mail errors ■ `w`: Use write to send errors ■ `e`: Mail errors and force zero return value

continues >>

ued >>

Option	Description
`f`	Save from headers (UNIX style).
`F` *`mode`*	File mode.
`g` *`n`*	Set group ID to *`n`*.
`H` *`file`*	Set the help file for the SMTP daemon.
`h` *`n`*	Set max hop count to *`n`*.
`i`	Ignore dots.
`I`	Nameserver must be running to send mail.
`j`	Send error messages in MIME format.
`J` *`path`*	Forward file (`.forward`) search path. Set to *`user`*`/.forward`.
`k` *`n`*	Set the maximum number of connections to *`n`*.
`K` *`time`*	Maximum time to allow a cached and inactive connection to live.
`l`	Use `Errors-To:` header.
`L` *`n`*	Set logging level. Default value is `9`.
`M` *`m val`*	Set the macro (*`m`*) to some value (*`val`*).
`n`	When the aliases database is rebuilt, also validate the RHS of addresses.
`o`	Treat headers as if they are old format.
`O` *`opt`*	SMTP server options as *`key`*`=`*`value`* pairs: ■ `Port=`*`n`*: Set port number ■ `Addr=`*`n`*: Set address mask ■ `Family=`*`n`*: Set address family ■ `Listen=`*`n`*: Set size of listen queue
`p` *`opt,opt,...`*	Privacy Options: ■ `public`: No privacy ■ `needmailhelo`: Require a `HELO` or `EHLO` ■ `needexpnhelo`: Require a `HELO` or `EHLO` before an `EXPN` command ■ `noexpn`: Disallow `EXPN` commands ■ `needvrfyhelo`: Require a `HELO` or `EHLO` before a `VRFY` command

continues >>

continued >>

Option	Description
	■ `novrfy`: Disallow `VRFY` ■ `restrictmailq`: Restrict access to the `mailq` command ■ `restrictqrun`: Restrict access to the `-q` option for `sendmail` command lines ■ `authwarnings`: Use X-Authentication ■ `Warning`: Headers
`P` *`pmaster`*	Define a postmaster to send copies of error messages to.
`Q` *`dir`*	Specify a different queue directory.
`q` *`n`*	Set map function multiplier to *`n`*, when deciding when to queue and when to run jobs. Default value is **`600000`**.
`s`	Super-Safe. The queue file is always instantiated.
`S` *`file`*	Statistics are to be logged to the specified file.
`T` *`rt/wt`*	Set the timeout after which mail is bounced (`rt`) and after which a warning is sent (`wt`). Default bounce time is five days.
`t` *`TZ`*	Set the timezone to *`TZ`*.
`u` *`n`*	Set the default mailer user identification number (`uid`) to *`n`*.
`v`	Verbose. Extra detail is provided displaying all mail delivery steps.
`V` *`fbh`*	Define a fall-back-host. If no other mail exchange host works, the fall-back-host is used.
`x` *`load`*	If the system average load is greater than *`load`*, messages are queued and not sent.
`X` *`load`*	If the system average load is greater than *`load`*, no more SMTP connections are allowed.
`Y`	Save memory by sending each queued message in a separate process.
`y` *`n`*	Lower the priority of jobs with many recipients. The default value is **`30000`**.

smapd

smapd

`smapd [`*`option`*`]`

`smapd` is started when the system boots and runs as a daemon, scanning the `smap` spool directory periodically and invoking `sendmail` to deliver the mail messages it finds in the spool directory.

Option	Description
-d	Indicate that the smapd program should display status messages as it processes the mail messages in the spool directory.

smapd reads configuration entries from the file /usr/local/etc/netperm-table. Configuration entries for smapd have the following format:

```
smapd: option
```

where *option* includes the following:

Option	Description
userid *name*	Specify the user name or UID under which smapd should run.
groupid *name*	Specify the group name or GID under which smapd should run.
directory *path*	Specify the path to which smap should perform a chroot(2) before invoking the mail delivery program.
baddir *path*	Specify the directory into which smapd places mail that it cannot deliver.
wakeup *seconds*	Specify the number of seconds smapd sleeps between scans of the spool directory.
executable_➥*prog*	Specify the program name that the smapd program uses to fork a copy of itself.
sendmail *prog*	Specify the name of the program smapd invokes to deliver the mail messages read from the spool directory.
maxchildren *n*	Specify the maximum number of processes smapd spawns concurrently to deliver the mail messages read from the spool directory.

Example

The /usr/local/etc/netperm-table entries

```
smapd: userid noaccess
smapd: groupid noaccess
smapd: directory /var/spool/smap
smapd: baddir /var/spool/smap/undelivered
smapd: executable /usr/local/bin/smapd
smapd: sendmail /usr/lib/sendmail
smapd: maxchildren 5
```

result in the smapd program running with the privileges of user and group noaccess, scanning the directory /var/spool/smap for mail every 60 seconds (the default), forking a maximum of five concurrent instances of itself, each of which invokes the /usr/lib/sendmail program to deliver the mail, and placing undeliverable messages in the directory /var/spool/smap/undelivered.

SMTP Application Proxy (smap)

smap

smap [-*daemon port*]

On systems that are not protected from electronic attack from untrustworthy users through the use of a network firewall, it may be deemed desirable to use a secure proxy application to avoid allowing remote systems to communicate directly with the sendmail program. In such cases, the SMTP Application Proxy (smap) can be used. smap is one component of the TIS Firewall Toolkit (fwtk), a collection of programs for enhancing the security of UNIX systems, written by Trusted Information Systems, Inc., and made available free of charge to anyone for non-commercial use. smap can either be run as a daemon listening for connection requests on the specified port (by default, smap uses the standard SMTP port 25), or it can be invoked by inetd for each SMTP connection request received.

smap consults a configuration file (/usr/local/etc/netperm-table) to determine the directory to make its root directory and to determine the user and group IDs to set itself to before accepting the SMTP connection with the remote system. smap then receives mail from the remote system, placing the mail in a spool directory within its restricted environment. It is then scanned periodically (by default, every 60 seconds) by the SMTP Proxy Server (smapd), which invokes the sendmail program to route or deliver each message. In this way, the remote system is prevented from communicating directly with the sendmail program, which must necessarily run with root privileges in an unrestricted environment.

Option	Description
-*daemon port*	Indicate that the smap program should act as a daemon, listening for connection requests on the specified port, rather than being invoked by inetd. *port* can be specified by name or number.

The configuration file /usr/local/etc/netperm-table is shared by all components of the TIS Firewall Toolkit. Configuration entries for smap have the following format:

smap: *option*

where *option* includes the following:

Option	Description
userid *name*	Specify the user name or UID under which smap should communicate with the remote system.
groupid *name*	Specify the group name or GID under which smap should communicate with the remote system.
directory *path*	Specify the path to which smap should perform a chroot(2) before communicating with the remote system.
timeout ➥*seconds*	Specify the number of seconds smap will keep an idle connection open before disconnecting from the remote system.

Example

The /etc/inetd.conf entry

```
smtp stream tcp nowait root /usr/local/bin/smap smap
```

accompanied by the /usr/local/etc/netperm-table entries

```
smap: userid noaccess
smap: groupid NOACCESS
smap: directory /var/spool/smap
```

results in the smap program communicating with remote systems with the privileges of user and group noaccess and with the directory /var/spool/smap as its root directory.

11 Filesystems

Filesystem Overview and Description

Solaris Filesystem Description File (vfstab)

vfstab

`/etc/vfstab`

All the Solaris filesystems are described in the `vfstab` file (`/etc/vfstab`). Each line in the `vfstab` file consists of seven space-delimited columns. The columns are as follows:

```
device to mount  device to fsck  mount point  FS type
➥fsck pass  mount at boot  mount options
```

Field	Description
`device to mount`	The name of the resource to mount. If a swap file is to be specified, the device to mount is the swap filename.
`device to fsck`	The raw device on which to perform a filesystem consistency check (`fsck`).
`mount point`	The default mount point.
`FS type`	The filesystem type (such as `ufs`, `pcfs`, `nfs`, or `hsfs`). If the resource is a swap file, the `FS` type is `swap`.
`fsck pass`	A number to determine when and in what order `fsck` will automatically check the filesystem.
`mount at boot`	Determine whether the filesystem should be mounted by `mountall` at boot time. If a swap file is being specified, `mount at boot` should be set to no.
`mount options`	Any mount options to be used when mounting the resource. See `mount`.

If a field does not apply or needs to be left blank, put a `-` in the column.

Solaris Filesystem Layout

Solaris Filesystem Layout

Under Solaris, hard disk storage is divided into *filesystems* (also known as *partitions*). Dividing the hard drive into sections allows common files to be grouped together. This makes sharing files over networks easier and generally improves the ability to manage the system.

The default Solaris installation is divided into three filesystems: `/`, `/usr`, and `/expor`.

Solaris Filesystems

Filesystem	Description
/	The root filesystem. Usually files on the root filesystem are not shared across the network and are kept only on the local machine. System configuration files, such as those kept in `/etc`, are on the root filesystem. The root filesystem should be kept as small as possible if there is a separate `/var` filesystem. If `/var` is simply a directory under the root filesystem, then / should be large because it will hold all the variable system logs and other variable size files.
`/usr`	The `/usr` filesystem. The `/usr` (pronounced "user") filesystem is usually much larger than the root filesystem and contains files that are to be shared across the network using NFS. Traditionally, the `/usr` filesystem was used to serve files that can be used on many computer architectures.
`/export`	If a Solaris system has a large amount of disk space available and is on a network, it can be used to share entire filesystems (such as root or swap space) with other diskless clients.

The Root Filesystem

Directory	Description
`/dev`	Device files for kernel and hardware
`/dev/dsk`	Disk devices
`/dev/pts`	Pseudo-terminal devices
`/dev/rdsk`	Raw disk devices (such as floppy drives)
`/dev/rmt`	Tape devices (such as tape backups)
`/dev/sad`	STREAMS administrative devices
`/dev/term`	Terminal devices
`/etc`	Configuration files that are unique to each host
`/etc/acct`	Accounting system configuration files
`/etc/cron.d`	`cron` configuration
`/etc/default`	Default configuration files for certain programs
`/etc/dfs`	Shared filesystem configuration
`/etc/fs`	Files used before `/usr` is mounted

continues >>

>>continued

Directory	Description
/etc/inet	Internet configuration files
/etc/init.d	Scripts for startup and shutdown, as well as change of run state
/etc/lib	Shared libraries
/etc/lp	Printer service configuration files
/etc/mail	Mail service configuration files
/etc/net	Network service configuration files
/etc/opt	Optional software package configurations
/etc/rc0.d	Startup and shutdown scripts for run state 0
/etc/rc1.d	Startup and shutdown scripts for run state 1
/etc/rc2.d	Startup and shutdown scripts for run state 2
/etc/rc3.d	Startup and shutdown scripts for run state 3
/etc/saf	Files for the Service Access Facility
/etc/skel	Files for new accounts created using the useradd utility
/etc/sm	Status monitor information
/etc/sm.bak	Status monitor information backup
/etc/tm	Trademark information shown at boot time
/etc/uucp	UUCP configuration files
/home	User files and home directories
/kernel	Platform-independent kernel modules
/mnt	Temporary mount point for mounting filesystems
/opt	Optional/third-party software packages and applications
/platform	Platform-dependent objects
/platform/*/ ➥kernel	Platform-dependent objects related to the UNIX kernel
/platform/*/ ➥lib	Platform-dependent objects related to shared libraries
/platform/*/ ➥sbin	Platform-dependent objects related to system binaries
/proc	Process information and tools
/sbin	System binaries required to boot and before /usr is mounted

continues >>

continued

Directory	Description
/tmp	Temporary files (all files are removed at boot time)
/var	Varying files that are host specific, yet are of an undetermined size, such as log files (/var/log/syslog or /var/adm/log)
/var/adm	Varying administrative files
/var/cron	cron log files
/var/mail	User mail files
/var/news	Files shown to users using the news command (not related to Usenet)
/var/nis	NIS+ databases
/var/opt	Varying files created by optional software packages or applications
/var/preserve	vi and ex backup files
/var/sadm	Software management databases
/var/saf	Logging and accounting files for the Service Access Facility
/var/spool	Files used by mail services, printer services, and cron
/var/spool/lp	Printer spool files
/var/spool/ ➥mqueue	Mail queue files (mail waiting to be sent)
/var/spool/pkg	Temporary space for packages being installed using the pkgadd utility
/var/spool/ ➥uucp	Queued UUCP processes
/var/spool/ ➥uucppublic	Files created by UUCP jobs
/var/tmp	Temporary files (not cleared at boot time)
/var/uucp	UUCP log files
/var/yp	Compatibility files for NIS and YP services
/var/spool/ ➥cron	Temporary files for cron and at
/var/spool/ ➥locks	Lock files

The usr Filesystem

Directory	Description
/usr/4lib	Binary Compatibility Package (BCP) libraries
/usr/bin	System utilities and binaries
/usr/bin/ ➥sunview1	Binary Compatibility Package (BCP) SunView executables
/usr/ccs	C Compiler System (CCS) files
/usr/ccs/bin	C compiler binaries
/usr/ccs/lib	Libraries for the C compiler
/usr/demo	Demonstration programs
/usr/dt	Common Desktop Environment (CDE) files
/usr/dt/bin	CDE binaries
/usr/dt/ ➥include	CDE include and header files
/usr/dt/lib	CDE libraries
/usr/dt/man	Online manual pages (man pages) for CDE
/usr/games	Game files
/usr/include	Header files for use with C compilers
/usr/kernel	Platform-independent kernel modules
/usr/platform	Platform-dependent objects
/usr/lib	Program-specific libraries and programs that are not directly executed by users (such as sendmail)
/usr/lib/acct	Accounting binaries
/usr/lib/dict	Dictionary files and spelling databases
/usr/lib/class	priocntrl and dispadmin files
/usr/lib/font	Description files for use with troff
/usr/lib/fs	Filesystem modules and programs that are not directly executed by users
/usr/lib/iconv	iconv conversion tables
/usr/lib/libp	Profiled libraries
/usr/lib/ ➥locale	Databases for localization of the system (languages, time zones, and so on)

continues >>

continued

Directory	Description
/usr/lib/lp	Printer service databases and binaries that are not directly executed by users
/usr/lib/mail	Mail service programs (including sendmail)
/usr/lib/ ➥netsvc	Internet files
/usr/lib/nfs	Network File System (NFS) files
/usr/lib/pics	Position Independent Code (PIC) files
/usr/lib/refer	Programs used by refer
/usr/lib/sa	System Activity Report (SAR) files
/usr/lib/saf	Service Access Facility (SAF) files
/usr/lib/ ➥spell	Binary Compatibility Package spelling files
/usr/lib/uucp	UUCP daemons
/usr/local	Local programs and utilities
/usr/net/ ➥servers	Entry points for the Listen daemon
/usr/oasys	Framed Access Command Environment (FACE) package files
/usr/old	Old programs
/usr/openwin	OpenWindows software
/usr/sadm	System administration files
/usr/sadm/bin	Form and Menu Language Interpreter (FMLI) files
/usr/sadm/ ➥install	Package management files
/usr/sbin	System administration binaries
/usr/sbin/ ➥static	Statically linked programs to recover from problems
/usr/share	Platform-independent shared files
/usr/share/man	Online manual pages
/usr/share/lib	Platform-independent libraries and databases
/usr/share/ ➥lib/keytables	Keyboard configuration files

continues >>

>>continued

Directory	Description
/usr/share/ ➥lib/mailx	mailx help files
/usr/share/ ➥lib/nterm	Terminal tables for nroff
/usr/share/ ➥lib/pub	Character sets
/usr/share/ ➥lib/spell	spell databases and files
/usr/share/ ➥lib/tabset	Tab-setting files
/usr/share/ ➥lib/terminfo	Terminal information files for use with terminfo
/usr/share/ ➥lib/tmac	nroff and troff macro files
/usr/share/ ➥lib/zoneinfo	Time zone information
/usr/share/src	Shared source code
/usr/snadm	SNAG files
/usr/ucb	University of California Berkeley (UCB) distribution files for compatibility
/usr/ ➥ucbinclude	University of California Berkeley (UCB) distribution header files
/usr/ucblib	University of California Berkeley (UCB) distribution library
/usr/vmsys	Framed Access Command Environment (FACE) files

The export Filesystem

Directory	Description
/export	The exported filesystem
/export/exec/ ➥*platform*	The /usr filesystem that is ready for export for the platform/architecture specified by *platform*
/export/exec/ ➥share	The /usr/share directory for export to all systems
/export/root/ ➥*hostname*	The root filesystem to be exported to the host specified by *hostname*

continues >>

ntinued

Directory	Description
`/export/root/` ➥`swap/`*`hostname`*	The swap file to be exported for the host specified by *`hostname`*
`/.export/var/` ➥*`hostname`*	The */var* filesystem to be exported to the host specified by *`hostname`*

Constructing and Mounting New Filesystems

Constructing a New Filesystem (mkfs)

`/usr/sbin/mkfs [`*`options`*`]` *`filesystem`*

The `mkfs` utility constructs new filesystems. All types of filesystems can be created using `mkfs`. Options that are common to all types of filesystems are specified, as usual, on the command line. Filesystem specific options are specified using the `-o` option.

Using the Front-End

The `newfs` utility has been added to Solaris to make the creation of new filesystems easier. It acts as a front-end for the `mkfs` utility. It is highly recommended that the `newfs` front-end be used to create new filesystems whenever possible. See "Constructing a New Filesystem (`newfs`)" (p. 233).

Options for All Filesystems

Option	Description
`-F`	Filesystem type. This option can be used to specify the filesystem type. If this option is omitted, the `/etc/vfstab` and `/etc/default/fs` files are checked to determine a filesystem type.
`-m`	Show the command line that was used to create the specified filesystem. No changes are made to the filesystem.
`-o`	Use filesystem-specific options. (See subsequent tables.)
`-V`	Verbose. Show the command line but do not execute anything.

Options for New UFS Filesystems

The options used to create a new UFS filesystem are specified by keywords set to a specified value. In each case, *n* is an integer.

Option	Description
`apc=`*n*	Reserved space for bad block replacement on SCSI devices. The default value is `0`.
`bsize=`*n*	Logical block size of either `4096` (4K) or `8192` (8K). The default is `8192`.
`cgsize=`*n*	Number of cylinders per cylinder group. The default value is `16`.
`fragsize=`*n*	The smallest amount of space allocated to a file. The value must be 2^b where *b* is a number from `512` to the local block size. The default value is `1024`.
`free=`*n*	The minimum amount of free space to maintain on the filesystem. The default value is `60`.
`gap=`*n*	Rotational delay, given in milliseconds. The default value depends on the drive type.
`maxcontig=`*n*	The maximum number of blocks that can be allocated together before a rotational delay is inserted. The default value depends on the filesystem: ■ 4K systems: `14` ■ 8K systems: `7` This parameter can be changed later using `tunefs`.
N	Do not construct the filesystem. Only show the parameters that would be used.
`nbpi=`*n*	Number of blocks per inode. The default value is `2048`.
`nrpos=`*n*	Rotational positions for each cylinder. The default value is `8`.
`nsect=`*n*	Number of sectors per track. The default value is `32`.
`ntrack=`*n*	Number of tracks per cylinder. The default value is `16`.
`opt=`*type*	Optimization type. The type can be one of the following: ■ `s`: Optimize for disk space. ■ `t`: Optimize for speed (time).
`rps=`*n*	Disk speed given in revolutions per second. The default value is `60`.

Constructing a New Filesystem (newfs)

`newfs [options] raw-device`

newfs

In previous versions of SunOS, new filesystems were created using the mkfs command. The newfs command has been added to ease the creation of UFS filesystems, acting as a front-end to the mkfs utility. The newfs command automatically determines all the necessary parameters to pass to mkfs to construct the new filesystem.

This command can only be used by the root user to create new file -systems, unless the new filesystem is on a removable floppy disk. If the new filesystem is on a disk, anyone use can use newfs. The following options can be used with the newfs utility.

Option	Description
-a *abpc*	Alternate blocks per cylinder. This option applies only to SCSI devices reserved for bad block placement. The default value is 0.
-b *blocksize*	Block size. Specify the logical block size of the filesystem in bytes. Must be either 4096 or 8192. The default value is 8192.
-c *cpg*	Cylinders per cylinder group. This value must be in the range of 1 to 32. The default value is 16.
-C *max*	The maximum number of blocks that can be allocated together before a rotational delay is inserted. The default value depends on the filesystem: ■ 4K FS = 14 ■ 8K FS = 7 This option can be changed later using tunefs.
-d *delay*	Rotational delay. Specify the rotational spacing between blocks in a file and give it in milliseconds. This value can be changed later using the tunefs command. The default value depends on the type of drive.
-f *size*	Fragment size. The smallest number of bytes to allocate to a file. The value must be 2^n, where *n* can be in the range from 512 to the logical block size.
-i *bpi*	Bytes per inode. The number determines the total number of inodes in the filesystem. To allow for fewer inodes, use a large number. For more inodes, use a small number. The default value is 2048.

continues >>

>>continued

Option	Description
-m *freepct*	Minimum free space. Specify the amount of free space (expressed as a percentage of the total) to be maintained on the disk. Only the root user can write to the disk to exceed the minimum free space allowance. The default value is **10%**.
-N	Display all parameters that would be used in creating the new filesystem, but do not actually create the filesystem or alter the disk in any way.
-n *rotpos*	Rotational positions. Specify the number of divisions in a cylinder group. The default value is **8**.
-o *optimize*	Optimization. Can be one of two options: ■ space: Minimize time spent allocating blocks. ■ time: Minimize space fragmentation on the disk. If the minimum free space (as given by -m) is less than 10%, space optimization is used.
-r *rpm*	Disk speed. Specify the speed of the disk in revolutions per minute. The default value is **3600**.
-s *sectors*	Disk sectors. Specify the size of the file system in sectors. The default is to use the entire filesystem.
-t *tpc*	Tracks per cylinder. Specify the number of tracks per cylinder on the disk. The default value depends on the drive.
-v	Verbose. All actions and informative messages are displayed.

Example	Description
newfs -v /dev/rdsk/c0t0d0s6	Create a new filesystem using all default values, showing all actions
newfs -Nv /dev/rdsk/c0t0d0s8	Display information about a raw device but do not create a filesystem

Mounting and Unmounting Filesystems (mount, mountall)

mount, mountall

```
/usr/sbin/mount [options] filesystem mountpoint
/usr/sbin/umount [options] mountpoint
```

The `mount` and `umount` commands are used to mount and unmount filesystems. Mounting a filesystem attaches it to the existing filesystem hierarchy so that it can be used. A table of mounted filesystems is kept in the `mnttab` (pronounced mount-tab) file at `/etc/mnttab`.

Options for All Filesystem Types

Option	Description
`-a`	Mount all filesystems specified in `/etc/vfstab` as "mount at boot" in parallel if possible. If the `umount` command is being used, all filesystems listed in `/etc/mnttab` are unmounted.
`-a` *`mountpoints`*	If the `umount` command is being used, only the mount points listed are unmounted.
`-F` *`type`*	Specify the type of filesystem to mount.
`-m`	Mount filesystem without adding an entry to `/etc/mnttab`.
`-o`	Specify filesystem-specific mount options. Options should be separated by commas.
`-O`	Overlay. The filesystem is mounted over a currently mounted mount point. The underlying filesystem will not be usable after this operation.
`-p`	Print the filesystems in `/etc/vfstab`. No other options can be used with this option.
`-r`	Mount the filesystem as read-only.
`-v`	Print the filesystems in `/etc/vfstab` showing all information (verbose). No other options can be used with this option.
`-V`	Print the command line, but do not execute anything.

Options for Mounting UFS Filesystems

Option	Description
`f`	Fake entry. Add an entry to `/etc/mnttab`, but do not actually mount the filesystem.
`intr`	Allow keyboard interrupts to kill processes waiting for locked filesystems.
`m`	Mount the filesystem but do not add an entry to `/etc/mnttab`.

continues >>

>>continued

Option	Description
nointr	Do not allow keyboard interrupts to kill processes waiting for locked filesystems.
nosuid	Disallow `suid` execution of programs.
onerror=*action*	Specify the action to take on errors. The action can be one of four options: ■ `panic`: Force a system shutdown. ■ `lock`: Lock the filesystem. ■ `umount`: Force the filesystem to be unmounted. ■ `repair`: Perform an automatic `fsck`. The default option is `panic`.
quota	Enable quotas for the specified filesystem.
remount	Remount a currently mounted filesystem. To be used to change filesystems from read-only to read-write.
ro	Mount filesystem as read-only.
rq	Mount filesystem as read and write with quotas enabled.
rw	Mount filesystem as read-write enabled.
toosoon=*time*	Specify the minimum time between filesystem inconsistencies that will signal a forced shutdown or repair. The time is specified in seconds (`s`), minutes (`m`), hours (`h`), days (`d`), weeks (`w`), or years (`y`), using the units shown. For example: `15h` is 15 hours.

Checking and Tuning Filesystems

Checking and Fixing Filesystems (fsck)

fsck

The `fsck` utility is an interactive tool to perform consistency checks and repair filesystems. By default, the user will be asked for confirmation before any corrective action takes place. Only the root user can fix disk problems using `fsck`.

Possible Loss of Data

The `fsck` utility can fix many common disk problems. It should be noted, however, that corrective actions can lead to loss of data on the filesystem. The amount of data lost depends on the severity of the problem and will be reported at the end of the `fsck` execution.

To prevent potential problems, unmount filesystems before performing a `fsck` whenever possible. If this is not possible, reboot immediately after running `fsck`.

Options for All Filesystems

Option	Description
`-F` *type*	Specify filesystem type.
`-m`	Perform a sanity check on the filesystem but no repairs are made. This option can be used as a quick check to see if a filesystem is ready to be mounted.
`-N`	Answer `no` to all corrective-action questions.
`-o`	Use filesystem-specific options. Options must be given in a comma-delimited list.
`-V`	Print command lines but do not perform any actions.
`-Y`	Answer `yes` to all corrective action questions.

Options for UFS Filesystems

Option	Description
`b=`*n*	Treat block *n* as the filesystem super block. Super blocks can be found using the `newfs` utility with the `-V`*n* option.
`c`	Convert table formats. Old format static tables are converted to new dynamic tables, and vice versa.
`f`	Force filesystem checks.
`p`	Preen. Check and fix filesystem without user interaction.
`w`	Perform `fsck` on writeable filesystems only.

Exit Codes

Exit Code	Description
0	No errors or filesystem problems.
1	Incorrect `fsck` usage.
32	Filesystem is unmounted and needs to be checked.
33	Filesystem is mounted.
34	Cannot check device.
36	Filesystem errors were found that cannot be corrected.
37	Signal encountered during execution.
39	Filesystem errors were found that cannot be corrected—abnormal termination.
40	No errors or filesystem problems.

Printing Filesystem Statistics and Filenames (ff)

ff

The `ff` utility can be used to print pathnames and inode numbers for all the files on a given filesystem. This command is similar to the `ncheck` utility.

Options for All Filesystems

Option	Description
`-a` *n*	Print files only if they have been accessed in *n* days.
`-c` *n*	Print files only if their status has changed in the last *n* days.
`-F` *type*	Specify the filesystem type.
`-I`	Print the inode numbers with associated pathnames.
`-i` *list*	Print only files with inodes given in *list*. The list must be a comma-delimited list of inumbers.
`-l`	Generate another list for file with multiple links.
`-m` *n*	Print files only if they have been written to or created in the last *n* days.
`-n` *filename*	Print files only if they have been modified in the last *n* days.
`-o`	Specify filesystem-specific options.

continues >>

ntinued

Option	Description
`-p prefix`	Prepend the prefix to each pathname listed.
`-s`	Show file sizes in bytes.
`-u`	Show file ownership.
`-V`	Print the command line, but do not perform any actions.

Options for UFS Filesystems Only

Option	Description
`a`	Print `.` and `..` as well as other files.
`m`	Show file modes.
`s`	Print only `setuid` and special files.

Checking Free Disk Space (df)

The `df` command can be used to check free disk space on a filesystem. Exported and remounted filesystems (such as `/export` or, sometimes, `./home`) can occasionally be listed twice.

df

Option	Description
`-a`	Show disk space for all filesystems.
`-b`	Show only free disk space, in kilobytes.
`-e`	Show only the number of files free on the filesystem.
`-F type`	Specify the filesystem type. Used only with unmounted filesystems.
`-g`	Show all information (entire `statvfs` structure) for mounted filesystems.
`-k`	Display all information with allocations and free space given in kilobytes.
`-l`	Show local filesystems only. NFS filesystems are not shown.
`-n`	Print the filesystem type only.
`-o options`	Specify filesystem-specific options given as a comma-delimited list.
`-P`	Show all information given in 512-byte units.
`-t`	Show totals for disk statistics.
`-v`	Print the command line, but do not execute any actions.

Example Output of df

```
/                (/dev/dsk/c0t0d0s0 ):  655122 blocks
➥461301 files
/proc            (/proc             ):       0 blocks
➥1959 files
/dev/fd          (fd                ):       0 blocks
➥0 files
/opt             (/dev/dsk/c0t1d0s0 ):  351948 blocks
➥366443 files
/export          (/dev/dsk/c1t0d0s6 ): 6318772 blocks
➥502588 files
/stuff           (/dev/dsk/c0t1d0s6 ): 5439788 blocks
➥397744 files
/spare1          (/dev/dsk/c0t0d0s7 ): 1984568 blocks
➥499453 files
/spare2          (/dev/dsk/c0t2d0s5 ): 7803320 blocks
➥470011 files
/music           (/dev/dsk/c0t2d0s6 ): 2957202 blocks
➥469375 files
/tmp             (swap              ):  866776 blocks
➥16166 files
/oldroot         (/dev/dsk/c0t2d0s0 ):  522688 blocks
➥340701 files
/home/marym      (/export/home/marym): 6318772 blocks
➥502588 files
```

Example Output of df -k

```
Filesystem            kbytes    used   avail capacity  Mounted
                                                       ➥on
/dev/dsk/c0t3d0s0     100935   27083   63762    30%    /
/dev/dsk/c0t2d0s6     384243  255164   90659    74%    /usr
/proc                      0       0       0     0%    /proc
fd                             0       0       0      0%
/dev/fd
/dev/dsk/c0t3d0s3     167631  129800   21071    87%    /var
/dev/dsk/c0t2d0s5      96048   11225   75223    13%    /tmp
/dev/dsk/c0t2d0s7     131718    1334  117214     2%
➥/var/tmp
/dev/dsk/c1t2d0s1    3939430 1348153 2197337    39%
➥/var/spool/news
/dev/dsk/c1t1d0s6     306418  142389  133389    52%    /home
/dev/dsk/c1t1d0s7     306418  261545   14233    95%
/home/staff
/dev/dsk/c0t0d0s6     306418  198473   77305    72%
➥/home/student
/dev/dsk/c0t0d0s7     306418  117572  158206    43%
➥/home/math
host2:/usr/local      631824  463824  104816    82%
➥/usr/local
```

```
host2:/opt              192416  154176   19000    90%    /opt
host2:/usr/share/man    631824  463824  104816    82%
➥/usr/share/man
host2:/usr/X11R6.1      631824  463824  104816    82%
➥/usr/X11R6.1
```

Labeling Filesystems (labelit)

The `labelit` utility is used to label filesystems and to print labels for current filesystems. The filesystem must be unmounted before it can be labeled. Disk labels are used by programs such as `volcopy`.

labelit

Option	Description
`-F` *type*	Specify the filesystem type.
`-V`	Print command line, but do not perform any actions.

List Pathnames and inumbers (ncheck)

The `ncheck` utility generates a list of pathnames with the associated inumbers for a block special device. A block special device can be specified on the command line; otherwise, `ncheck` is run on all devices marked as special in `/.etc/vfstab`. Some options can be used for all filesystem types, whereas other options are filesystem specific.

ncheck

Options for All Filesystem Types

Option	Description
`-a`	Show `.` and `..` when listing filenames.
`-F`	Specify the filesystem type on which to perform an `ncheck` on.
`-i` *list*	Show only those files associated with the list of inumbers given. The list must be comma-delimited.
`-o`	Specifies filesystem-specific options. Given in a comma-delimited list.
`-s`	Show only `setuid` and special files. This option can be used to check the security of the system.
`-V`	Print the command line, but do not perform any actions.

Options for Use with UFS Filesystems

Option	Description
`m`	Print mode information for files.

Tuning a Filesystem (tunefs)

tunefs

After a filesystem has been unmounted, `tunefs` can be used to tune the performance and parameters of the disk. The filesystem must be in `/etc/vfstab` to be tuned.

Option	Description
`-a` *max*	Set the maximum number of blocks that will be written continuously before a rotational delay is inserted.
`-d` *delay*	Set the size of the rotational delay (in milliseconds) to insert between blocks.
`-e` *bpg*	Set the maximum number of blocks per cylinder group.
`-m` *free*	Set the minimum amount of free space to maintain on the filesystem.
`-o` *type*	Set the type of filesystem optimization: ■ `space`: Optimize for space. ■ `time`: Optimize for speed (access time reduction).

Example	Description
`tunefs -o time /home`	Optimize the `/home` filesystem for speed.

Backups

Backing Up a Filesystem (ufsdump)

ufsdump

The `ufsdump` utility is used to back up filesystems. Either specific files or entire filesystems can be dumped to the backup device (such as a tape backup). By default, the backup is dumped to `/dev/rmt/0`.

Devices Must Be Inactive When Backing Up

It is very important that the filesystem being backed up is not active (being read or written to). It should be either unmounted or in single-user mode when `ufsdump` is running. Attempting to back up an active filesystem will lead to data corruption and it may be impossible to restore files from the backup.

Option	Description
`a`	Archive file. Create an archive table of contents to be used by `ufsrestore` to check if a file has been backed up.
`b` *`factor`*	Blocking factor. Specify the blocking factor to be used for tape devices. The default value is **`20`** blocks per write for tapes of 6,250 bytes/inch or less. Blocks are 512-byte blocks.
`c`	Use default values for cartridge backups rather than half-inch reel.
`D`	Dump to disk.
`d` *`bpi`*	Tape density. Set the tape density to *`bpi`*, or bytes per inch.
`dumplevel`	Dump level. The dump level is an integer (`0...9`) that is used to decide what files are backed up during incremental backups. A level `0` dump backs up all files on the filesystem. If a non-zero dump level is given, all files that were modified since the last dump level that was lower than the current level will be backed up. For example, a level `2` dump would back up all files that were modified since the last `1` or `0` backup.
`file`	Dump file. Backup is dumped to the specified file rather than to `/dev/rmt/0`.
`l`	Autoload. At the end of the tape, the drive is taken offline and waits two minutes before going back online. This allows autoloaders to perform correctly.
`n`	Notify. All users in the `sys` group are notified of any problems encountered during a backup.
`o`	Offline. The tape drive is taken offline after the backup is complete or the end of the tape is reached—whichever comes first.
`S`	Do not perform the backup—only print an estimate of the space needed to perform the dump.

continues >>

>>continued

Option	Description
s *size*	Specify the size of the backup device media (tapes). This option is not required. Values are given in feet and should be slightly less than the actual tape length.
t *tracks*	Specify the number of tracks for a cartridge tape. Not usually needed. The default value is 9.
u	Add an entry (filesystem name, date, dump level) to the /etc/dumpdates file.
v	Verify. Check the dumped filesystem against the backup copy.
w	Warn. Print filesystems that have not been backed up in more than a day.
W	Warn with highlight. Print all filesystems in /etc/dumpdates, highlighting filesystems that have not been backed up in more than a day.

Restoring a Filesystem from a Backup (ufsrestore)

ufsrestore

The ufsrestore utility is used to restore filesystems from backups.

Backup Modes

Mode	Function Letter	Description
Extract	x	Extract the files specified from the media to the filesystem.
Interactive	i	The ufsrestore utility runs in interactive mode, prompting for responses from the user, after reading the initial information from the backup media. In this mode, commands can be used (given later in this section).
Recursive	r	Recursively restore an entire filesystem into the current top-level directory.

continues >>

ntinued

Mode	Function Letter	Description
Resume	`R`	Resume restoring at a particular volume of a backup after it was interrupted.
Table-of-Contents	`t`	Print a table of contents of the backup media, showing all files.

Modifiers

Modifier	Description
`a` *`file`*	Use the table of contents in the specified file rather than from the backup media.
`b` *`factor`*	Blocking factor. Specify the blocking factor for a tape backup in 512-byte blocks.
`c`	Convert old format media to new `ufs` format.
`d`	Debug. Print debugging information.
`f` *`file`*	Use the file specified by *`file`* rather than `/dev/rmt/0` as the source from which to restore.
`h`	Restore the actual directory from the backup rather than from the files referenced by it.
`m`	Restore by inode number rather than by filename.
`s` *`n`*	Extract from the backup media starting at the nth file.
`v`	Verbose. Show extra information when restoring from a backup.
`y`	Force `ufsrestore` to continue when errors are encountered.

Commands

Command	Description
`add` *`file`*	Add the specified file to the list of files to be extracted from the backup media.
`cd` *`directory`*	Change to the specified directory in the dump file.
`delete` *`file`*	Delete the specified file (or directory) from the list of files to be extracted from the backup media.

continues >>

>>continued

Command	Description
`extract`	Extract all files on list to be restored. The list is created using the `add` and `delete` commands.
`help`	Print a summary of commands.
`ls`	List files and directories in the current working directory in the dump file.
`pwd`	Print the current working directory.
`quit`	Exit immediately.
`setmodes`	Interactively ask for modes to set "`.`".
`verbose`	Toggle the verbose flag. If verbose is on, inode numbers are shown when the `ls` command is used.
`what`	Print the media dump header.

Copying Filesystems

Copying Volumes (volcopy)

volcopy

The `volcopy` command can be used by the root user to make a copy of a labeled filesystem. This command works with ufs filesystems, but may not work with other filesystem types. Unless the `-a` option is specified on the command line, the `volcopy` utility will pause 10 seconds before making the copy.

Use `dd` for Copying to Tape Devices

Use the `volcopy` utility for copying between disks. To copy a volume to a tape device, use the `dd` utility.

Option	Description
`-a`	Prompt the user for confirmation before copy is made.
`-F` *`type`*	Specify the filesystem type.
`-o` *`options`*	Specify filesystem-specific options as a comma-delimited list.
`-V`	Print the command line but do not perform any actions.

Copying and Converting Files (cpio, dd)

Two main utilities exist to copy and convert files or entire filesystems. The cpio utility is used to copy file archives, and the dd utility is used to copy and convert files (to tape drives, especially). The cpio utility preserves file modes and permissions.

cpio, dd

cpio Modes

cpio Mode	Mode Letter	Description
Copy In	-i	Read from standard input, creating the extracted files and directories and preserving file modes and permissions. If the user is the root user, file user and group ownerships will be preserved as well.
Copy Out	-o	Read from standard input to create a list of files and paths to copy. This information is sent to standard output along with path and status information.
Pass	-p	Read a list of pathnames and copy the associated files and directories to the specified destination.

Option	Description
-a	Reset access times of copied files.
-A	Add files to an archive file.
-B	Block input and output to 5,120 bytes per record.
-c	Keep header information in ASCII format when reading or writing.
-C *size*	Set the input/output buffer size to *size*. The default buffer size is 512 bytes.
-d	Directories are created if needed.
-E *file*	Read filenames to be copied from the specified file.
-H *header*	Set the header format to *header*. Valid header values are Bar, crc, odc, tar, and ustar.

continues >>

>>continued

Option	Description
`-I file`	Treat the specified file as an input file, reading filenames from the file. The file can also be a special device.
`-k`	Skip corrupted file headers and continue.
`-l`	Link rather than copy files.
`-L`	Symbolic links are followed.
`-m`	Do not change file modification times.
`-M msg`	Define the message that is printed when it is time to change media when using the `-O` or `-I` option.
`-O file`	Send output of `cpio` to the specified file. The file can also be a special device.
`-P`	Preserve access control lists (ACLs).
`-r`	The user is prompted to rename each file as it is read.
`-R uid`	Interactively change the *uid* of each file. You must be the root user to do this.
`-t`	Print input table of contents.
`-u`	Unconditional copy. By default (without `-u`), older files will not replace newer files of the same name.
`-v`	Verbose. Print informational messages.
`-V`	Special Verbose. Print only files that are copied.

`cpio` Example

Example	Description
`Find . -print | cpio -dump{output}`	Copy one directory tree to another.

`dd`

An alternative to using `cpio` is `dd`, which can be used to copy and convert files. This utility is especially useful for copying to tape drives. The block size of input and output streams can be converted.

Operand	Description
`bs=`*n*	Set the output and input block sizes to the same value.
`cbs=`*n*	Set the conversion block size. Only used with ASCII and EBCDIC conversions.
`conv=` ➥*conversion*	Convert the input using the specified conversion format. Conversions are given in the subsequent table.
`count=`*n*	Copy *n* input blocks.
`files=`*n*	Copy *n* files before exiting.
`ibs=`*n*	Set the input block size.
`if=`*file*	Use ***file*** as the input path. The default value is standard input.
`iseek=`*n*	Seek, rather than skip, *n* blocks of the input file before copying and converting (faster than skipping for disk files).
`obs=`*n*	Set the output block size.
`of=`*file*	Use ***file*** as the out path. The default value is standard output.
`oseek=`*n*	Seek, rather than skip, *n* blocks from the beginning of the output file before copying.
`skip=`*n*	Skip *n* blocks and then begin to copy and convert.

Conversions

Option	Description
`ascii`	EBCDIC to ASCII conversion.
`block`	Treat newlines as the end of records rather than depending on block lengths.
`ebcdic`	ASCII to EBCDIC conversion.
`ibm`	Different ASCII to EBCDIC.
`lcase`	Uppercase to lowercase conversion.
`noerror`	Do not stop if an error occurs.
`notrunc`	Do not truncate the output file.
`swab`	If the number of bytes in the input record is odd, ignore the last byte.
`sync`	Input blocks are made to be the size of `ibs=`*buffer* by appending null characters.
`ucase`	Lowercase to uppercase conversion.
`unblock`	Fixed-length to variable-length conversion. Remove trailing spaces and add terminating newlines.

Example	Description
`dd if=/dev/rmt/0 ➥of=outfile conv=ebcdic`	Convert an ASCII tape to an EBCDIC file.
`dd if=/dev/rmt/0 ➥of=/dev/rmt/.1`	Copy from one tape drive to another.

▶ **See Also** tar (250)

Creating and Extracting Tape Archives (tar)

tar

```
/usr/bin/tar [options] [function][modifier] [tarfile] [file]
```

One common way to transmit and store files is as a tape archive, commonly called a `tar` file. Traditionally, `tar` files were magnetic tape files; however, tar files can now be any file on any filesystem. Most source code is distributed as a compressed `tar` file. `tar` files usually have a `.tar` filename extension. The `tar` command is used to create, list, and extract `tar` files.

Option	Description
`-C` *`dir file`*	Use the `chdir` command on the directory specified by *`dir`*. Then create a tar file specified by *`file`*.
`-I` *`file`*	Use a file containing a list of filenames and run the `tar` command line on each filename. Do not leave any trailing space characters at the end of each line. Do not leave any blank lines at the end of the file.

Function Letter	Description
`c`	Create. Create a new `tar` file archive.
`r`	Replace. Write the new files to the end of the existing specified file.
`t`	Table of Contents. Print a listing of all of the filenames and pathnames for the tar file.
`u`	Update. The specified files to be added to the `tar` file are appended to the end of the file if and only if they are not already in the `tar` file. This process is slow.
`x`	Extract. The files stored in the tape archive are extracted. The `tar` file can contain directory names. Any directory names not already existing on the system and specified in the `tar` file will be created. It is recommended that a table of contents be printed before extracting files to check where they will be extracted to.

Solaris 1.x and 2.x Incompatibilities When Using tar

It should be noted that the update function (u) depends on the system on which the tar file was created. If the tar file was created on a Solaris 1.x system, it can be updated only on a Solaris 1.x system. If the tar file was created on a Solaris 2.x system, it can be updated only on a Solaris 2.x system.

Function Modifier	Description
b	Blocking Factor. Specify the blocking factor (in 512-byte blocks) for writing to raw magnetic devices.
B	Block. Read multiple times when reading from standard input or across an ethernet.
e	Error. If an error occurs, exit immediately.
f	Filename. Specify a filename rather than a device name. This is used when creating a new tar file.
F	Exclude all directories named SCCS and RCS.
FF	Exclude all directories named SCCS and RCS and all files ending in .o.
h	Treat symbolic links as files and follow them.
i	Ignore checksum errors.
l	Link-Error. Print error messages in the event a link cannot be resolved.
m	Modify. When used with the extract function, the modification time of the tar file is set to the time of the last extraction.
number	Specify the drive number for the tape drive. This value must be a number between 0 and 7. The default drive number is stored in /etc/default/tar.
o	Set the ownership of the extracted files to the user running the tar command.
p	Keep the original file modes and permissions of the files in the tar archive when extracting files.
P	Do not add a trailing slash to directory names.
v	Verbose. Print extra information when running, especially when printing the table of contents.
w	Confirm the requisition function. The user must respond with a single y to confirm and continue.

continues >>

>>continued

Function Modifier	Description
X	Exclude. Specify a text file containing a list of files to exclude from being placed in a new `tar` file or extracted from an existing `tar` file. When used with the `t` function, the filenames will not be printed.

Example	Task
`tar vxf source.tar`	Extract the files from the tape archive called `source.tar`, showing all files extracted.
`tar cvf source.tar ./dev`	Create a tar file called `source.tar`, including all the files and pathnames in the dev subdirectory.

▸ **See Also** "Copying and Converting Files (`cpio`, `dd`)," p. 247.

Device Configuration

drvconfig

drvconfig

`/usr/sbin/drvconfig [options]`

The `drvconfig` utility is used to configure the `/devices` directory. Alternatively, the `devfsadmin` utility can be used to configure devices using a graphical user interface. The kernel major number binding is stored in `/etc/name_to_major`. Driver class bindings are stored in `/etc/driver_classes`.

Option	Description
`-i` *driver*	Configure the devices for the specified driver only.
`-n`	Do not load or attach any drivers. If used with the `-i` option, it means that the specified driver is not loaded or attached.
`-a` *alias*	Add the specified alias name to the list of aliases for a driver.
`-c` *number*	Add the specified major number to the kernel `name_to_major` binding tables.
`-r` *dir*	Build the devices directory in the root directory specified rather than under the default of `/devices`.

continues >>

ntinued

Option	Description
`-b`	Add a major number to the name binding in the kernel `name_to_major` tables. It is not recommended that this option be used when manually calling `drvconfig` from the command line.
`-c` *`class`*	Export the named class for the added driver. This option is only meaningful when used with `-b`.

▶ **See Also** "Modules" (284) for more information on the `modinfo` and `modload` commands, `rem_drv` (253)

rem_drv

`/usr/sbin/rem_drv`

rem_drv

Invalidate a currently installed driver. The driver is then unloaded (if possible) from memory. The `/devices` entry is deleted, and the system driver configuration files are updated. After the `rem_drv` utility has been used, the next reboot will automatically be a reconfiguration reboot (`boot -r`).

Option	Description
`-b dir`	Removes a driver for a diskless client, where *`dir`* is the root directory of the client. The driver removal will not take place until the diskless client is rebooted.

▶ **See Also** "Modules" (284) for more information on the `modinfo` and `modload` commands.

12 Security

continues >>

System Auditing

The Audit Daemon

The Audit Daemon

The Audit daemon can be used only after the Solaris Basic Security Module has been enabled using the `bsmconv` script. After the BSM has been enabled, the Audit daemon generates audit trail files, which can be used to enhance the security of a system. The Audit daemon is controlled through the audit control file (`/etc/security/audit/audit_control`).

The daemon will use the `audit_warn` utility to warn of potential problems under the following conditions.

Auditing Conditions

Auditing Condition	Description
`allhard`	All filesystems are full or are unavailable. No audit trail files are written. Warnings are issued every 20 seconds.
`allsoft`	All filesystems have exceeded their minimum free space requirements. A new audit trail is created anyway.
`auditoff`	The Audit daemon has exited.
`ebusy`	An Audit daemon is already running.
`getacdir`	A problem with the directory list in `/etc/security/audit/audit_control` has been found. The Audit daemon waits until this problem has been corrected.
`hard`	A filesystem has become full or is unable to be written to. A new Audit trail is created on a different filesystem if possible.
`nostart`	The Audit daemon cannot be started. Reboot and try again.
`postsigterm`	A problem was encountered while attempting to shut down the Audit daemon.
`soft`	A filesystem minimum free space limit has been exceeded. A new audit trail file is created on a different file system.
`tmpfile`	A temporary audit file already exists. This indicates that the daemon was not properly shut down the last time it was run.

Current Audit daemon information is stored in a file in `./etc/security` called `audit_data`. The `/etc/security/audit_data` file has the following format:

```
pid:logpath
```

pid is the Audit daemon process identification number, and *logpath* is the path and filename of the Audit daemon log file.

Audit Warnings

Audit Warnings

Audit warnings are handled by the `audit_warn` script. These warnings are sent from the Audit daemon (`auditd`). Also, users can be specified as `audit_warn` in the mail aliases file. These users receive email concerning any warnings.

Warning	Description	Default Action
`allhard count`	The hard limit for all filesystems has been exceeded the number of times specified by *count*.	Send mail to the `audit_warn` alias the first time the warning is logged (`count=1`). Write a message to the console every time.
`allsoft`	The soft limit for all filesystems has been exceeded.	Send mail to `audit_warn` alias and write a message to the console.
`auditoff`	The system audit state was changed from `AUC_AUDITING` by someone other than `auditd`.	Send mail to `audit_warn` alias and write a message to the console.
`ebusy`	The Audit daemon is already running.	Send mail to `audit_warn` alias and write a message to the console.
`getacdir count`	There is a problem with the directory list in the `audit_control` file.	Send mail to `audit_warn` alias the first time a message is logged. Write a message to the console every time.
`hard filesystem`	Hard limit for the filesystem has been exceeded.	Send mail to `audit_warn` alias and write a message to the console.

continues >>

ontinued

Warning	Description	Default Action
nostart	Auditing could not be started.	Send mail to audit_warn alias and write a message to the console.
postsigterm	The Audit daemon was improperly shut down.	Send mail to audit_warn alias and write a message to the console.
soft filesystem	The soft limit of a filesystem has been exceeded.	Send mail to audit_warn alias and write a message to the console.
tmpfile	The temporary audit file already exists. This is an indication of a previous error.	Send mail to audit_warn alias and write a message to the console.

Controlling the Audit Daemon

The Audit daemon (auditd) is controlled by editing the /etc/security/audit_control file. The file is a plain text file and can be manually edited. Comment lines begin with # and are ignored.

Controlling the Audit Daemon

Audit Parameter	audit_control Line	Description
Audit	minfree:*percent*	Specify the minimum free threshold space. If the allowed free space goes below this amount, an audit_warn warning is sent.
Audit trail file directories	dir:*directory*	Specify the directory in which audit trail files are written. More than one dir: line can be specified, in order of preference.

continues >>

>>continued

Flags	`flags:` *`flags`*	Define what events are audited. These flags can be overridden by the `audit_user` file.
Non-attributable flags	`naflags:` *`flags`*	Define what events are audited that cannot be associated with a specific user.

The audit daemon can also be controlled to log specific events for individual users on the system. This is done by adding lines to the `/etc/security/audit_user` file. The format of the file is as follows:

```
username:flags-to-audit:flags-not-to-audit
```

The `audit_user` file always overrides the `audit_control` file.

Event	**Flag**	**Long Name**
Access of object attributes	`fa`	`file_attr_acc`
Admin actions	`ad`	`administrative`
All	`all`	`all`
Application auditing	`ap`	`application`
Change of object attributes	`fm`	`file_attr_mod`
Creation of object	`fc`	`file_creation`
Deletion of object	`fd`	`file_deletion`
Everything else	`ot`	`other`
`exec` calls	`ex`	`exec`
File close	`cl`	`file_close`
`ioctl` calls	`io`	`ioctl`
IPC calls	`ip`	`ipc`
Login/logout	`lo`	`login_logout`
Network events	`nt`	`network`
Non-attributable events	`na`	`non_attrib`
Process operations	`pc`	`process`
Read of data, open for read	`fr`	`file_read`
Write of data, open for write	`fw`	`file_write`

Event Flag Modifiers

Modifier	Description
-	Audit if event failed.
+	Audit only if event was successful.

Task	Example
`dir: /etc/security/argus/➥audit`	Set up directory to store audit trail files
`dir: /etc/security/➥argus.aux/audit`	Set up directory to store audit trail files, as well as a backup directory.
`flags: -fw`	Audit all failed attempts to write to files.

Enabling the Basic Security Module (BSM)

BSM

The Solaris Basic Security Module (BSM) is enabled or disabled on a system by using two scripts in the `/etc/security` directory. The BSM increases the security of a system in many respects.

Actions

Action	Command
Enable BSM	`/etc/security/bsmconv`
Disable BSM	`/etc/security/bsmunconv`

Executing `bsmconv` with no options or arguments will enable the BSM on the host machine as well as any diskless clients being served by the host machine. It is important to reboot after enabling the BSM.

The BSM must be enabled to use any of the Solaris auditing facilities.

Diskless clients can enable the BSM by running `bsmconv` on the server system and specifying the exported root directory.

Example	Task
`bsmconv`	Enable the BSM on the local host and all diskless clients supported by the host.
`bsmconv /export/➥root/host3`	Enable the BSM on the diskless client called `host3`.

Printing Audit Trail Files

Printing Audit Trail Files

Audit log files are commonly called *audit trail files*. They contain information gathered by the Audit daemon as specified in the `/etc/security/audit_control` file. The location of the audit trail files is defined in the `audit_control` file using the `dir:` lines.

Audit trail files must be read using the `praudit` utility. If no filename is given, the input from standard input is assumed to be in the format of an audit trail file. Up to 100 audit trail files can be listed on the command line for printing.

Options	Description
`-d`*`char`*	Use the character specified by *`char`* as the delimiter.
`-l`	Print one line per record.
`-r`	Print records in raw format. All times, ID numbers, and events are shown as integers.
`-s`	Print records in short format. All times, ID numbers, and events are converted to a readable ASCII format.

Example	Task
`praudit -r audit001`	Print the audit trail file called `audit001` in raw format.
`praudit -s audit002`	Print the audit trail file called `audit002`, converting to ASCII format.

Starting the Auditing System

Starting the Auditing System

The `audit_startup` script must be executed before the audit daemon (`auditd`) is started. The script is located at

```
/etc/security/audit_startup
```

It is available only after the Solaris BSM has been enabled using the `bsmconv` script.

The `audit_startup` script is a plain text file and can be manually edited by the system administrator.

Example

Use the following to initialize the audit system:

```
audit_startup
```

System Logging Daemon (syslogd)

/usr/bin/syslogd [options]

The system logging daemon (syslogd) handles system messages, sending them to the appropriate log files or users based on priority. The main syslog file is located at /var/log/syslog. The syslog daemon is configured by editing the /etc/syslog.conf file.

Option	Description
-d	Enable debugging mode. Do not use this option in startup scripts.
-f file	Use the specified configuration file. The default configuration file is /etc/syslog.conf.
-m interval	Use the specified interval between mark messages.
-p logdevice	Use the specified log device. The default is /dev/log.
-t	Disable the syslog port (UDP). If this option is used, remote messages will not be logged.

Priority	Description
LOG_EMERG	Panic condition
LOG_ALERT	Alert condition
LOG_CRIT	Critical condition
LOG_ERR	Errors
LOG_WARNING	Warning messages
LOG_NOTICE	Notices less severe than errors
LOG_INFO	Informational messages
LOG_DEBUG	Debugging information

Facility	Description
LOG_KERN	Kernel messages
LOG_USER	User messages
LOG_MAIL	Mail messages (default)
LOG_DAEMON	Daemon/server process messages

continues >>

>>continued

Facility	Description
LOG_AUTH	Authorization messages
LOG_LPR	Printer messages
LOG_NEWS	USENET messages (reserved)
LOG_UUCP	UUCP messages (reserved)
LOG_CRON	Cron/at messages
LOG_LOCAL0	Local use
LOG_LOCAL1	Local use
LOG_LOCAL2	Local use
LOG_LOCAL3	Local use
LOG_LOCAL4	Local use
LOG_LOCAL5	Local use
LOG_LOCAL6	Local use
LOG_LOCAL7	Local use

▶ **See Also** `at` (57), `crontab` (59)

Third-Party Tools

Third-Party Tools

Some third-party tools may provide similar or better security. Some of these security tools (most are freeware) to consider are provided in the following sections with a short synopsis.

COPS

`ftp://coast.cs.purdue.edu/pub/tools/unix/cops/1.04/`

The Computer Oracle and Password System (COPS) is a proactive security tool for UNIX systems. It checks the local system for common security flaws and weaknesses and then reports them. Suggestions are given for fixing the problems, or the problems can be automatically fixed.

Internet Security Scanner (ISS)

`http://www.iss.net`

Much like COPS, this is a proactive security tool that attempts to "crack" the system. This tool can, however, be used to check remote systems. In many ways, this is similar to the SATAN tool that was released (and gained much media hype). New versions of the ISS security tools have a very nice graphical user interface.

TAMU Tiger

`ftp://coast.cs.purdue.edu/pub/tools/unix/TAMU/`

The TAMU Tiger scripts from Texas A&M University are Perl scripts that perform security checks on UNIX systems. It works, in many ways, like COPS. The scripts are extremely easy to use and configure. Tiger is a good security check to run on a regular basis.

Tripwire

`ftp://coast.cs.purdue.edu/pub/tools/unix/Tripwire/`

The Tripwire program creates digital signatures of selected and important files, routinely checking the signatures against new checksums. If a difference is found, it means that an intruder has changed one of the files and the system administrator is notified. This program might not be necessary for most systems, but it does increase the security of the system.

ASET

ASET Environment File

`/usr/aset/asetenv`

The ASET environment file (`/usr/aset/asetenv`) is used to manually configure the Automatic Security Enhancement Tool. There are two types of parameters listed in the file: *User Configurable Parameters* and *ASET Internal Environment Variables*. Only the User Configurable Parameters should be changed.

Parameters

ASET Parameter	Description

`CKLISTPATH_LOW`
`CKLISTPATH_MED`
`CKLISTPATH_HIGH`
	Set files to have checksums generated during a `cklist` task. Each security level can be individually customized.

`PERIODIC_SCHEDULE`	Set how often period ASET checks are performed.

continues >>

>>continued

ASET Parameter	Description
TASK	Set the tasks that will be performed by ASET. Valid tasks include the following: ■ `tune`: Restrict access to system files. ■ `usrgrp`: Perform checks on user account and group information. ■ `sysconf`: Perform checks on system configuration files. ■ `env`: Check user environment variables. ■ `cklist`: Perform checksum consistency checks. ■ `eeprom`: Set secure parameter for `eeprom`s. ■ `firewall`: Set up system to be used as a firewall host.
UID_ALIASES	Set the filename for a file to define allowable duplicate UIDs.
YPCHECK	If this is set to `true`, NIS equivalents are checked as well.

Example

```
CKLISTPATH_HIGH=$CKLISTPATH_MED:/usr/lib:/usr/sbin
CKLISTPATH_LOW=/etc/:/
CKLISTPATH_MED=$CKLISTPATH_LOW:/usr/bin:/usr/ucb
PERIODIC_SCHEDULE="0 0 * * *"
TASKS="env sysconf usrgrp"
UID_ALIASES=/usr/aset/masters/uid_aliases
YPCHECK=false
```

ASET Masters

ASET Masters

`/usr/aset/masters/`

The Automated Security Enhancement Tool (ASET) can be configured by editing the files in the `./usr/aset/masters` directory. By default, the files are set to provide a reasonable amount of security and do not need to be modified. However, system administrators can edit the files to properly tune the ASET system.

Master Files

Master File	Description
cklist.low cklist.med cklist.high	cklist task. The checksums generated by the cklist task are stored in these files. To configure the cklist task, consult the ASET master files.
tune.low tune.med tune.high	tune task. These files set the mode, owner, group, and type of the files specified. Three files exist, so each security level can be individually customized. The wildcard character can be used in the pathname field. Valid types include symlink, directory, and file. Format: *pathname mode owner group type*
uid_alias	usrgrp task. Defines UIDs that can be duplicated for accounts. Usually duplicate UIDs are not allowed by ASET. This file can override that security check for specific UIDs. Format: *uid=username1=username2=username3=...*

ASET Restore

/usr/aset/aset.restore [*options*]

ASET Restore

The aset.restore utility exists to undo all of the security enhancements made by the Automated Security Enhancement Tool (ASET). All files, file permissions, and other objects are returned to the same state they were before ASET was initially run. This is helpful if ASET removed the functionality of some part of the system while attempting to increase security.

Option	Description
-d *directory*	Specifies the ASET working directory. By default, the working directory is set to /usr/aset.

Automated Security Enhancement Tool (ASET) Overview

aset [*options*]

ASET

Solaris comes with a built-in security tool called the Automated Security Enhancement Tool (ASET). ASET is a security suite that can be used to increase the general security of the system. It does not fix all security problems, but it can prevent some of the more common problems associated with the administration of Solaris systems.

ASET restricts access to important system files and directories. The amount of protection depends on the security level chosen when ASET is started. Specific definitions of what tasks are performed at each security level are stored in the `asetenv` and `aset` master files. Reports generated from ASET are stored in the `/usr/aset/reports` directory.

ASET Security Levels

Level	Description
`low`	No system changes are made. System security checks are per formed and weaknesses are reported.
`med`	Some system changes are made to restrict access to key system files. System security checks are performed and weaknesses are reported.
`high`	Many system changes are made to restrict access to key system files and directories. Some applications and services may change in functionality due to increased security. System security checks are performed, and weaknesses are reported.

Option	Description
`-d` *`directory`*	Set the working directory for the ASET system. This must be the directory in which ASET has been installed. The default value for the working directory is `/usr/aset`.
`-l` *`level`*	Specify the security level at which to run ASET. Valid levels include `low`, `med`, and `high`.
`-n` *`user@host`*	Mail the output of the ASET execution to the user specified. The output is in summary format.
`-p`	Run ASET periodically via the `cron` service. The time period is defined by the `PERIODIC_SCHEDULE` environment variable in the `/usr/aset/asetenv` file.
`-u` *`userlist`*	Check the environments of the users listed in the file specfied by *`userlist`*. By default, only the root account is checked.

ASET Tasks

Task	Description
`cklist`	A checksum is generated for specified system files the first time this task is executed. Subsequent executions compare the previous checksum against a new checksum generated from the file. Any inconsistencies (evidence that the file has been modified) are reported. This task can be customized by changing the ASET environment file `CKLISTPATH` parameters.
`eeprom`	Set the secure parameter on newer `eeprom` versions.
`env`	Check environment variables defined in `.rc` files for the root user (and any other users specified with the `-u` option). Common problems such as a dot in the `PATH` environment variable and `UMASK` problems are reported.
`firewall`	Set up the system to be used as a firewall (AKA bastion) host. IP forwarding is disabled, as well as other tasks to make the system more secure.
`sysconf`	Check system configuration files for common security problems. The following files are checked: ■ `/etc/hosts.equiv` ■ `/etc/inetd.conf` ■ `/etc/aliases` ■ `/etc/default/login` ■ `/etc/vfstab` ■ `/etc/dfs/dfstab` ■ `/etc/ftpusers` ■ `/var/adm/utmp` ■ `/var/adm/utmpx` ■ `/.rhosts`
`tune`	Increase security by setting more restrictive file permissions on system files. The amount and type of file permission changes can be customized by editing the ASET master files.
`usrgrp`	User accounts and groups are checked for common problems. This task is similar to the `grpck` and `pwck` commands.

▸ **See Also** ASET Environment File (265), ASET Masters (266)

Printing ASET Status

Printing ASET Status

`/usr/aset/util/taskstat [options]`

The `taskstat` utility can be used to check the status of the Automatic Security Enhancement Tool (ASET) while it is running in the background. The output of `taskstat` shows a list of all security tasks being executed, noting which have been completed and which are still running. When all tasks have been completed, the report is stored in `/usr/aset/reports`.

Option	Description
`-d directory`	Set the working directory for ASET.

Role Based Access Control (RBAC)

Role Based Access Control (RBAC) is a new security feature in Solaris 8. RBAC allows administrators to create "roles" for users. A role can have specific privileges including setUID to applications. Authorizations are stored in the `/etc/auth_attr` file. Authorizations are checked using the `user_attr`, `prof_attr`, and `policy.conf` files. The main commands used to manage the RBAC system are: `roleadd`, `roledel`, `rolemod`, and `roles`.

roleadd

roleadd

`/usr/bin/roleadd [options] [role]`

Add a new role to the system. The `/etc/passwd`, `/etc/shadow`, and `/etc/user_attr` files are modified. Option arguments are limited to 512 characters.

Option	Description
`-b basedir`	Set the base directory for the system for use if the `-d` option is not given.
`-c comment`	Set a short text description of the role, placed in `/etc/passwd`.
`-d homedir`	Set the home directory of the new role.

continues >>

ntinued

Option	Description
-D	If this option is used with no other options, the default values for group, base directory, skeleton directory, shell, inactivity limit, and expire date are shown. If this option is given with the -g, -b, or -f options, the default values of the respective options are changed.
-e expire	Set the expiration date for the role.
-f days	Set the number of days of inactivity for a role before it is invalidated.
-g group	Set the primary group for a role.
-G group	Set the supplementary group for the role.
-k skeletondir	Use the skeleton information in the specified directory when creating the new role.
-m	Create a new home directory for the role if one does not exist.
-o	Allow duplicate UIDs.
-s shell	Set the role's login shell.
-u uid	Set the UID of the role.

▶ **See Also** roledel (271), rolemod (271), roles (272)

roledel

/usr/bin/roledel [*options*] [*role*]

This command is used to delete roles from the RBAC system.

Option	Description
-r	Remove the role's home directory along with the role. All files in the directory are permanently deleted.

▶ **See Also** roleadd (270), rolemod (271), roles (272)

rolemod

/usr/bin/rolemod [*options*] [*role*]

The rolemod utility is used to modify a role used in the RBAC system. All option arguments must be less than 512 characters.

Option	Description
`-A auth`	Use the specified authorization. Multiple authorizations can be specified as a comma delimited list.
`-c comment`	Set a comment to be stored in the `/etc/password` file with the user's entry.
`-d homedir`	Set the role's home directory.
`-e expire`	Set a role expiration date using any format in `/etc/datemsk`.
`-f days`	Set a maximum number of days of inactivity. After this number of days has been exceeded, the login is invalidated.
`-g group`	Set the role's primary group membership. The group can be specified as a group ID or the group name.
`-l login`	Change the login name for the role to the one specified.
`-m`	Move the role's current home directory to the directory specified by the `-d` option.
`-o`	Allow duplicate UIDs.
`-p profile`	Replace any existing profile settings with the specified profile.
`-s shell`	Set the shell for the role. The shell must be specified with its full path.
`- uid`	Change the role UID to the one specified.

▸ **See Also** `roleadd` (270), `roledel` (271), `roles` (272)

roles

`/usr/bin/roles [username]`

The `roles` utility shows the granted roles of the given user or users. Multiple users can be checked at a time by giving multiple usernames (separated by spaces) on the command line. If no username is specified, the roles of the user executing the command are shown. All output is sent to standard output. Valid roles are stored in the `/etc/user_attr` file.

▸ **See Also** `roleadd` (270), `roledel` (271), `rolemod` (271)

Network Sniffing

snoop

In many ways, network *sniffers* are used as system-cracking tools or network troubleshooting tools. However, it is good to understand network sniffing in order to have a firm grasp on the security of the system. The `snoop` utility comes with Solaris and provides a good way to learn about network sniffing.

Network packets can be captured and displayed using the Solaris `snoop` utility. The packets can be filtered, capturing only packets of interest. Several formats are available for displaying captured packets. Many of the options also apply to previously captured packets stored in files.

Option	Description
`-a`	Convert packets to audio using `/dev/audio`. This option is not very useful on a busy network.
`-C`	Print filter expression code.
`-c` *`n`*	Capture *`n`* packets and quit.
`-D`	Print the number of packets dropped in summary format.
`-d` *`dev`*	Capture packets from the device specified by *`dev`*. The default value is `/dev/le0`.
`-i` *`file`*	Read packets from the capture file specified by *`file`*.
`-N`	Create an IP/DNS-name mapping file that lists all IP addresses and associated names. Must be used with the `-i` option.
`-n` *`file`*	Use the file specified by *`file`* to convert IP addresses to names. The file must be of the following format: *`ip-addr hostname`*
`-o` *`file`*	Write captured packets to *`file`*.
`-P`	Non-promiscuous mode. Only show packets addressed to host (plus broadcast and multicast packets).
`-p` *`list`*	Display the packets specified in the comma delimited *`list`*.

continues >>

>>continued

Option	Description
`-S`	Show Ethernet frame size.
`-s` *`snaplength`*	Capture only a part of packets. Packets are shortened to the specified *`snaplength`*.
`-t` *`stamp`*	Timestamp packets with one of three modes. The stamp is specified by *`stamp`*, which is one of the following: ■ `r`: Relative—Based on the time of the first packet ■ `a`: Absolute—Wall-clock time ■ `d`: Delta—Time between packets
`-v`	Verbose. Use extra detail when displaying packets, including full packet headers.
`-V`	Verbose Summary. More detail than normal mode, but less detail than verbose mode.
`-x` *`offset`*	Print packet contents in hex and ASCII format, using *`offset`* as the offset. An offset of `0` prints the entire packet.

Filter Expressions

Expression	Description
`apple`	Print all Apple Ethertalk packets.
`broadcast`	Print all broadcast packets.
`decnet`	Print all DECNET packets.
`ether`	Resolve hosts to Ethernet addresses.
`etheraddr`	Print all packets that have `etheraddr` as their source or destination Ethernet address (such as `aa:0:54:53:65:23`). A zero (`0`) must be prepended to the Ethernet address.
`ethertype` *`n`*	Print packets that have *`n`* as the Ethernet type field number.
`from`	Can be added to `host`, `net`, `ipaddr`, `etheraddr`, `port`, or `rpc` to specify that the packet must be from that expression (source).
`gateway` *`host`*	Print all packets that used the specified host as a gateway.
`greater` *`length`*	Print all packets longer than *`length`*.

continues >>

tinued

Expression	Description
`host` *`hostname`*	Print packets with *`hostname`* as their source address.
`ipaddr`	Print all packets with `ipaddr` as their source or destination.
`less` *`length`*	Print all packets smaller than *`length`*.
`multicast`	Print all multicast packets.
`net` *`net`*	Print all packets to or from the specified network number.
`nofrag`	Print only unfragmented packets.
`packet-type`	Print all packets of a specific type. This can be one of three types: `ip`, `arp`, or `rarp`.
`port` *`port`*	Print all packets to or from the specified port number.
`protocol`	Print all packets of a specific protocol type: `udp`, `tcp`, or `icmp`.
`rpc` *`prog`*	Print all packets to or from the specified RPC program.
`to`	Can be added to `host`, `net`, `ipaddr`, `etheraddr`, `port`, or `rpc` to specify what the packet must be to that expression (destination).

Kerberos

Kerberos Overview

Kerberos Overview

The Kerberos authentication and authorization system can be used for increased security on a computer network. When logged in to the system, users can authenticate themselves with the Kerberos daemon and then use the Kerberos functions of services (such as NFS). A major advantage of using Kerberos is that when authenticated, `.rhosts` are no longer needed for services such as `rlogin` and `rsh`. Users must first be registered with the Kerberos system before they can properly use it; the system administrator must perform this registration task. When registered, users log in to the Kerberos system using the `kinit` command.

Kerberos Name Parts

Part	Description
Principal name	The user's username or the service name.
Instance	For users, this is `NULL`. For services, this is the name of the machine that the service is running on.
Realm	The service providing authentication for the principal.

When authenticated, the user or service is given a *Kerberos ticket*, an encrypted protocol that can be used for authentication. These tickets expire after a predetermined amount of time. After they expire, new tickets can be issued by re-running the `kinit` command.

Kerberos Daemon (kerbd)

kerbd

The Kerberos daemon (`kerbd`) is the process that controls the entire Kerberos system by creating and validating tickets for kernel remote procedure calls. The daemon works between the kernel RPC calls and the key distribution center (KDC). The daemon is automatically started in normal multiuser run states.

Option	Description
`-d`	Debug. Extra output is provided concerning ticket generation and validation.
`-g`	Do not initialize the grouplist. Only the group in the password file (`/etc/passwd`) for each use is used in mapped credentials.

Configuring Kerberos

Configuring Kerberos

`/etc/krb.conf`

The Kerberos system can be configured by editing the Kerberos configuration file (`/etc/krb.conf`). This file stores information about Kerberos realms and key distribution centers (KDCs). The Kerberos daemon (`kerbd`) must be restarted whenever the Kerberos configuration file is changed.

```
local-realm-name
realm-name realm-KDC-host
realm-name realm-KDC-host
realm-name realm-KDC-host
```

Administrative databases can be specified by adding `admin server` to the end of the `realm` lines in the file.

Destroying Kerberos Tickets

`/usr/bin/kdestroy [options]`

Destroying Kerberos Tickets

The `kdestroy` utility is used to destroy the user's active Kerberos authorization tickets. This is accomplished by overwriting the ticket file with zeros and then deleting the file. Also, any Kerberos credentials stored in the kernel are removed. If, for some reason, `kdestroy` is unable to properly destroy the user ticket, a warning message is displayed along with a terminal beep. Only the current ticket file is destroyed. Other ticket files are not removed. Therefore, it is recommended that all tickets be kept in one file.

Option	Description
-f	Suppress status messages.
-n	Destroy tickets, but do not remove credentials from the kernel.
-q	Quiet. Do not beep the terminal if `kdestroy` fails to properly destroy the tickets.

Automatically Destroying Tickets

If the `/usr/bin/kdestroy` command is added to a user's `.logout` file, the tickets automatically are destroyed when the user logs out of the system. This makes the user's Kerberos system slightly more secure. However, because all Kerberos credentials stored in the kernel are removed, it is possible that NFS operations started by the user will fail after the user logs out.

Kerberos realms File

Kerberos realms File

The Kerberos system must translate hostnames to the corresponding realm name for each service provided by the host. This is done using the `/etc/krb.realms` file. Domain names must begin with a leading dot, such as the following:

```
.cs.university.edu
```

File Format

```
hostname kerberos-realm
domainname kerberos-realm
```

The following table elaborates on the file format and the conditions that can be met.

Condition	Result
hostname matches *hostname* field.	Kerberos realm of the matching field is used.
hostname does not match any *hostname* field, but domain name matches a *domainname* field.	Kerberos realm of the matching domain name field is used.
hostname does not match any *hostname* field, and domain name does not match any *domainname*.	The host's domain name (uppercase) is used as the realm field.

Listing Kerberos Tickets

Listing Kerberos Tickets

It is possible to list all tickets in a user's ticket file by using the `klist` utility. The ticket principal identity, principal names of all tickets, issue times, and expire times for all tickets are printed. The `KRBTKFILE` environment variable is consulted to find the ticket file. If this variable is not set, the `/tmp` directory is checked for a ticket file for the user.

Option	Description
`-file` *file*	Use the file specified by *file* as the user ticket file.
`-s`	Silent. Only output the principal names of user tickets.
`-srvtab`	Treat the ticket file like a service key file.
`-t`	Check for a non-expired ticket-granting ticket. The exit status returns the results: ■ `1`: Ticket exists. ■ `0`: No ticket exists.

Logging In to the Kerberos Authentication System

Logging In to the Kerberos Authentication System

`kinit [options] [username]`

Initialize and log in to the Kerberos authentication system. Before logging in, the user must first be registered with the Kerberos system. Running `kinit` prompts the user for a username and password, unless the username is given on the command line. When the user is logged in, a ticket-granting ticket is created in `/tmp` for the user. The location of this ticket can be changed by putting a different path/filename in the `KRBTKFILE` environment variable. The ticket expires in eight hours.

To destroy tickets at any time after logging in, use the `kdestroy` command. See the section "Destroying Kerberos Tickets, page 277" for more information.

Option	Description
`-i`	Prompt the user for a Kerberos instance.
`-l`	Prompt the user for a ticket lifetime. Times are given in minutes and must be between 5 and 1,275 minutes and are rounded to the closest multiple of 5. The default lifetime is 8 hours.
`-r`	Prompt the user for a Kerberos realm to authenticate with a remote server.
`-v`	Verbose. Print status messages.

Retrieving a Ticket-Granting Ticket

`/usr/bin/ksrvtgt` *`name instance`* `[`*`realm`*`]`

Retrieving a Ticket-Granting Ticket

The `ksrvgt` utility retrieves a ticket-granting ticket and stores it in the ticket cache. This is done in three steps, as follows:

1. A ticket with a five-minute lifetime is fetched for the principal.
2. The response is decrypted using the /etc/srvtab file.
3. The ticket is stored in the standard ticket cache.

13 System Configuration and Tuning

Page *Contents*

System Identification

Changing the System Hostname

Changing the System Hostname

It is possible to change the system hostname by using the `sys-unconfig` utility (see "Reconfiguring the System," p. 283). However, the `sys-unconfig` utility reconfigures almost all system parameters, rather than just the hostname. Therefore, in some cases, it may be preferable to simply manually change the hostname. This can be done with the following script:

```
#/bin/sh
# Change the system hostname
# Usage:  newname <newhostname>
#
# Backup files and substitute new name in place
# of the old name
OLDNAME='uname -n'
echo "Changing hostname from $OLDNAME to $1"
for FILE in /etc/hosts        \
            /etc/nodename     \
            /etc/hostname.*l  \
            /etc/net/tic*/hosts ;
do
        cp $FILE $FILE.bak;
        echo "$FILE backed up as $FILE.bak"
        sed 's/$OLDNAME/$1/g' $FILE.bak > $FILE;
done
echo "Rebooting..."
/usr/sbin/reboot
```

Editing the Message of the Day (MOTD)

MOTD

The Message of the Day, or MOTD, is the system's message that is displayed to each user at login. The message is only displayed after the user has successfully logged in (supplying the correct username and password).

If users do not want to see the MOTD when they log in, they can create an empty `.hushlogin` file in their home directory.

The message is stored in a plain text file called `/etc/motd` that can be edited by the root user at any time. This can be done with any text editor (such as `vi`, `pico`, and so on). No rebooting is needed. The following is an example of an MOTD:

```
------------------------------------------------------------
Sun Microsystems Inc.   SunOS 5.5      Generic November 1995
------------------------------------------------------------
DISK QUOTAS
System will be shutdown for maintenance on 10/12/98 from 8AM
➥until 11 AM.

Send questions to John Doe <doej@somehost.com>
------------------------------------------------------------
```

Reconfiguring the System (sys-unconfig)

sys-unconfig

1. Back up all files that will be changed:
   - `cp /etc/hostname /etc/hostname.old`
   - `mkdir /etc/net.backup`
   - `cp /etc/net/* /etc/net.backup`
   - `cp /etc/nodename /etc/nodename.old`
   - `cp /etc/shadow /etc/shadow.old`
   - `chmod 600 /etc/shadow`
   - `cp /etc/TIMEZONE /etc/TIMEZONE.old`
   - `cp /etc/hostname.hme0 /etc/hostname.hme0.old`
   - `cp /etc/hostname.le0 /etc/hostname.le0.old`
   - `cp /etc/hosts /etc/hosts.old`
2. Reconfigure the system:
   - `/usr/sbin/sys-unconfig`
3. Reboot the system after it halts.
4. Answer configuration questions when prompted.
5. Wait while the system reboots.

Although it may be possible to change the hostname of a Solaris system by manually editing the required files, it is recommended that the `sys-unconfig` utility be used instead. Upon running `sys-unconfig`, the system will halt. The next time it is booted, the administrator will be prompted for configuration information. This utility will edit the following files when run:

File	Result
`/etc/hostname`	Remove the hostname.
`/etc/inet/hosts`	Copy the current hosts file to `/etc/inet/hosts.saved` and replace it with the default hosts file.

continues >>

>>continued

File	Result
/etc/inet/netmasks	Delete the file.
/etc/net/*/hosts	Remove all entries for local host.
/etc/nodename	Remove the hostname.
/etc/shadow	Remove the root password.
/etc/TIMEZONE	Reset the timezone to PST8PDT.

Along with the listed files, all NIS/NIS+ services are disabled. When complete, the system will be configured the same as a new "out-of-the-box" system.

This procedure cannot be used on diskless or dataless clients. If the hostname of a diskless or dataless client must be changed, manually edit the files listed above. This task should be performed from the console rather than a remote workstation connected via the network.

Modules

In previous versions of the SunOS operating system, the kernel had to be rebuilt to load or unload certain sections or modules. In Solaris 2.x, the modules are dynamically loaded and unloaded as needed. Therefore, there is no need to rebuild the kernel, and most times there is no need to manually configure/load modules at all. In spite of this, there may be a few occasions when a module must be unloaded manually to prevent problems. An example of this can sometimes be found when using the SunPC product from Sun Microsystems.

If, for some reason, a module must be manually manipulated, the following commands apply:

Command	Description
mod_info	Query a module.
mod_install	Install a module.
mod_remove	Remove a module.
modinfo	Display information about modules that are currently loaded.
modlinkage	Module linkage structure.
modload	Load a kernel module.

Modules can be forced to load upon boot by adding a `forceload` line to `/etc/system`. The general form of a `forceload` line is as follows:

```
forceload: modulename
```

▶ **See Also** Kernel Parameters (p. 288) for more information on editing `/etc/system`

General Configuration

Adding a Device

Adding a Device

Solaris automatically detects most hardware devices. When adding SCSI devices, the system must be rebooted. To do this, shutdown to `init` state 0, and then reboot using the `boot -r` command. Make sure that all peripheral devices are turned on before booting the system. If booting from somewhere other than the default boot device, an alternate device can be specified by using the following:

```
boot device -r
```

Alternatively, `/reconfigure` can be used, followed by a regular reboot. This accomplishes the same task. The advantage is that the reboot can be left unattended and the system should come back up properly on its own.

Adding Swap Space

Adding Swap Space

It is possible to add swap space to an already configured system. To do so, use the following three steps:

1. Create the new swap file where *size* is the new size of the swap file expressed in megabytes (MB). It is recommended that this be double the amount of new physical RAM. The name of the file is specified as *`swap.file`*:

   ```
   mkfile sizem /swap.file
   ```

2. Set the new file as the swap file:

   ```
   swap -a /swap.file
   ```

3. Create a file called `/etc/rc2.d/S99swap` with the following contents:

   ```
   swap -a /swap.file
   ```

Bus Performance Monitoring (busstat)

busstat

```
/usr/bin/busstat [options]
```

Show system bus performance information. Devices must support the bus-related performance counters for this utility to work properly. To get a list of devices that support bus-related performance counters, use the -l option.

Option	Description
`-a`	Show absolute counter values rather than delta values.
`-e device-instance`	Show the list of supported events for the given device. The device name must be followed by an instance number. If an instance is not specified, the first instance is used.
`-h`	Show usage.
`-l`	Show devices that support bus-related performance counters.
`-n`	Suppress output of titles.
`-r device-instance`	Show all PIC values for the given device(s).
`-w device-instance [,pic0=event] [,picn=event]`	Write the specified devices to count the given events. Only the root user may use this option. Use the `-e` option to get a list of valid event names for a given device.)

Changing the Console Terminal Type

Changing the Console Terminal Type

The `inittab` file is read each time the system is booted. The line that controls the console setup starts with `co:` and is similar to the following:

```
co:234:respawn:/usr/lib/saf/ttymon -g -h -p "'uname -n'
console login: " -T sun -d /dev/console -l console -m
ldterm,ttcompat
```

The `/usr/lib/saf/ttymon -T` option controls the terminal type of the console, setting the `TERM` environment variable. To change the console terminal type, simply change the `-T` option parameter.

Changing the Root Login Shell

Changing the Root Login Shell

The root login shell is actually `/sbin/sh`. If the shell is not carefully changed, a mistake such as making the shell `/usr/bin/tcsh` can cause major problems. In some cases, `/usr` may not be mounted, leaving the root account with no shell to use. Therefore, always confirm that the root shell is statically linked and in the `/sbin` directory.

The root shell can be changed with the following command:

```
passwd -e shell root
```

Again, it is recommended that the root shell not be changed. An alternative approach would be to create a second account with the UID of 0 with an alternate shell. However, this too presents some security concerns.

A low-risk way of using a different shell when logging in to the system as root is to add a line to the `.profile` file that executes the desired shell. This can be done by adding the following lines to the `.profile`:

```
if [ -x /usr/bin/csh -a -r /.cshrc -a -n 'tty' ] ; then
            /usr/bin/csh;
            exit;
        fi
```

Disabling Automounting of /home

Disabling Automounting of /home

1. Edit the `/etc/auto_master` file, commenting out the `/home` line by placing a # as the first character of the line.
2. Reload automount:

   ```
   /usr/sbin./automount
   ```

Solaris 2.x comes "out-of-the-box" with automounting enabled for use with NFS. By default, `automount` uses `/home` for home directories. This causes one of the most frequently experienced problems of new Solaris users. With automounting of `/home` enabled, no user home directories can be written to the directory. To fix this, the `/home` directory is removed from automounter control.

SunOS 4.x and SunOS 5.x Automounter Naming

In Solaris 1.x (including the SunOS 4.x series), the automounter files were called `auto.*` rather than `auto_*`. This is something to note when migrating systems from Solaris 1.x to Solaris 2.x. If, after an upgrade, there are automounting and NIS problems, check the filenames to make sure they have been properly changed to the new naming convention. The first file you should check is `auto_home`, making sure it is no longer called `auto.home`.

Kernel Tuning

Kernel Parameters

Kernel Parameters

1. Edit the /etc/system file to reflect the desired changes.
2. Touch the reconfigure file:
   ```
   touch /reconfigure
   ```
3. Reboot the system:
   ```
   /usr/sbin/shutdown -i5
   ```

The kernel parameters are kept in `/etc/system`. This file is read once each time the system is booted. This is a plain text file that can be manually edited. There are few reasons why the `/etc/system` file should be changed. Some database and Java tools, however, do require modification of the system file.

The `set` command can be used to change parameters. These `set` commands are in the following form:

```
set parameter = value
```

Editable parameters are listed in the following table.

Parameter	Description
`hires_tick`	Set this to `1` to have a higher resolution system clock. Sets system Hz value to 1000.
`hz`	Manually set the clock resolution instead of using the `hires_tick` parameter. The value of this parameter must be an integer.
`maxuprc`	Maximum number of user processes.
`maxusers`	Maximum number of users.
`nfssrv: nfs_portmon`	NFS fileserver security. Set to `1` for increased security.
`ngroups_max`	Set the maximum number of groups per user. Default is 16.
`noexec_user_ ➥stack`	*Solaris 2.6 only*. Set this parameter to `1` to prevent some simple forms of buffer overrun exploits.
`noexec_user_ ➥stack_log`	*Solaris 2.6 only*. Set this parameter to `1` to log possible attempts to exploit the system using buffer overruns.

continues >>

tinued

Parameter	Description
pt_cnt	Number of System V pseudo-terminals (ptys). Default is 48. Use boot -r after changing this instead of shutdown.
rlim_fd_cur	Set the soft limit on the maximum number of file descriptors. It is not recommended to increase this number past 256, and definitely not past 1024, when using Solaris 2.5 or earlier versions. This is not a problem in Solaris 2.6.
rlim_fd_max	Set hard limit on the maximum number of file descriptors.
rstchown	Set this parameter to 0 to allow all users to chown their own files. This is not recommended for security reasons.
sd:sd_max_ ➥throttle	Maximum number of queued commands. Decreasing this to 10 may fix some SCSI/RAID problems.

Manually editing /etc/system is for experienced users only. It is possible to damage the system to the point that it will not boot. If this happens, halt the system and boot with the following:

```
boot -as
```

This reconfigures the entire system. If prompted for a system filename, specify /dev/null or the name of the backed up /etc/system file.

IV

Appendices

A
Solaris Version Changes

Solaris 2.2

- AnswerBook access over networks
- Multithreaded Library Interface
- New interface for installation
- OpenWindows improvements
- Volume Management (automatically mounts removable media)
- XGL Runtime Environment
- XIL 1.0 Imaging Runtime Libraries

Solaris 2.3

- Asynchronous PPP
- Automatic mounting of filesystems
- Direct Xlib 3.0 (MIT DDX)
- Improved disk caching
- NIS+ Setup Scripts
- PEX Runtime Environment 3D graphics support
- POSIX 1003.2
- Serial Port Manager
- X11R5–based OpenWindows
- XGL Runtime Environment graphics API

Solaris 2.4

- Added four European, four Asian, Latin American Spanish, and U.S. English languages
- Direct Xlib 3.1 (DGA Drawable Interface and multiple frame buffer support)
- Kodak PhotoCD support
- OSF/Motif Runtime Environment
- PEX 2.2 Runtime Environment 3D graphics API
- Graphical installation procedure
- Transparent Overlays API
- Wider range of hardware configurations
- XGL 3.1 Runtime Environment
- XIL 1.2 Imaging Library Runtime Environment

Solaris 2.5

- AdminTools and Solstice AdminSuite for managing systems in a network
- Better conformance to XCU4 and POSIX standards
- Enhanced hardware support
- Filesystem (UFS)-improved error detection, access control lists
- Improved compatibility with Solaris 1.x
- Improved PPP security
- Name Service Cache Daemon
- NFS v.3: NFS over TCP, NFS Lock Manager, X/Open Federated Naming
- NIS+ Password Aging
- PEX 3.0 Runtime Environment
- Proc Tools for detailed process management
- Telnet client, rlogind/telnetd improved
- Time-sharing workload performance enhancements
- XGL 3.2 Runtime Environment
- XIL 1.2.1 Runtime Environment

Solaris 2.5.1

- 64-bit KAIO
- Improved support for Ultra series of workstations
- Large UID support
- Support for up to 3.75GB of virtual memory

Solaris 2.6

- Additional languages, Unicode 2.0, and TrueType fonts
- Changeable system boot device
- Documentation via a Web browser (AnswerBook2)
- Dynamic host configuration protocol (DHCP) support added
- HotJava Web browser included
- Java Virtual Machine (JVM) included, integrating Solaris and Java
- Large file support (1TB)
- Network time protocol (NTP) support added
- Solaris Software Development Kit (SDK) included
- Variable length subnet masks
- Web browser-based installation tool for initial installation
- WebNFS for file access via the Web using the Network Filesystem protocol
- Year 2000-compliant (previous versions are not completely Y2K-compliant)

Solaris 7

- Free for non-commercial developer or educational use
- Support for 64-bit operating system
- SNMP support included
- Improved PPP software
- Unzip program included
- Integrated UFS logging

- Sendmail 8.9.1b
- Fully year 2000-compliant
- Centralized software management
- New commands: `plimit`, `pkill`, `pgrep`, `traceroute`
- SACK—support of selective acknowledgments (RFC 2018)
- Special packages available for ISPs and PC interaction
- Upgraded directory name lookup cache
- Dedicated dump partitions for crashes
- BIND 8.1.2 including dynamic updates (RFC 2136)
- Improved priority memory paging
- Processes are allowed to have address spaces greater than 4GB

Solaris 8

- Automated Dynamic Reconfiguration/Reconfiguration Coordination Manager
- IEEE 1394 support
- Improved crash dump analysis
- Improved DHCP support
- IPSec for IPv4 and IPv6
- IPv6 support
- Lightweight Directory Access Protocol (LDAP)
- Network installation using DHCP
- Perl 5.005_03 included and preinstalled
- Role-Based Access Control
- Sendmail 8.9.3
- Solaris Software Companion CD (includes GNU utilities)
- Palm HotSync Utilities

B
Common Startup Problems and Solutions

After initially installing Solaris on a new system, there are a few common problems that most people encounter within the first few hours or days. These problems, and their possible solutions, are listed below. Note that there may be other solutions in addition to the ones given.

Problem	Solution
Cannot create user home directories under `/home`.	Comment out `/home` line in `/etc/auto_master` by placing a `#` as the first character of the line. Run the `/usr/sbin/automount` program to make the change take effect. Note: If disk space is an issue, consider making `/home` a link to `/export/home` or some other directory instead.
Hostnames resolve correctly using `/etc/hosts`, but hostname lookups using DNS servers fail.	Edit the `hosts:` line in `/etc/nsswitch.conf` to read: *`hosts: files dns`* Note: Other name services such as NIS can be specified as well. Create a `/etc/resolv.conf` file with the following contents: `domain` *`domainname`* `nameserver` *`ipaddr`* `nameserver` *`ipaddr`*

continues >>

>>continued

Problem	Solution
	domainname is the domain name (such as `sun.com`) and *ipaddr* is the IP address of the nameserver. Other `nameserver` lines can be added to provide backup servers in the event the first server in the list cannot be contacted.
Some users cannot FTP to the host even though they can log properly via telnet.	Check to make sure the user's shell is included in the `/etc/shells` file. If it is not listed, edit the file to add it.
C compiler does not appear to work. Running cc gives anerror similar to: `language optional software package not installed.`	Sun Solaris does not ship with a compiler included. The SunPro C compiler can be ordered from Sun Microsystems, or the free GNU Gcc compiler can be down loaded from the Internet.
Unable to perform keyword searches of the online manual pages using `man -k`.	The index files required to perform keyword searches are not automatically built. To build these files, use the following command: `catman -w -M` *`directory`* *`directory`* is the manual page directory—usually `/usr/share/man`.

C
Linux Compatibility

Linux binaries cannot be run, by conventional means, on a Solaris system. However, Michael Davidson has created a utility that can map system calls "on-the-fly" on an x86 based system. In effect, this allows users to run Linux binaries on Solaris x86 systems. This utility, called lxrun, is available for free at the lxrun Web site: `http://ugcs.caltech.edu/~steven/lxrun/`.

lxrun does require the Linux dynamic loader (`ld.so`) to be present on the system, as well as any shared libraries that may be required by the program.

It is recommended that you keep all Linux binaries in a separate directory such as `/usr/local/linux/bin`. You can then set the `LINUX_ROOT` environment variable to `/usr/local/linux` and execute the Linux binaries by using lxrun *`linuxcommand`*.

Currently, a Sparc version of lxrun is not available, but it may be available in the future.

D
GNU Public License

GNU General Public License

This license can be found online at `http://www.fsf.org/copyleft/gpl.html`.

GNU GENERAL PUBLIC LICENSE

Version 2, June 1991

Preamble

The licenses for most software are designed to take away your freedom to share and change it. By contrast, the GNU General Public License is intended to guarantee your freedom to share and change free software—to make sure the software is free for all its users. This General Public License applies to most of the Free Software Foundation's software and to any other program whose authors commit to using it. (Some other Free Software Foundation software is covered by the GNU Library General Public License instead.) You can apply it to your programs, too.

When we speak of free software, we are referring to freedom, not price. Our General Public Licenses are designed to make sure that you have the freedom to distribute copies of free software (and charge for this service if you wish), that you receive source code or can get it if you want it, that you can change the software or use pieces of it in new free programs; and that you know you can do these things.

To protect your rights, we need to make restrictions that forbid anyone to deny you these rights or to ask you to surrender the rights. These restrictions translate to certain responsibilities for you if you distribute copies of the software, or if you modify it.

For example, if you distribute copies of such a program, whether gratis or for a fee, you must give the recipients all the rights that you have. You must make sure that they, too, receive or can get the source code. And you must show them these terms so they know their rights.

We protect your rights with two steps: (1) copyright the software, and (2) offer you this license which gives you legal permission to copy, distribute and/or modify the software.

Also, for each author's protection and ours, we want to make certain that everyone understands that there is no warranty for this free software. If the software is modified by someone else and passed on, we want its recipients to know that what they have is not the original, so that any problems introduced by others will not reflect on the original authors' reputations.

Finally, any free program is threatened constantly by software patents. We wish to avoid the danger that redistributors of a free program will individually obtain patent licenses, in effect making the program proprietary. To prevent this, we have made it clear that any patent must be licensed for everyone's free use or not licensed at all.

The precise terms and conditions for copying, distribution and modification follow.

Terms and Conditions for Copying, Distribution and Modification

0. This License applies to any program or other work which contains a notice placed by the copyright holder saying it may be distributed under the terms of this General Public License. The "Program", below, refers to any such program or work, and a "work based on the Program" means either the Program or any derivative work under copyright law: that is to say, a work containing the Program or a portion of it, either verbatim or with modifications and/or translated into another language. (Hereinafter, translation is included without limitation in the term "modification".) Each licensee is addressed as "you".

Activities other than copying, distribution and modification are not covered by this License; they are outside its scope. The act of running the Program is not restricted, and the output from the Program is covered only if its contents constitute a work based on the Program (independent of having been made by running the Program). Whether that is true depends on what the Program does.

1. You may copy and distribute verbatim copies of the Program's source code as you receive it, in any medium, provided that you conspicuously and appropriately publish on each copy an appropriate copyright notice and disclaimer of warranty; keep intact all the notices that refer to this License and to the absence of any warranty; and give any other recipients of the Program a copy of this License along with the Program.

   You may charge a fee for the physical act of transferring a copy, and you may at your option offer warranty protection in exchange for a fee.

2. You may modify your copy or copies of the Program or any portion of it, thus forming a work based on the Program, and copy and distribute such modifications or work under the terms of Section 1 above, provided that you also meet all of these conditions:

   a) You must cause the modified files to carry prominent notices stating that you changed the files and the date of any change.

   b) You must cause any work that you distribute or publish, that in whole or in part contains or is derived from the Program or any part thereof, to be licensed as a whole at no charge to all third parties under the terms of this License.

   c) If the modified program normally reads commands interactively when run, you must cause it, when started running for such interactive use in the most ordinary way, to print or display an announcement including an appropriate copyright notice and a notice that there is no warranty (or else, saying that you provide a warranty) and that users may redistribute the program under these conditions, and telling the user how to view a copy of this License. (Exception: if the Program itself is interactive but does not normally print such an announcement, your work based on the Program is not required to print an announcement.)

These requirements apply to the modified work as a whole. If identifiable sections of that work are not derived from the Program, and can be reasonably considered independent and separate works in themselves, then this License, and its terms, do not apply to those sections when you distribute them as separate works. But when you distribute the same sections as part of a whole which is a work based on the Program, the distribution of the whole must be on the terms of this License, whose permissions for other licensees extend to the entire whole, and thus to each and every part regardless of who wrote it.

Thus, it is not the intent of this section to claim rights or contest your rights to work written entirely by you; rather, the intent is to exercise the right to control the distribution of derivative or collective works based on the Program.

In addition, mere aggregation of another work not based on the Program with the Program (or with a work based on the Program) on a volume of a storage or distribution medium does not bring the other work under the scope of this License.

3. You may copy and distribute the Program (or a work based on it, under Section 2) in object code or executable form under the terms of Sections 1 and 2 above provided that you also do one of the following:

   a) Accompany it with the complete corresponding machine-readable source code, which must be distributed under the terms of Sections 1 and 2 above on a medium customarily used for software interchange; or,

   b) Accompany it with a written offer, valid for at least three years, to give any third party, for a charge no more than your cost of physically performing source distribution, a complete machine-readable copy of the corresponding source code, to be distributed under the terms of Sections 1 and 2 above on a medium customarily used for software interchange; or,

   c) Accompany it with the information you received as to the offer to distribute corresponding source code. (This alternative is allowed only for noncommercial distribution and only if you received the program in object code or executable form with such an offer, in accord with Subsection b above.)

The source code for a work means the preferred form of the work for making modifications to it. For an executable work, complete source code means all the source code for all modules it contains, plus any associated interface definition files, plus the scripts used to control compilation and installation of the executable. However, as a special exception, the source code distributed need not include anything that is normally distributed (in either source or binary form) with the major components (compiler, kernel, and so on) of the operating system on which the executable runs, unless that component itself accompanies the executable.

If distribution of executable or object code is made by offering access to copy from a designated place, then offering equivalent access to copy the source code from the same place counts as distribution of the source code, even though third parties are not compelled to copy the source along with the object code.

4. You may not copy, modify, sublicense, or distribute the Program except as expressly provided under this License. Any attempt otherwise to copy, modify, sublicense or distribute the Program is void, and will automatically terminate your rights under this License. However, parties who have received copies, or rights, from you under this License will not have their licenses terminated so long as such parties remain in full compliance.
5. You are not required to accept this License, since you have not signed it. However, nothing else grants you permission to modify or distribute the Program or its derivative works. These actions are prohibited by law if you do not accept this License. Therefore, by modifying or distributing the Program (or any work based on the Program), you indicate your acceptance of this License to do so, and all its terms and conditions for copying, distributing or modifying the Program or works based on it.
6. Each time you redistribute the Program (or any work based on the Program), the recipient automatically receives a license from the original licensor to copy, distribute or modify the Program subject to these terms and conditions. You may not impose any further restrictions on the recipients' exercise of the rights granted herein. You are not responsible for enforcing compliance by third parties to this License.
7. If, as a consequence of a court judgment or allegation of patent infringement or for any other reason (not limited to patent issues), conditions are imposed on you (whether by court order, agreement or otherwise) that contradict the conditions of this License, they do not excuse you from the conditions of this License. If you cannot distribute so as to satisfy simultaneously your obligations under this License and any other pertinent obligations, then as a consequence you may not distribute the Program at all. For example, if a patent license would not permit royalty-free redistribution of the Program by all those who receive copies directly or indirectly through you, then the only way you could satisfy both it and this License would be to refrain entirely from distribution of the Program.

If any portion of this section is held invalid or unenforceable under any particular circumstance, the balance of the section is intended to apply and the section as a whole is intended to apply in other circumstances.

It is not the purpose of this section to induce you to infringe any patents or other property right claims or to contest validity of any such claims; this section has the sole purpose of protecting the integrity of the free software distribution system, which is implemented by public license practices. Many people have made generous contributions to the wide range of software distributed through that system in reliance on consistent application of that system; it is up to the author/donor to decide if he or she is willing to distribute software through any other system and a licensee cannot impose that choice.

This section is intended to make thoroughly clear what is believed to be a consequence of the rest of this License.

8. If the distribution and/or use of the Program is restricted in certain countries either by patents or by copyrighted interfaces, the original copyright holder who places the Program under this License may add an explicit geographical distribution limitation excluding those countries, so that distribution is permitted only in or among countries not thus excluded. In such case, this License incorporates the limitation as if written in the body of this License.

9. The Free Software Foundation may publish revised and/or new versions of the General Public License from time to time. Such new versions will be similar in spirit to the present version, but may differ in detail to address new problems or concerns.

   Each version is given a distinguishing version number. If the Program specifies a version number of this License which applies to it and "any later version", you have the option of following the terms and conditions either of that version or of any later version published by the Free Software Foundation. If the Program does not specify a version number of this License, you may choose any version ever published by the Free Software Foundation.

10. If you wish to incorporate parts of the Program into other free programs whose distribution conditions are different, write to the author to ask for permission. For software which is copyrighted by the Free Software Foundation, write to the Free Software Foundation; we sometimes make exceptions for this. Our decision will be guided by the two goals of preserving the free status of all derivatives of our free software and of promoting the sharing and reuse of software generally.

NO WARRANTY

11. BECAUSE THE PROGRAM IS LICENSED FREE OF CHARGE, THERE IS NO WARRANTY FOR THE PROGRAM, TO THE EXTENT PERMITTED BY APPLICABLE LAW. EXCEPT WHEN OTHERWISE STATED IN WRITING THE COPYRIGHT HOLDERS AND/OR OTHER PARTIES PROVIDE THE PROGRAM "AS IS" WITHOUT WARRANTY OF ANY KIND, EITHER EXPRESSED OR IMPLIED, INCLUDING, BUT NOT LIMITED TO, THE IMPLIED WARRANTIES OF MERCHANTABILITY AND FITNESS FOR A PARTICULAR PURPOSE. THE ENTIRE RISK AS TO THE QUALITY AND PERFORMANCE OF THE PROGRAM IS WITH YOU. SHOULD THE PROGRAM PROVE DEFECTIVE, YOU ASSUME THE COST OF ALL NECESSARY SERVICING, REPAIR OR CORRECTION.

12. IN NO EVENT UNLESS REQUIRED BY APPLICABLE LAW OR AGREED TO IN WRITING WILL ANY COPYRIGHT HOLDER, OR ANY OTHER PARTY WHO MAY MODIFY AND/OR REDISTRIBUTE THE PROGRAM AS PERMITTED ABOVE, BE LIABLE TO YOU FOR DAMAGES, INCLUDING ANY GENERAL, SPECIAL, INCIDENTAL OR CONSEQUENTIAL DAMAGES ARISING OUT OF THE USE OR INABILITY TO USE THE PROGRAM (INCLUDING BUT NOT LIMITED TO LOSS OF DATA OR DATA BEING RENDERED INACCURATE OR LOSSES SUSTAINED BY YOU OR THIRD PARTIES OR A FAILURE OF THE PROGRAM TO OPERATE WITH ANY OTHER PROGRAMS), EVEN IF SUCH HOLDER OR OTHER PARTY HAS BEEN ADVISED OF THE POSSIBILITY OF SUCH DAMAGES.

E Web Resources

Administration and Management

Resource Name	Location
Frequently Asked Questions About Sun NVRAM/hostid	http://www.squirrel.com/squirrel/sun-nvram-hostid.faq.html
NIS+ Frequently Asked Questions	http://www.eng.auburn.edu/users/rayh/solaris/NIS+_FAQ.html
Printing Under Solaris	http://www.ebsinc.com/solaris/printfaq.html
Questions and Answers on OpenBoot	http://www.sunworld.com/swol-10-1995/swol-10-openboot.html
Solaris and PPP FAQ	http://www.sunhelp.org/faq/sunppp.html
Sun Administration FAQ	http://www.sunhelp.org/faq/sunadm.html
Sun Managers Summaries Archives	http://www.latech.edu/sunman.html
SunSolve Online Public Patch Access	http://access1.sun.com
Useful Tools for Sun Workstations and Solaris	http://www.squirrel.com/squirrel/sun-stuff.html
What are the tunable kernel parameters for Solaris 2?	http://www.sunworld.com/swol-01-1996/swol-01-perf.html
ZD Solaris Tip of the Week	http://www.elementkjournals.com/zdtips/sun/zdt-f.htm

Common Desktop Environment/OpenLook

Name	Location
Colormap FAQ List	http://tarl.net/FAQ/ColormapFAQ.html
Common Desktop Environment FAQ	http://www.laxmi.net/cde.htm
Open Look FAQs	http://step.polymtl.ca/~coyote/open look/index.html

Developer Resources

Name	Location
Access1 Technical Information	http://access1.sun.com/techroom.html
IPv6 Development	http://playground.sun.com/pub/solaris2-ipv6/html/
Solaris Developer Support Center	http://www.sun.com/developers
Sun Solaris ABI Tools	http://www.sun.com/software/dev-progs/abi/

Hardware

Name	Location
Frame Buffer FAQ	http://bul.eecs.umich.edu/~crowej/sunfaq/FrameBuffer.html
How do I install my Zip Drive on a Sun Workstation?	http://www.iomega.com/support/documents/2019.html
How to install an Iomega Jaz Drive on a Sun Workstation	http://www.iomega.com/support/documents/4019.html
SparcBook FAQ	http://home.kabelfoon.nl/~hvdkooij/SparcBook-FAQ/sparcbook-faq.html
Sun CD-ROM FAQ	http://saturn.tlug.org/suncdfaq/

Lists of Resources

Name	Location
Solaris Central	http://www.solariscentral.org/
Solaris WWW Resources	http://oak.ece.ul.ie/~griffini/solaris.html
Sun FAQs, Patches, & Other Information	http://www.stokely.com/unix.sysadm.resources/faqs.sun.html
SunHELP	http://www.sunhelp.org/
SunWHERE	http://www.sunworld.com/sunwhere.html
The Sun Shack	http://lios.apana.org.au/~cdewick/sun_ark.html
The Suns at Home Page	http://www.net-kitchen.com/~sah/
The Unofficial Guide to Solaris	http://sun.icsnet.com

Magazines (Online and Print)

Name	Location
Inside Solaris	http://www.zdjournals.com/sun/
	http://www.elementkjournals.com/sun/
SunExpert	http://www.hillside.co.uk/articles/sunexpert.html
SunWorld	http://www.sunworld.com/

Online Documentation

Name	Location
RTFM	http://www.solarisguide.com/rtfm.shtml
Sun Product Documentation	http://docs.sun.com

Security

Name	Location
Computer Incident Advisory Capability (CIAC)	http://ciac.llnl.gov/
Passwd+	ftp://ftp.dartmouth.edu/pub/security/
Securing Solaris	http://www.securityfocus.com/focus/sun/articles/securing.htm
TAMU Tiger Security Scripts	ftp://coast.cs.purdue.edu/pub/tools/unix/TAMU/
TCP Wrappers	http://www.porcupine.org
The Solaris Security FAQ	http://www.sunworld.com/common/security-faq.html

Software

Name	Location
Access1 Sun Software Support	http://access1.sun.com/
CERT Coordination Center	http://www.cert.org
Crack - Proactive Password Security	ftp://coast.cs.purdue.edu/pub/tools/unix/crack/
Free Software from Sun Microsystems	http://www.sun.com/products-n-solutions/promotions.html
Solaris Porting Project (This site is an excellent place to find source code as well as precompiled binaries for most Sun freeware packages.)	http://www.sunfreeware.com
The "ready-to-go" Solaris Helpers Page	http://home1.swipnet.se/%7Ew-10694/helpers.html

Solaris x86

Name	Location
Hardware Compatibility List	`http://soldc.sun.com/support/drivers/hcl/`
Solaris x86 FAQ	`http://sun.drydog.com/faq/`
Solaris x86 Software	`http://www.sun.com/software/Products/x86.html`

Solaris PPP/NAT

Name	Location
Solaris ISDN PPP	`http://www.mcgeonet.com/solaris_external_isdn_ppp.html`
Celeste's Tutorial on Solaris 2.x Modems & Terminals	`http://www.stokely.com/unix.serial.port.resources/tutorials.html`
IP Filter (free firewall/NAT software)	`http://www.ipfilter.org`
Configuring PPP dial-in on Solaris 7 and Solaris 8	`http://www.kempston.net/solaris/pppserver.html`
Configuring high-speed dialup on Solaris 7 and Solaris 8	`http://www.kempston.net/solaris/dialup.html`
Connecting to Any ISP with Solaris 7 and Solaris 8	`http://www.kempston.net/solaris/connectanyisp.html`
Solaris ipfilter/NAT Configs	`http://www.riddleware.com/solx86/nat-config.html`

F Signals

Signals by Value

Name	Value	Default	Event
SIGHUP	1	Exit	Hangup.
SIGINT	2	Exit	Interrupt. This is the default signal sent by the kill command.
SIGQUIT	3	Dump Core	Quit. SIGINT should always be sent to a process before sending a SIGQUIT.
SIGILL	4	Dump Core	Illegal Instruction.
SIGTRAP	5	Dump Core	Trace/Breakpoint Trap.
SIGABRT	6	Dump Core	Abort.
SIGEMT	7	Dump Core	Emulation Trap.
SIGFPE	8	Dump Core	Arithmetic Exception.
SIGKILL	9	Exit	Killed.
SIGBUS	10	Dump Core	Bus Error.
SIGSEGV	11	Dump Core	Segmentation Fault.
SIGSYS	12	Dump Core	Bad System Call.
SIGPIPE	13	Exit	Broken Pipe.
SIGALRM	14	Exit	Alarm Clock.
SIGTERM	15	Exit	Terminated.
SIGUSR1	16	Exit	User Signal 1.
SIGUSR2	17	Exit	User Signal 2.

continues >>

>>continued

Name	Value	Default	Event
SIGCHLD	18	Ignore	Child Status Changed.
SIGPWR	19	Ignore	Power Fail/Restart.
SIGWINCH	20	Ignore	Window Size Change.
SIGURG	21	Ignore	Urgent Socket Condition.
SIGPOLL	22	Exit	Pollable Event.
SIGSTOP	23	Stop	Stopped.
SIGTSTP	24	Stop	User Stopped.
SIGCONT	25	Ignore	Continued.
SIGTTIN	26	Stop	TTY Input Stopped.
SIGTTOU	27	Stop	TTY Output Stopped.
SIGVTALRM	28	Exit	Virtual Timer Expired.
SIGPROF	29	Exit	Profiling Timer Expired.
SIGXCPU	30	Dump Core	CPU Time Limit Exceeded.
SIGXFSZ	31	Dump Core	File Size Limit Exceeded.
SIGWAITING	32	Ignore	Threads Wait Signal.
SIGLWP	33	Ignore	Lightweight Process (LWP) Signal.
SIGFREEZE	34	Ignore	Check Point Freeze.
SIGTHAW	35	Ignore	Check Point Thaw.
SIGCANCEL	36	Ignore	Cancellation Signal.

Commonly Used Signals

Task	Signal
Kill a process and all processes started by it.	`kill -9 pid`
Restart a process.	`kill -HUP pid`
Kill all processes owned by the user `smithj`.	`/usr/ucb/ps -aux | grep smithj| grep -v grep | awk '{print$1}' | xargs kill -9`

G
TCP/UDP Port List

Some ports have certain security issues related to them. Ports marked as "disable" are a major security concern and should be disabled if at all possible (via `inetd.conf`). Ports marked as "log" are possible security issues, but can still be used if some form of logging functionality is added. The best way to do this is to use TCP Wrappers written by Wietse Venema. It allows TCP ports to be logged ("wrapped") via `inetd`. It also provides host- and user-based access control for TCP ports. It can be downloaded for free from the following URL:

`ftp://coast.cs.purdue.edu/pub/tools/unix/tcp_wrappers/`

TCP/UDP Ports by Service

Service	Port	Security
biff	512/udp	Disable unless used
chargen	19/tcp	Log
chargen	19/udp	
courier	530/tcp	
csnet-ns	105/tcp	
daytime	13/tcp	Log
daytime	13/udp	
discard	9/tcp	Log
discard	9/udp	
domain	53/udp	
domain	53/tcp	
dtspc	6112/tcp	
echo	7/tcp	Log
echo	7/udp	
exec	512/tcp	Disable unless necessary
finger	79/tcp	Disable
fs	7100/tcp	
ftp	21/tcp	Log
ftp-data	20/tcp	
hostnames	101/tcp	
ident	113/tcp	Wrap
imap	143/tcp	Disable unless used
ingreslock	1524/tcp	Disable
iso-tsap	102/tcp	
kerberos	750/udp	
kerberos	750/tcp	
link	87/tcp	
listen	2766/tcp	
lockd	4045/udp	
lockd	4045/tcp	
login	513/tcp	
monitor	561/udp	
name	42/udp	
netstat	15/tcp	Disable
new-rwho	550/udp	Disable

Service	Port	Security
NeWS	144/tcp	Disable
nfsd	2049/udp	
nfsd	2049/tcp	
nntp	119/tcp	
ntalk	518/udp	
ntp	123/tcp	
ntp	123/udp	
pcserver	600/tcp	
pop-2	109/tcp	Log
pop3	110/tcp	Log
printer	515/tcp	
rje	77/tcp	
rmonitor	560/udp	Disable
route	520/udp	
shell	514/tcp	Disable unless necessary
smtp	25/tcp	Log
sunrpc	111/udp	
sunrpc	111/tcp	
supdup	95/tcp	
syslog	514/udp	
systat	11/tcp	
talk	517/udp	
tcpmux	1/tcp	
telnet	23/tcp	Consider using ssh instead
tftp	69/udp	Disable
time	37/tcp	Log
time	37/udp	
ufsd	1008/tcp	
ufsd	1008/udp	
uucp	540/tcp	Disable
uucp-path	117/tcp	Disable
who	513/udp	Disable
whois	43/tcp	Disable
x400	103/tcp	
x400-snd	104/tcp	

TCP/UDP Ports by Port

Service	Port
tcpmux	1/tcp
echo	7/tcp
echo	7/udp
discard	9/tcp
discard	9/udp
systat	11/tcp
daytime	13/tcp
daytime	13/udp
netstat	15/tcp
chargen	19/tcp
chargen	19/udp
ftp-data	20/tcp
ftp	21/tcp
ssh	22/tcp
telnet	23/tcp
smtp	25/tcp
time	37/tcp
time	37/udp
name	42/udp
whois	43/tcp
domain	53/udp
domain	53/tcp
tftp	69/udp
rje	77/tcp
finger	79/tcp
link	87/tcp
supdup	95/tcp
hostnames	101/tcp
iso-tsap	102/tcp
x400	103/tcp
x400-snd	104/tcp
csnet-ns	105/tcp
poppassd	106/tcp
pop-2	109/tcp
pop3	110/tcp
sunrpc	111/udp
sunrpc	111/tcp
ident	113/tcp

Service	Port
uucp-path	117/tcp
nntp	119/tcp
ntp	123/tcp
ntp	123/udp
imap	143/tcp
NeWS	144/tcp
masqdialer	224/tcp
exec	512/tcp
biff	512/udp
login	513/tcp
who	513/udp
shell	514/tcp
syslog	514/udp
printer	515/tcp
talk	517/udp
ntalk	518/udp
route	520/udp
courier	530/tcp
uucp	540/tcp
new-rwho	550/udp
rmonitor	560/udp
monitor	561/udp
pcserver	600/tcp
kerberos	750/udp kdc
kerberos	750/tcp
ufsd	1008/tcp
ufsd	1008/udp
ingreslock	1524/tcp
radius	1645/tcp
radacct	1645/tcp
nfsd	2049/udp
nfsd	2049/tcp
listen	2766/tcp
lockd	4045/udp
lockd	4045/tcp
dtspc	6112/tcp
irc	6667/tcp
fs	7100/tcp

Index

Symbols

A

B

C

D

E

F

G–H

I

J–K

N

O

P

Q

R

S

U

V

W–Z

Advanced Information on Networking Technologies

New Riders Books Offer Advice and Experience

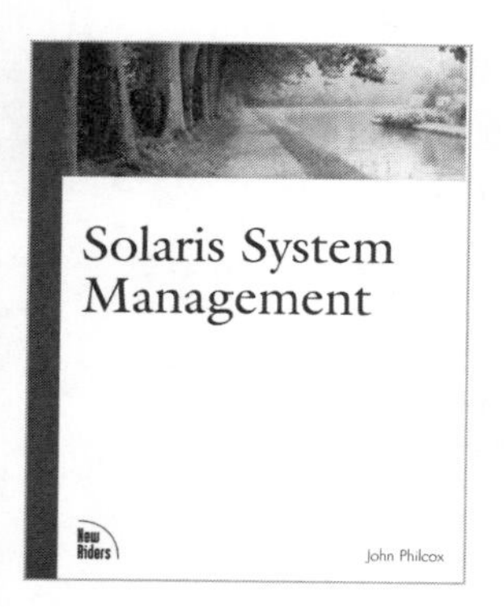

LANDMARK

We know how important it is to have access to detailed, solution-oriented information on core technologies. *Landmark Series* books contain the essential information you need to solve technical problems. Written by experts and subjected to rigorous peer and technical reviews, our *Landmark* books are hard-core resources for practitioners like you.

ESSENTIAL REFERENCE

The *Essential Reference* series from New Riders provides answers when you know what you want to do but need to know how to do it. Each title skips extraneous material and assumes a strong base of knowledge. These are indispensable books for the practitioner who wants to find specific features of a technology quickly. Avoiding fluff and basic material, these books present solutions in an innovative, clean format—and at a great value.

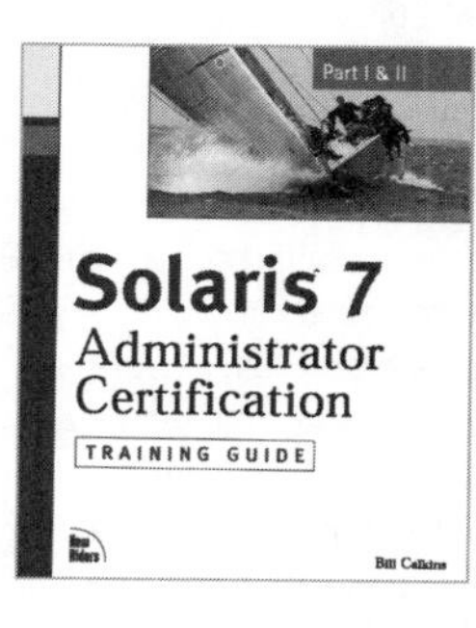

CERTIFICATION

New Riders offers a complete line of test preparation materials to help you achieve your certification. With books like the *Training Guide* and software like the revolutionary *ExamGear*, New Riders offers comprehensive products built by experienced professionals who have passed the exams and instructed hundreds of candidates.

Selected titles from New Riders

Microsoft Technologies

Inside Windows 2000 Server

By William Boswell
1st Edition
1515 pages, $49.99
ISBN: 1-56205-929-7

Taking the author-driven, no-nonsense approach we pioneered with our *Landmark* books, New Riders proudly offers something unique for Windows 2000 administrators—an interesting, discriminating book on Windows 2000 Server written by someone who can anticipate your situation and give you workarounds that won't leave a system unstable or sluggish.

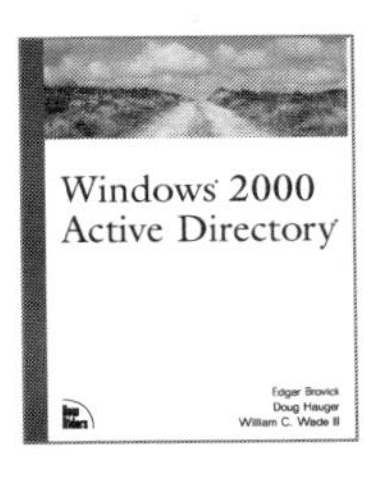

Windows 2000 Active Directory

By Ed Brovick, Doug Hauger, and William Wade III
1st Edition
416 pages, $29.99
ISBN: 0-7357-0870-3

Written by three of Microsoft's key premium partners, with high-level access to people, information, and resources, this book offers a concise, focused, and informative *Landmark* format, filled with case studies and real-world experience for Windows 2000's most anticipated and most complex feature—the Active Directory.

Windows 2000 Essential Reference

By Steven Tate, et al.
1st Edition
670 pages, $35.00
ISBN: 0-7357-0869-X

Architected to be the most navigable, useful and value-packed reference for Windows 2000, this book uses a creative "telescoping" design that you can adapt to your style of learning. The authors give you answers based on their hands-on experience with Windows 2000 and apply their formidable credentials toward giving you the answers you won't find anywhere else.

Windows 2000 Routing and Remote Access Service

By Kackie Charles
1st Edition
400 pages, $34.99
ISBN: 0-7357-0951-3

Ideal for system administrators looking to create cost-effective and secure remote access across the network. Author Kackie Charles uses concrete examples to demonstrate how to smoothly integrate Windows 2000 routing with your existing routing infrastructure, and connect users to the network while maxmizing available bandwidth. Featured coverage includes new authentication models, routing protocols, configuration of the Windows 2000 router, design issues, security, and troubleshooting.

Windows 2000 Deployment & Desktop Management

By Jeffrey A. Ferris
1st Edition
408 pages, $34.99
ISBN: 0-7357-0975-0

More than a simple overview of new features and tools, this solutions-driven book is a thorough reference to deploying Windows 2000 Professional to corporate workstations. The expert real-world advice and detailed exercises make this a one-stop, easy-to-use resource for any system administrator, integrator, engineer, or other IT professional planning rollout of Windows 2000 clients.

Windows 2000 DNS

By Herman Knief, Jeffrey Graham, Andrew Daniels, and Roger Abell
2nd Edition
480 pages, $39.99
ISBN: 0-7357-0973-4

Focusing on such key topics as designing and securing DNS services, planning for interoperation, and installing and using DHCP and WINS services, *Windows 2000 DNS* is a comprehensive guide to the newest iteration of Microsoft's DNS. The authors provide you with real-world advice, best practices, and strategies you will need to design and administer DNS for optimal performance.

Windows 2000 User Management

By Lori Sanders
1st Edition
240 pages, $34.99
ISBN: 1-56205-886-X

With the dawn of Windows 2000, it has become even more difficult to draw a clear line between managing the user and managing the user's environment and desktop. This book, written by a noted trainer and consultant, provides a comprehensive, practical guide to managing users and their desktop environments with Windows 2000.

Windows 2000 Professional

By Jerry Honeycutt
1st Edition
330 pages, $34.99
ISBN: 0-7357-0950-5

Windows 2000 Professional explores the power available to the Windows workstation user on the corporate network and Internet. The book is aimed directly at the power user who values the security, stability, and networking capabilities of NT alongside the ease and familiarity of the Windows 9X user interface. This book covers both user and administration topics, with a dose of networking content added for connectivity.

Windows NT/2000 Thin Client Solutions

By Todd Mathers
2nd Edition
840 pages, $45.00
ISBN: 1-57870-239-9

A practical and comprehensive reference to MetaFrame 1.8 and Terminal Server Edition, this book should be the first source for answers to the tough questions on the TSE/MetaFrame platform. Building on the quality of the previous edition, additional coverage of installation of Terminal Services and MetaFrame on a Windows 2000 Server, as well as chapters on TSE management, remote access, and application integration, are included.

Windows 2000 Active Directory Design & Deployment

By Gary Olsen
1st Edition
648 pages, $45.00
ISBN: 1-57870-242-9

This book focuses on the design of a Windows 2000 Active Directory environment, and how to develop an effective design and migration plan. The reader is lead through the process of developing a design plan by reviewing each pertinent issue, and then provided expert advice on how to evaluate each issue as it applies to the reader's particular environment. Practical examples illustrate all of these issues.

Windows 2000 Virtual Private Networking

By Thaddeus Fortenberry
1st Edition
350 pages, $45.00
ISBN 1-57870-246-1

Because of the ongoing push for a distributed workforce, administrators must support laptop users, home LAN environments, complex branch offices, and more—all within a secure and effective network design. The way an administrator implements VPNs in Windows 2000 is different than that of any other operating system. In addition to discussions about Windows 2000 tunneling, new VPN features that can affect Active Directory replication and Network Address Translation are also covered.

Windows 2000 and Mainframe Integration

By William Zack
1st Edition
390 pages, $40.00
ISBN:1-57870-200-3

Windows 2000 and Mainframe Integration provides mainframe computing professionals with the practical know-how to build and integrate Windows 2000 technologies into their current environment.

Windows 2000 Server: Planning and Migration

By Sean Deuby
1st Edition
480 pages, $40.00
ISBN:1-57870-023-X

Windows 2000 Server: Planning and Migration can quickly save the NT professional thousands of dollars and hundreds of hours. This title includes authoritative information on key features of Windows 2000 and offers recommendations on how to best position your NT network for Windows 2000.

Windows 2000 Quality of Service

By David Iseminger
1st Edition
264 pages, $45.00
ISBN:1-57870-115-5

As the traffic on networks continues to increase, the strain on network infrastructure and available resources has also grown. *Windows 2000 Quality of Service* teaches network engineers and administrators to how to define traffic control patterns and utilize bandwidth on their networks.

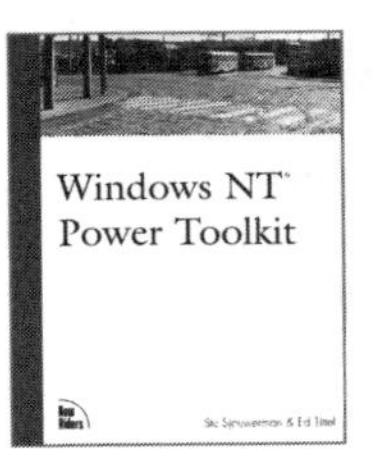

Windows NT Power Toolkit

By Stu Sjouwerman and Ed Tittel
1st Edition
848 pages, $49.99
ISBN: 0-7357-0922-X

A unique offering from New Riders, this book covers the analysis, tuning, optimization, automation, enhancement, maintenance, and troubleshooting of both Windows NT Server 4.0 and Windows NT Workstation 4.0. *Windows NT Power Toolkit* includes comprehensive coverage of all service packs and security updates, IE5 upgrade issues, recent product additions, third-party tools and utilities.

Windows NT Terminal Server and Citrix MetaFrame

By Ted Harwood
1st Edition
746 pages, $29.99
ISBN: 1-56205-944-0

This technical reference details all aspects of planning, installing, administering, and troubleshooting Microsoft Terminal Server and Citrix MetaFrame systems. MetaFrame greatly enhances the usability of NT as a thin-client solution, but the heterogeneous networking issues involved in its integration will be a significant source of information pain.

Windows NT/2000 Native API Reference

By Gary Nebbett
1st Edition
528 pages, $50.00
ISBN: 1-57870-199-6

This book is the first complete reference to the API functions native to Windows NT and covers the set of services that are offered by the Windows NT to both kernel- and user-mode programs. Coverage consists of documentation of the 210 routines included in the NT Native API, and the functions that will be added in Windows 2000. Routines that are either not directly accessible via the Win32 API or offer substantial additional functionality are described in especially great detail. Services offered by the NT kernel—mainly the support for debugging user mode applications—are also included.

Windows NT Device Driver Development

By Peter Viscarola and W. Anthony Mason
1st Edition
704 pages, $50.00
ISBN: 1-57870-058-2

This title begins with an introduction to the general Windows NT operating system concepts relevant to drivers, then progresses to more detailed information about the operating system, such as interrupt management, synchronization issues, the I/O Subsystem, standard kernel mode drivers, and more.

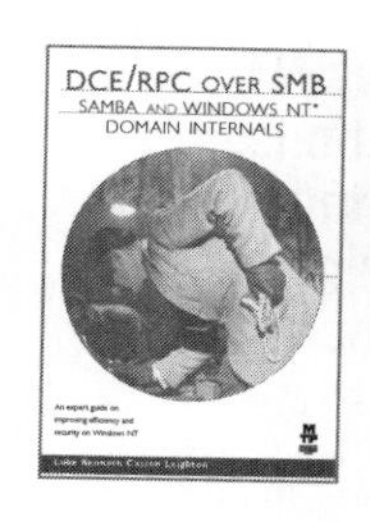

DCE/RPC over SMB: Samba and Windows NT Domain Internals

By Luke Leighton
1st Edition
312 pages, $45.00
ISBN: 1-57870-150-3

Security people, system and network administrators, and those writing tools for them all need to be familiar with the packets flowing across their networks. Authored by a key member of the Samba team, this book describes how Microsoft has taken DCE/RPC and implemented it over SMB and TCP/IP.

Delphi COM Programming

By Eric Harmon
1st Edition
500 pages, $45.00
ISBN: 1-57870-221-6

Delphi COM Programming is for all Delphi 3, 4, and 5 programmers. After providing readers with an understanding of the COM framework, it offers a practical exploration of COM to enable Delphi developers to program component-based applications. Typical real-world scenarios, such as Windows Shell programming, automating Microsoft Agent, and creating and using ActiveX controls, are explored. Discussions of each topic are illustrated with detailed examples.

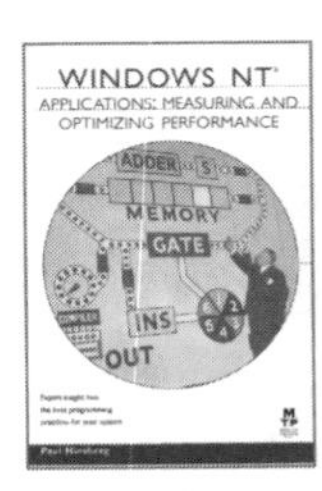

Windows NT Applications: Measuring and Optimizing Performance

By Paul Hinsberg
1st Edition
288 pages, $40.00
ISBN: 1-57870-176-7

This book offers developers crucial insight into the underlying structure of Windows NT, as well as the methodology and tools for measuring and ultimately optimizing code performance.

Applying COM+

By Gregory Brill
1st Edition
450 pages, $49.99
ISBN: 0-7357-0978-5

By pulling a number of disparate services into one unified technology, COM+ holds the promise of greater efficiency and more diverse capabilities for developers who are creating applications—either enterprise or commercial software—to run on a Windows 2000 system. *Applying COM+* covers the features of the new tool, as well as how to implement them in a real case study. Features are demonstrated in all three of the major languages used in the Windows environment: C++, VB, and VJ++.

Exchange & Outlook: Constructing Collaborative Solutions

By Joel Semeniuk and Duncan Mackenzie
1st Edition
576 pages, $40.00
ISBN 1-57870-252-6

The authors of this book are responsible for building custom messaging applications for some of the biggest Fortune 100 companies in the world. They share their expertise to help administrators and designers use Microsoft technology to establish a base for their messaging system and to lay out the tools that can be used to help build those collaborative solutions. Actutal planning and design solutions are included along with typical workflow/collaborative solutions.

Windows Script Host

By Tim Hill
1st Edition
448 pages, $35.00
ISBN: 1-57870-139-2

Windows Script Host is one of the first books published about this powerful tool. The text focuses on system scripting and the VBScript language, using objects, server scriptlets, and ready-to-use script solutions.

Windows NT Shell Scripting

By Tim Hill
1st Edition
400 pages, $32.00
ISBN: 1-57870-047-7

A complete reference for Windows NT scripting, this book guides you through a high-level introduction to the Shell language itself and the Shell commands that are useful for controlling or managing different components of a network.

Win32 Perl Programming: The Standard Extensions

By Dave Roth
1st Edition
640 pages, $40.00
ISBN:1-57870-067-1

Discover numerous proven examples and practical uses of Perl in solving everyday Win32 problems. This is the only book available with comprehensive coverage of Win32 extensions, where most of the Perl functionality resides in Windows settings.

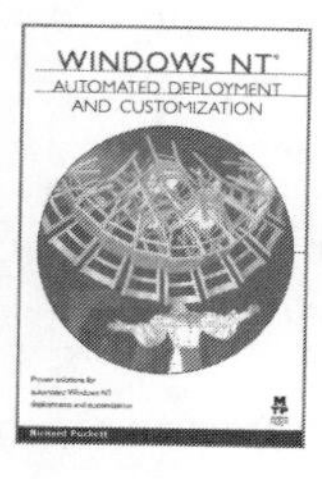

Windows NT Automated Deployment and Customization

By Richard Puckett
1st Editon
300 pages, $32.00
ISBN: 1-57870-045-0

This title offers time-saving advice that helps you install, update and configure software on each of your clients, without having to visit each client. Learn how to control all clients remotely for tasks, such as security and legal software use. Reference material on native NT tools, registry edits, and third-party tools is included.

Windows NT/2000 ADSI Scripting for System Administration

By Thomas Eck
1st Edition
700 pages, $45.00
ISBN: 1-57870-219-4

Active Directory Scripting Interfaces (ADSI) allow administrators to automate administrative tasks across their Windows networks. This title fills a gap in the current ADSI documentation by including coverage of its interaction with LDAP and provides administrators with proven code samples that they can adopt to effectively configure and manage user accounts and other usually time-consuming tasks.

SMS 2 Administration

By Darshan Doshi and Mike Lubanski
1st Edition
448 pages, $39.99
ISBN: 0-7357-0082-6

SMS 2 Administration offers comprehensive coverage of how to design, deploy, and manage SMS 2.0 in an enterprise environment. This book follows the evolution of a software management system from the initial design through the implementation life cycle, to day-to-day management and usage of the system. Packed with case studies and examples pulled from the author's extensive experience, this book makes this complex product seem almost simple.

Web Application Development with PHP 4.0

By Till Gerken, Tobias Ratschiller, et al.
1st Edition
416 pages, $39.99
ISBN: 0-7357-0997-1

Web Application Development with PHP 4.0 explains PHP's advanced syntax including classes, recursive functions, and variables. The authors present software development methodologies and coding conventions, which are a must-know for industry quality products and make software development faster and more productive. Included is coverage on Web applications and insight into user and session management, e-commerce systems, XML applications, and WDDX.

PHP Functions Essential Reference

By Landon Bradshaw, Till Gerken, Graeme Merrall, and Tobias Ratschiller
1st Edition
500 pages, $35.00
ISBN: 0-7357-0970-X
April 2001

This carefully crafted title covers the latest developments through PHP 4.0, including coverage of Zend. These authors share their knowledge not only of the development of PHP, but also how they use it daily to create dynamic Web sites. Covered as well is instruction on using PHP alongside MySQL.

Python Essential Reference

By David Beazley
1st Edition
352 pages, $34.95
ISBN: 0-7357-0901-7

Avoiding the dry and academic approach, the goal of *Python Essential Reference* is to concisely describe the Python programming language and its large library of standard modules, collectively known as the Python programming environment. This informal reference covers Python's lexical conventions, datatypes, control flow, functions, statements, classes, and execution model—a truly essential reference for any Python programmer!

GNU Autoconf, Automake, and Libtool

By Gary V. Vaughan, et al.
1st Edition
432 pages, $40.00
ISBN: 1-57870-190-2

This book is the first of its kind, authored by Open Source community luminaries and current maintainers of the tools, teaching developers how to boost their productivity and the portability of their applications using GNU Autoconf, Automake, and Libtool.

Linux/UNIX

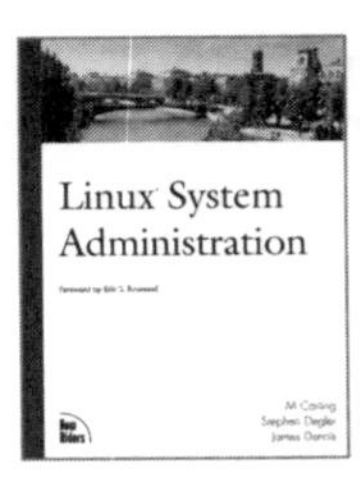

Linux System Administration

By M. Carling, James T. Dennis, and Stephen Degler
1st Edition
368 pages, $29.99
ISBN: 1-56205-934-3

Today's overworked sysadmins are looking for ways to keep their networks running smoothly and achieve enhanced performance. Users are always looking for more storage, more services, and more Speed. *Linux System Administration* guides the reader in the many intricacies of maintaining a secure, stable system.

Linux Firewalls

By Robert Ziegler
1st Edition
496 pages, $39.99
ISBN: 0-7357-0900-9

This book details security steps that a small, non-enterprise business user might take to protect his system. These steps include packet-level firewall filtering, IP masquerading, proxies, tcp wrappers, system integrity checking, and system security monitoring with an overall emphasis on filtering and protection. The goal of *Linux Firewalls* is to help people get their Internet security measures in place quickly, without the need to become experts in security or firewalls.

Linux Essential Reference

By Ed Petron
1st Edition
368 pages, $24.95
ISBN: 0-7357-0852-5

This title is all about getting things done by providing structured organization to the plethora of available Linux information. Providing clear and concise instructions on how to perform important administration and management tasks, as well as how to use some of the more powerful commands and more advanced topics, the scope of *Linux Essential Reference* includes the best way to implement the most frequently used commands, manage shell scripting, administer your own system, and utilize effective security.

UnixWare 7 System Administration

By Gene Henriksen and Melissa Henriksen
1st Edition
560 pages, $39.99
ISBN: 1-57870-080-9

In great technical detail, this title presents the latest version of SCO UnixWare and is the definitive operating system resource for SCO engineers and administrators. SCO troubleshooting notes and tips are integrated throughout the text, as are tips specifically designed for those who are familiar with other UNIX variants.

Developing Linux Applications with GTK+ and GDK

By Eric Harlow
1st Edition
512 pages, $34.99
ISBN: 0-7357-0021-4

This handbook is for developers who are moving to the Linux platform, and those using the GTK+ library, including Glib and GDK using C. All the applications and code the author developed for this book have been released under the GPL.

GTK+/Gnome Application Development

By Havoc Pennington
1st Edition
528 pages, $39.99
ISBN: 0-7357-0078-8

More than one million Linux users are also application developers. *GTK+/Gnome Application Development* provides the experienced programmer with the knowledge to develop X Windows applications with the popular GTK+ toolkit. It contains reference information for more experienced users who are already familiar with usage, but require function prototypes and detailed descriptions.

KDE Application Development

By Uwe Thiem
1st Edition
190 pages, $39.99
ISBN: 1-57870-201-1

KDE Application Development offers a head start on KDE and Qt. The book covers the essential widgets available in KDE and Qt, and offers a strong start without the "first try" annoyances which sometimes make strong developers and programmers give up.

Grokking the GIMP

By Carey Bunks
1st Edition
342 pages, $45.00
ISBN: 0-7357-0924-6

Grokking the GIMP is a technical reference that covers the intricacies of the GIMP's functionality. The material gives the reader the ability to get up to speed quickly and start creating great graphics using the GIMP. Included as a bonus are step-by-step cookbook features used entirely for advanced effects.

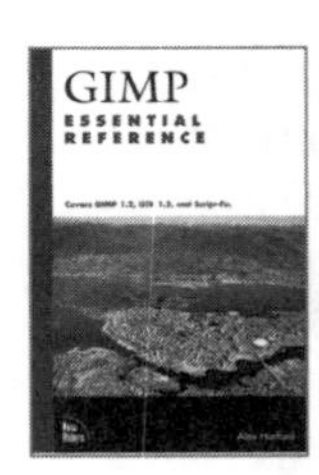

GIMP Essential Reference

By Alex Harford
1st Edition
400 pages, $24.95
ISBN: 0-7357-0911-4

As the use of the Linux OS gains steam, so does the use of the GIMP. Many Photoshop users are starting to use the GIMP, recognized for its power and versatility. Taking this into consideration, GIMP Essential Reference has shortcuts exclusively for Photoshop users and puts the power of this program into the palm of the reader's hand.

Solaris System Administrator's Guide

By Janice Winsor
2nd Edition
324 pages, $34.99
ISBN: 1-57870-040-X

Designed to work as both a practical tutorial and quick reference, this book provides UNIX administrators complete, detailed descriptions of the most frequently performed tasks for Solaris. Learn how to employ the features of Solaris to meet these needs of your users, and get tips on how to make administration easier.

Solaris Advanced System Administrator's Guide

By Janice Winsor
2nd Edition
587 pages, $39.99
ISBN: 1-57870-039-6

This officially authorized tutorial provides indispensable tips, advice, and quick-reference tables to help you add system components, improve service access, and automate routine tasks. this book also includes updated information on Solaris 2.6 topics.

Networking

Cisco Router Configuration &Troubleshooting

By Mark Tripod
2nd Edition
330 pages, $39.99
ISBN: 0-7357-0999-8

A reference for the network and system administrator who finds himself having to configure and maintain existing Cisco routers, as well as get new hardware up and running. By providing advice and preferred practices, instead of just rehashing Cisco documentation, this book gives networking professionals information they can start using today.

Understanding Directory Services

By Beth Sheresh and Doug Sheresh
1st Edition
390 pages, $39.99
ISBN: 0-7357-0910-6

Understanding Directory Services provides the reader with a thorough knowledge of the fundamentals of directory services: what Directory Services are, how they are designed, and what functionality they can provide to an IT infrastructure. This book provides a framework to the exploding market of directory services by placing the technology in context and helping people understand what directories can, and can't, do for their networks.

Understanding the Network: A Practical Guide to Internetworking

By Michael Martin
1st Edition
690 pages, $39.99
ISBN: 0-7357-0977-7

Understanding the Network addresses the audience in practical terminology, and describes the most essential information and tools required to build high-availability networks in a step-by-step implementation format. Each chapter could be read as a standalone, but the book builds progressively toward a summary of the essential concepts needed to put together a wide-area network.

Understanding Data Communications

By Gilbert Held
6th Edition
620 pages, $39.99
ISBN: 0-7357-0036-2

Gil Held's book is ideal for those who want to get up to speed on technological advances as well as those who want a primer on networking concepts. This book is intended to explain how data communications actually work. It contains updated coverage on hot topics like thin client technology, x2 and 56Kbps modems, voice digitization, and wireless data transmission. Whatever your needs, this title puts perspective and expertise in your hands.

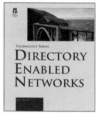

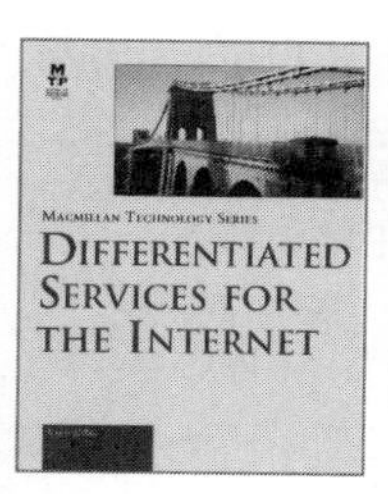

Differentiated Services for the Internet

By Kalevi Kilkki
1st Edition
400 pages, $50.00
ISBN: 1-57870-132-5

This book offers network architects, engineers, and managers of packet networks critical insight into the continuing development of Differentiated Services. It addresses the particular needs of a network environment as well as issues that must be considered in its implementation. Coverage allows networkers to implement DiffServ on a variety of networking technologies, including ATM, and to solve common problems related to TCP, UDP, and other networking protocols.

Quality of Service in IP Networks

By Grenville Armitage
1st Edition
310 pages, $50.00
ISBN: 1-57870-189-9

Quality of Service in IP Networks presents a clear understanding of the architectural issues surrounding delivering QoS in an IP network, and positions the emerging technologies within a framework of solutions. The motivation for QoS is explained with reference to emerging real-time applications, such as Voice/Video over IP, VPN services, and supporting Service Level Agreements.

Designing Addressing Architectures for Routing and Switching

By Howard Berkowitz
1st Edition
500 pages, $45.00
ISBN: 1-57870-059-0

One of the greatest challenges for a network design professional is making the users, servers, files, printers, and other resources visible on their network. This title equips the network engineer or architect with a systematic methodology for planning the wide area and local area network "streets" on which users and servers live.

Understanding and Deploying LDAP Directory Services

By Tim Howes, Mark Smith, and Gordon Good
1st Edition
850 pages, $50.00
ISBN: 1-57870-070-1

This comprehensive tutorial provides the reader with a thorough treatment of LDAP directory services. Minimal knowledge of general networking and administration is assumed, making the material accessible to intermediate and advanced readers alike. The text is full of practical implementation advice and real-world deployment examples to help the reader choose the path that makes the most sense for his specific organization.

Switched, Fast, and Gigabit Ethernet

By Sean Riley and Robert Breyer
3rd Edition
615 pages, $50.00
ISBN: 1-57870-073-6

Switched, Fast, and Gigabit Ethernet, Third Edition is the one and only solution needed to understand and fully implement this entire range of Ethernet innovations. Acting both as an overview of current technologies and hardware requirements as well as a hands-on, comprehensive tutorial for deploying and managing switched, fast, and gigabit ethernet networks, this guide covers the most prominent present and future challenges network administrators face.

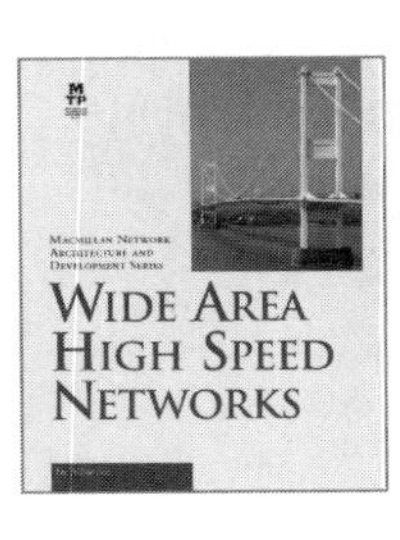

Wide Area High Speed Networks

By Dr. Sidnie Feit
1st Edition
624 pages, $50.00
ISBN: 1-57870-114-7

Networking is in a transitional phase between long-standing conventional wide area services and new technologies and services. This book presents current and emerging wide area technologies and services, makes them understandable, and puts them into perspective so that their merits and disadvantages are clear.

Local Area High Speed Networks

By Dr. Sidnie Feit
1st Edition
655 pages, $50.00
ISBN: 1-57870-113-9

There is a great deal of change happening in the technology being used for local area networks. As Web intranets have driven bandwidth needs through the ceiling, inexpensive Ethernet NICs and switches have come into the market. As a result, many network professionals are interested in evaluating these new technologies for implementation. This book provides real-world implementation expertise for these technologies, including traces, so that users can realistically compare and decide how to use them.

The DHCP Handbook

By Ralph Droms and Ted Lemon
1st Edition
535 pages, $55.00
ISBN: 1-57870-137-6

The DHCP Handbook is an authoritative overview and expert guide to the setup and management of a DHCP server. This title discusses how DHCP was developed and its interaction with other protocols. Learn how DHCP operates, its use in different environments, and the interaction between DHCP servers and clients. Network hardware, inter-server communication, security, SNMP, and IP mobility are also discussed. Also, included in the book are several appendices that provide a rich resource for networking professionals working with DHCP.

Wireless LANs: Implementing Interoperable Networks

By Jim Geier
1st Edition
432 pages, $40.00
ISBN: 1-57870-081-7

Wireless LANs covers how and why to migrate from proprietary solutions to the 802.11 standard, and explains how to realize significant cost savings through wireless LAN implementation for data collection systems.

Designing Routing and Switching Architectures for Enterprise Networks

By Howard Berkowitz
1st Edition
992 pages, $55.00
ISBN: 1-57870-060-4

This title provides a fundamental understanding of how switches and routers operate, enabling the reader to use them effectively to build networks. The book walks the network designer through all aspects of requirements, analysis, and deployment strategies, strengthens readers' professional abilities, and helps them develop skills necessary to advance in their profession.

Network Performance Baselining

By Daniel Nassar
1st Edition
736 pages, $50.00
ISBN: 1-57870-240-2

Network Performance Baselining focuses on the real-world implementation of network baselining principles and shows not only how to measure and rate a network's performance, but also how to improve the network performance. This book includes chapters that give a real "how-to" approach for standard baseline methodologies along with actual steps and processes to perform network baseline measurements. In addition, the proper way to document and build a baseline report will be provided.

The Economics of Electronic Commerce

By Soon-Yong Choi, Andrew Whinston, Dale Stahl
1st Edition
656 pages, $49.99
ISBN: 1-57870-014-0

This is the first electronic commerce title to focus on traditional topics of economics applied to the electronic commerce arena. While all other electronic commerce titles take a "how-to" approach, this focuses on what it means from an economic perspective.

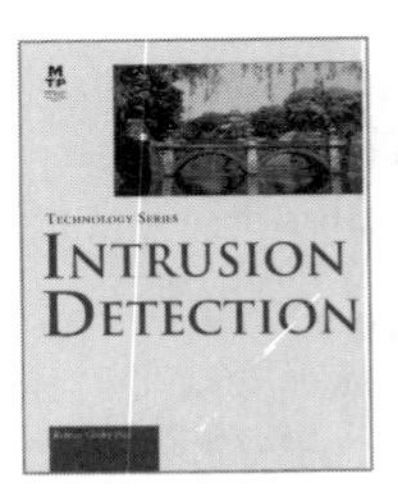

Intrusion Detection

By Rebecca Gurley Bace
1st Edition
340 pages, $50.00
ISBN: 1-57870-185-6

Intrusion detection is a critical new area of technology within network security. This comprehensive guide to the field of intrusion detection covers the foundations of intrusion detection and system audit. *Intrusion Detection* provides a wealth of information, ranging from design considerations to how to evaluate and choose the optimal commercial intrusion detection products for a particular networking environment.

Understanding Public-Key Infrastructure

By Carlisle Adams and Steve Lloyd
1st Edition
300 pages, $50.00
ISBN: 1-57870-166-X

This book is a tutorial on, and a guide to the deployment of, Public-Key Infrastructures. It covers a broad range of material related to PKIs, including certification, operational considerations and standardization efforts, as well as deployment issues and considerations. Emphasis is placed on explaining the interrelated fields within the topic area, to assist those who will be responsible for making deployment decisions and architecting a PKI within an organization.

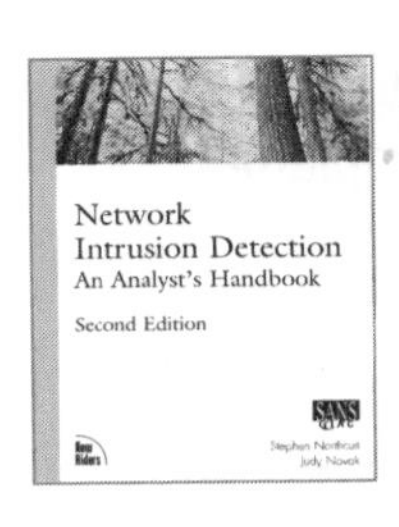

Network Intrusion Detection: An Analyst's Handbook

By Stephen Northcutt and Judy Novak
2nd Edition
480 pages, $45.00
ISBN: 0-7357-1008-2

Get answers and solutions from someone who has been in the trenches. Author Stephen Northcutt, original developer of the Shadow intrusion detection system and former Director of the United States Navy's Information System Security Office, gives his expertise to intrusion detection specialists, security analysts, and consultants responsible for setting up and maintaining an effective defense against network security attacks.

Domino System Administration

By Rob Kirkland
1st Edition
860 pages, $49.99
ISBN: 1-56205-948-3

Need a concise, practical explanation about the new features of Domino, and how to make some of the advanced stuff really work? *Domino System Administration* is the first book on Domino that attacks the technology at the professional level, with practical, hands-on assistance to get Domino 5 running in your organization.

Lotus Notes & Domino Essential Reference

By Dave Hatter and Tim Bankes
1st Edition
675 pages, $45.00
ISBN: 0-7357-0007-9

If you need something to facilitate your creative and technical abilities—something to perfect your Lotus Notes and Domino programming skills—this is the book for you. This title includes all of the objects, classes, functions, and methods found if you work with Lotus Notes and Domino. It shows the object hierarchy and the overlying relationship between each one, organized the way the language is designed.

Software Architecture and Engineering

Designing Flexible Object-Oriented Systems with UML

By Charles Richter
1st Edition
416 pages, $40.00
ISBN: 1-57870-098-1

Designing Flexible Object-Oriented Systems with UML details the UML, which is a notation system for designing object-oriented programs. The book follows the same sequence that a development project might employ, starting with requirements of the problem using UML case diagrams and activity diagrams. The reader is shown ways to improve the design as the author moves through the transformation of the initial diagrams into class diagrams and interaction diagrams.

Constructing Superior Software

By Paul Clements, et al.
1st Edition
285 pages, $40.00
ISBN: 1-57870-147-3

Published in cooperation with the Software Quality Institute at the University of Texas, Austin, this title presents a set of fundamental engineering strategies for achieving a successful software solution, with practical advice to ensure that the development project is moving in the right direction. Software designers and development managers can improve the development speed and quality of their software, and improve the processes used in development.

A UML Pattern Language

By Paul Evitts
1st Edition
260 pages, $40.00
ISBN: 1-57870-118-X

While other books focus only on the UML notation system, this book integrates key UML modeling concepts and illustrates their use through patterns. It provides an integrated, practical, step-by-step discussion of UML and patterns, with real-world examples to illustrate proven software modeling techniques.

NETWORKING

STANDARDS & PROTOCOLS

Cisco Router Configuration & Troubleshooting, Second Edition
0-7357-0999-8 • $34.99 US
Understanding Directory Services
0-7357-0910-6 • $39.99 US
Understanding the Network: A Practical Guide to Internetworking
0-7357-0977-7 • $39.99 US
Understanding Data Communications, Sixth Edition
0-7357-0036-2 • $39.99 US
LDAP: Programming Directory Enabled Applications
1-57870-000-0 • $44.99 US
Gigabit Ethernet Networking
1-57870-062-0 • $50.00 US
Supporting Service Level Agreements on IP Networks
1-57870-146-5 • $50.00 US
Directory Enabled Networks
1-57870-140-6 • $50.00 US
Differentiated Services for the Internet
1-57870-132-5 • $50.00 US
Policy-Based Networking: Architecture and Algorithms
1-57870-226-7 • $50.00 US
Networking Quality of Service and Windows Operating Systems
1-57870-206-2 • $50.00 US
Quality of Service on IP Networks
1-57870-189-9 • $50.00 US
Designing Addressing Architectures for Routing and Switching
1-57870-059-0 • $45.00 US
Understanding & Deploying LDAP Directory Services
1-57870-070-1 • $50.00 US
Switched, Fast and Gigabit Ethernet, Third Edition
1-57870-073-6 • $50.00 US
Wireless LANs: Implementing Interoperable Networks
1-57870-081-7 • $40.00 US
Wide Area High Speed Networks
1-57870-114-7 • $50.00 US
The DHCP Handbook
1-57870-137-6 • $55.00 US
Designing Routing and Switching Architectures for Enterprise Networks
1-57870-060-4 • $55.00 US
Local Area High Speed Networks
1-57870-113-9 • $50.00 US
Network Performance Baselining
1-57870-240-2 • $50.00 US
Economics of Electronic Commerce
1-57870-014-0 • $49.99 US

SECURITY

Intrusion Detection
1-57870-185-6 • $50.00 US
Understanding Public-Key Infrastructure
1-57870-166-X • $50.00 US
Network Intrusion Detection: An Analyst's Handbook, 2E
0-7357-1008-2 • $45.00 US
Linux Firewalls
0-7357-0900-9 • $39.99 US
Intrusion Signatures and Analysis
0-7357-1063-5 • $39.99 US

LOTUS NOTES/DOMINO

Domino System Administration
1-56205-948-3 • $49.99 US
Lotus Notes & Domino Essential Reference
0-7357-0007-9 • $45.00 US

PROFESSIONAL CERTIFICATION

TRAINING GUIDES

MCSE Training Guide: Networking Essentials, 2nd Ed.
1-56205-919-X • $49.99 US
MCSE Training Guide: Windows NT Server 4, 2nd Ed.
1-56205-916-5 • $49.99 US
MCSE Training Guide: Windows NT Workstation 4, 2nd Ed.
1-56205-918-1 • $49.99 US
MCSE Training Guide: Windows NT Server 4 Enterprise, 2nd Ed.
1-56205-917-3 • $49.99 US
MCSE Training Guide: Core Exams Bundle, 2nd Ed.
1-56205-926-2 • $149.99 US
MCSE Training Guide: TCP/IP, 2nd Ed.
1-56205-920-3 • $49.99 US
MCSE Training Guide: IIS 4, 2nd Ed.
0-7357-0865-7 • $49.99 US
MCSE Training Guide: SQL Server 7 Administration
0-7357-0003-6 • $49.99 US
MCSE Training Guide: SQL Server 7 Database Design
0-7357-0004-4 • $49.99 US
MCSD Training Guide: Visual Basic 6 Exams
0-7357-0002-8 • $69.99 US
MCSD Training Guide: Solution Architectures
0-7357-0026-5 • $49.99 US
MCSD Training Guide: 4-in-1 Bundle
0-7357-0912-2 • $149.99 US
A+ Certification Training Guide, Second Edition
0-7357-0907-6 • $49.99 US
A+ Certification Training Guide, Third Edition
0-7357-1088-0 • $49.99 US
Available April 2001
Network+ Certification Guide
0-7357-0077-X • $49.99 US
Solaris 2.6 Administrator Certification Training Guide, Part I
1-57870-085-X • $40.00 US
Solaris 2.6 Administrator Certification Training Guide, Part II
1-57870-086-8 • $40.00 US
Solaris 7 Administrator Certification Training Guide, Part I and II
1-57870-249-6 • $49.99 US
MCSE Training Guide: Windows 2000 Professional
0-7357-0965-3 • $49.99 US
MCSE Training Guide: Windows 2000 Server
0-7357-0968-8 • $49.99 US
MCSE Training Guide: Windows 2000 Network Infrastructure
0-7357-0966-1 • $49.99 US
MCSE Training Guide: Windows 2000 Network Security Design
0-73570-984X • $49.99 US
MCSE Training Guide: Windows 2000 Network Infrastructure Design
0-73570-982-3 • $49.99 US
MCSE Training Guide: Windows 2000 Directory Svcs. Infrastructure
0-7357-0976-9 • $49.99 US
MCSE Training Guide: Windows 2000 Directory Services Design
0-7357-0983-1 • $49.99 US
MCSE Training Guide: Windows 2000 Accelerated Exam
0-7357-0979-3 • $69.99 US
MCSE Training Guide: Windows 2000 Core Exams Bundle
0-7357-0988-2 • $149.99 US

FAST TRACKS

CLP Fast Track: Lotus Notes/Domino 5 Application Development
0-73570-877-0 • $39.99 US
CLP Fast Track: Lotus Notes/Domino 5 System Administration
0-7357-0878-9 • $39.99 US
Network+ Fast Track
0-7357-0904-1 • $29.99 US
A+ Fast Track
0-7357-0028-1 • $34.99 US
MCSD Fast Track: Visual Basic 6, Exam #70-175
0-7357-0019-2 • $19.99 US
MCSD FastTrack: Visual Basic 6, Exam #70-175
0-7357-0018-4 • $19.99 US

SOFTWARE ARCHITECTURE & ENGINEERING

Designing for the User with OVID
1-57870-101-5 • $40.00 US
Designing Flexible Object-Oriented Systems with UML
1-57870-098-1 • $40.00 US
Constructing Superior Software
1-57870-147-3 • $40.00 US
A UML Pattern Language
1-57870-118-X • $45.00 US

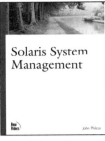

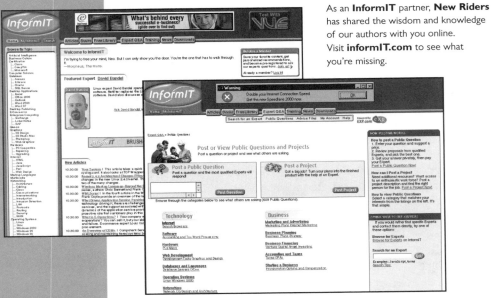

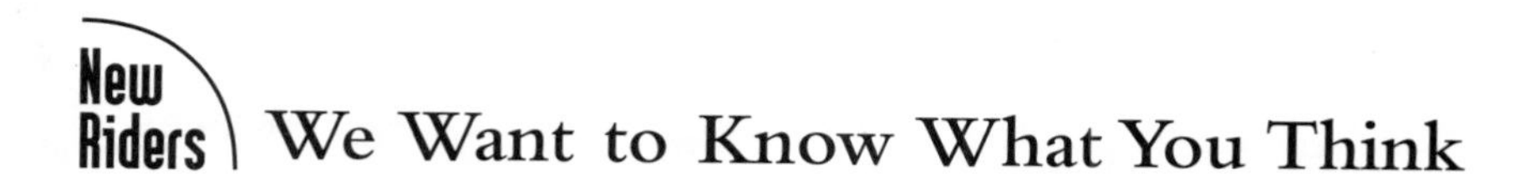

We Want to Know What You Think

To better serve you, we would like your opinion on the content and quality of this book. Please complete this card and mail it to us or fax it to 317-581-4663.

Name ______________________________

Address ______________________________

City __________ State __________ Zip __________

Email Address ______________________________

Occupation ______________________________

What influenced your purchase of this book?

- ❑ Recommendation
- ❑ Cover Design
- ❑ Table of Contents
- ❑ Index
- ❑ Magazine Review
- ❑ Advertisement
- ❑ New Rider's Reputation
- ❑ Author Name

How would you rate the contents of this book?

- ❑ Excellent
- ❑ Very Good
- ❑ Good
- ❑ Fair
- ❑ Below Average
- ❑ Poor

How do you plan to use this book?

- ❑ Quick reference
- ❑ Self-training
- ❑ Classroom
- ❑ Other

What do you like most about this book?
Check all that apply.

- ❑ Content
- ❑ Writing Style
- ❑ Accuracy
- ❑ Examples
- ❑ Listings
- ❑ Design
- ❑ Index
- ❑ Page Count
- ❑ Price
- ❑ Illustrations

What do you like least about this book?
Check all that apply.

- ❑ Content
- ❑ Writing Style
- ❑ Accuracy
- ❑ Examples
- ❑ Listings
- ❑ Design
- ❑ Index
- ❑ Page Count
- ❑ Price
- ❑ Illustrations

Can you name a similar book that you like better than this one, or one that is as good? Why?

____

____

How many New Riders books do you own? ______________________________

What are your favorite computer books? ______________________________

____

What other titles would you like to see us develop? ______________________________

____

Any comments for us? ______________________________

____

____

____

____

Solaris 8 Essential Reference, 0-7357-1007-4

www.newriders.com • Fax 317-581-4663

Fold here and tape to mail

Place
Stamp
Here

New Riders Publishing
201 W. 103rd St.
Indianapolis, IN 46290

How to Contact Us

Visit Our Web Site

www.newriders.com

On our Web site you'll find information about our other books, authors, tables of contents, indexes, and book errata.

Email Us

Contact us at this address:

nrfeedback@newriders.com

- If you have comments or questions about this book
- To report errors that you have found in this book
- If you have a book proposal to submit or are interested in writing for New Riders
- If you would like to have an author kit sent to you
- If you are an expert in a computer topic or technology and are interested in being a technical editor who reviews manuscripts for technical accuracy
- To find a distributor in your area, please contact our international department at this address.

nrmedia@newriders.com

- For instructors from educational institutions who want to preview New Riders books for classroom use. Email should include your name, title, school, department, address, phone number, office days/hours, text in use, and enrollment, along with your request for desk/examination copies and/or additional information.
- For members of the media who are interested in reviewing copies of New Riders books. Send your name, mailing address, and email address, along with the name of the publication or Web site you work for.

Bulk Purchases/Corporate Sales

If you are interested in buying 10 or more copies of a title or want to set up an account for your company to purchase directly from the publisher at a substantial discount, contact us at 800-382-3419 or email your contact information to corpsales@pearsontechgroup.com. A sales representative will contact you with more information.

Write to Us

New Riders Publishing

201 W. 103rd St.

Indianapolis, IN 46290-1097

Call Us

Toll-free (800) 571-5840 + 9 + 7477

If outside U.S. (317) 581-3500. Ask for New Riders.

Fax Us

(317) 581-4663

Colophon

The image on the cover of this book is a Landsat image of Easton, Pennsylvania, taken circa 1997.

Easton was founded in 1752 by Thomas Penn, the lesser-known son of William Penn. William was perhaps best known as the urban planner of Philadelphia (the plan from which, not coincidentally, Easton was designed) and one of the few colonial Americans to treat native Americans with some degree of respect. In 1682, he enacted the "Great Treaty," a land for goods quid pro quo, with the Leni Lenape (Delaware) tribe in the town of Shackamaxon.

After its founding, Easton thrived and played a role in the Industrial Revolution. Nestled between the Delaware and Lehigh rivers, it was part of an important trade route, and eventually became a stopping ground for five major railways to and from New York and Philadelphia. As a result of this economic prosperity, Easton's commerce and culture began to flourish. Continuing this trend, Lafayette College was organized in Easton by its citizens in 1826, led by James Madison Porter and Joel Jones. It eventually received its charter and opened in 1832, specializing in military science, literature, and general science.

One of the most colorful additions to the Easton landscape was the Crayola Crayon Factory, which was founded in 1900. Originally interested in making slate pencils, the founding company, Binney & Smith, settled in Easton because of the ready access to slate (for slate pencils, *natch*) and power from the Bushkill Creek. Crayola eventually manufactured the colorful drawing sticks now known as Crayons, which are made from paraffin wax and colored pigments. Some interesting Crayola factoids: The name is derived from the French word "craie" and the English "oleaginous," truncated to "ole" (translated literally: oily chalk). 100 billion Crayola crayons have been produced over the years, which is about five million crayons *a day*! Amazingly, the smell of Crayola crayons ranked 18th in a worldwide survey of the most recognized smells. The only colors that have ever changed names, (or are scheduled to do so) are "Prussian Blue," which changed to "Midnight Blue," "Flesh," which changed to "Peach," and "Indian Red," which has not been renamed yet.

One of the spookiest sites in Easton would have to be the State Theater, which is supposed to house *Fred the Ghost*. This paranormal presence is said to be the ghost of J. Fred Osterstock, manager of the theater from 1936-1965. Although there is no empirical evidence for the existence of Fred, several ostensibly reliable witnesses have had the luck to gander the ghost, including members of the State Board of Directors and the historian Ken Klabunde.

Today, Easton is home to nearly 27,000 industrious inhabitants. The local police station receives nearly 21,000 service calls per year. When 27 is added to 21, it equals 48, a popular number of crayons found in a specific type of Crayola box, rivaled only by the 64 box with built-in sharpener. Numerological coincidence, or cosmic concurrence? The editors withhold judgment, awaiting more evidence.

John P. Mulligan, author of this book and environmental engineer, lives and works in Spring Grove.